ALSO BY DENNIS PRAGER AND JOSEPH TELUSHKIN

The Nine Questions People Ask About Judaism

WHY

The Reason
for
Antisemitism

THE
JEWS?

DENNIS PRAGER
and JOSEPH TELUSHKIN

SIMON AND SCHUSTER · NEW YORK

Copyright © 1983 by Dennis Prager and Joseph Telushkin
All rights reserved
including the right of reproduction
in whole or in part in any form
Published by Simon and Schuster
A Division of Simon & Schuster, Inc.
Simon & Schuster Building
Rockefeller Center
1230 Avenue of the Americas
New York, New York 10020
SIMON AND SCHUSTER and colophon
are registered trademarks of Simon & Schuster, Inc.
Manufactured in the United States of America

10   9   8   7   6   5   4   3

Library of Congress Cataloging in Publication Data

Prager, Dennis.
  Why the Jews?

  Includes index.
    1. Antisemitism—History.   I. Telushkin,
Joseph   II. Title.
DS145.P484   1983   305.8'924   83-4723
ISBN 0-671-45270-3

To Raoul Wallenberg

Contents

9

Preface

Ask almost anyone—Jew or non-Jew, scholar or lay-person—why Jews have been hated so deeply and for so long, and you are likely to be told that people need scapegoats, or that Jews are affluent, or that antisemitism is yet another sad example of racism or religious bigotry, or that antisemites are simply sick. In fact, you are likely to be given every reason for antisemitism except, amazingly, that it is a response to anything distinctly Jewish.

We have devoted a good part of seven years to writing this book in order to counteract this dejudaization of Jew-hatred, this universalization of a unique phenomenon. Until recently and throughout their history Jews have believed that they have been hated because Judaism made them different and challenging, not because they were rich, or convenient scapegoats, or but another bullied minority, or for any other reason unrelated to their being Jews.

The purpose of this book is to substantiate this age-old Jewish understanding of antisemitism and to refute modern attempts to deny the distinctly Jewish reasons for Jew-hatred and its contemporary manifestation, anti-Zionism. The historical record clearly indicates, we believe, that Jew-hatred is

11

unique. The very word *Jew* continues to arouse passions as does no other religious or national name. Why this hatred? Why this passion? That is the subject of our inquiry.

We wish to express our gratitude to Dr. Max Vorspan, professor of history at the University of Judaism of the Jewish Theological Seminary of America, to Dr. William Brinner, professor of Near Eastern Studies at the University of California, Berkeley, and to Jewish historian Dr. Gilbert Graff. Each of these scholars has given us very valuable advice and criticisms. We also wish to thank David Lehrer and Mildred Marcus of the Los Angeles office of the Anti-Defamation League. Needless to say, we take all responsibility for any errors of fact or interpretation that remain.

Our editor, Fred Hills, senior vice president of Simon and Schuster, deserves special recognition for his simply indispensable advice and constant encouragement. His faith in the significance of this book made the book possible. We are also indebted to Fred Hills' assistant, Hilary Sares, for her insightful criticisms and suggestions which ensured a tighter manuscript.

To Kathy Phipps, wherever she is in Oregon, go our thanks for her patient and excellent typing of the manuscript.

This book was written during our seven years as director and education director respectively of the Brandeis-Bardin Institute. To the thousands of the Institute's members and BCI alumni, thank you for your support and encouragement. We are particularly grateful to David Woznica and Pat Havins.

This book was written in California: at Brandeis-Bardin, in Los Angeles, Mammoth Lakes, and Palm Springs. We are especially indebted to Romy and Flora Rosman for the use of their idyllic retreat in Palm Springs, and to Ira and Betty Weiner for their beautiful cottage in Mammoth Lakes. All writers should be blessed with such settings in which to think and write.

Finally, *akharon akharon khaviv*, our thanks to Janice Prager who, despite her time-consuming work on a book on Jewish moral values for children, was the single greatest source of suggestions, criticisms, and morale boosting. As this book goes to press, Janice has just given birth. May her and my (D.P.) son grow up in a world that will regard the subject of this book as history.

Dennis Prager and Joseph Telushkin

PART ONE

Why the Jews?
The Explanation

ONE

Why Jew-Hatred Is Unique

HATRED OF THE JEW has been humanity's greatest hatred. While hatred of other groups has always existed, no hatred has been as universal, as deep, or as permanent as antisemitism.[1]

The Jews have been objects of hatred in pagan, religious, and secular societies. Fascists have accused them of being Communists, and Communists have branded them capitalists. Jews who live in non-Jewish societies have been accused of having dual loyalties, and Jews who live in the Jewish state have been condemned as "racists." Poor Jews are bullied, and rich Jews are resented. Jews have been branded as both rootless cosmopolitans and ethnic chauvinists. Jews who assimilate are often called a fifth column, while those who stay together often spark hatred for remaining different. Literally hundreds of millions of people have believed that the Jews drink the blood of non-Jews, that they cause plagues and poison wells, that they plan to conquer the world, and that they murdered God Himself.

The *universality* of antisemitism is attested to by innumerable facts, the most dramatic being that Jews have been expelled from nearly every country in which they have resided.

Jews were expelled from England in 1290, France in 1306 and 1394, Hungary between 1349 and 1360, Austria in 1421, numerous localities in Germany between the fourteenth and sixteenth centuries, Lithuania in 1445 and 1495, Spain in 1492, Portugal in 1497, and Bohemia and Moravia in 1744–45. Between the fifteenth century and 1772, Jews were not allowed into Russia, and when finally admitted, they were restricted to one area, the Pale of Settlement. Between 1948 and 1967 nearly all the Jews of Aden, Algeria, Egypt, Iraq, Syria, and Yemen, though not officially expelled, fled these countries, fearing for their lives.

The *depth* of antisemitism is evidenced by the frequency with which hostility against Jews has gone far beyond discrimination and erupted into sustained violence. In nearly every country where Jews have lived, they have at some time been subjected to beatings, torture, and murder, solely because they were Jews. In the Russian Empire during the nineteenth and twentieth centuries, mass beatings and murders of Jews were so common that a word, *pogrom*, was coined to describe such incidents.[2] And these pogroms were viewed by their antisemitic perpetrators as being of such significance that they were equated with the saving of Russia.[3]

On a number of occasions even beating and murdering Jewish communities were not deemed sufficient. Antisemitic passions have run so deep that only the actual annihilation of the Jewish people could solve what came to be called the "Jewish Problem." The basic source of ancient Jewish history, the Bible, depicts two attempts to destroy the Jewish people, the attempt by Pharaoh and the Egyptians (*Exodus* 1:15–22) and that of Haman and the Persians (*Book of Esther*). While it is true that the historicity of these biblical accounts has not been proven or disproven by nonbiblical sources,[4] few would dispute the supposition that in ancient times attempts were made to destroy the Jews. Indeed the first recorded reference to Jews in non-Jewish sources, the Mernephta stele, written by an Egyptian king about 1220 B.C.E.,* states "Israel

* Many contemporary scholars use the universal B.C.E. (Before the Common Era), rather than the Christian-based B.C. (before Christ),

is no more." Jewish writings from the earliest times until the present are replete with references to attempts by non-Jews to destroy the Jewish people. *Psalms* 83:5 describes the enemies of the Jews as proponents of genocide: "Come, and let us cut them off from being a nation, that the Name of Israel may no more be remembered." Just how precarious Jews have viewed their survival is reflected in a statement from the ancient and still recited Passover Haggadah: "In every generation they rise against us in order to annihilate us."

On two occasions in the last 350 years annihilation campaigns have been waged against the Jews:[5] the Chmelnitzky massacres in Eastern Europe in 1648–49, and the Nazi destruction of Jews throughout Europe between 1939 and 1945.

For various reasons the Chmelnitzky massacres are today not well known among Jews and virtually unknown among non-Jews; perhaps the Holocaust tends to overshadow all previous Jewish sufferings. Yet without denying the unique aspects of the Nazi Holocaust, we are obliged to cite a number of significant similarities between it and the Chmelnitzky massacres. In both instances all Jews, including infants, were targeted for murder; the general populaces nearly always joined in the attacks; and the torture and degradation of Jews were an integral part of the murderers' procedures. These characteristics are evidenced by the following contemporaneous description of a typical Chmelnitzky massacre:

> Some of them [the Jews] had their skins flayed off them and their flesh was flung to the dogs. The hands and feet of others were cut off and they were flung onto the roadway where carts ran over them and they were trodden underfoot by horse. . . . And many were buried alive. Children were slaughtered in their mothers' bosoms and many children were torn apart like fish. They ripped up the bellies of pregnant women, took out the unborn children, and flung them in their faces. They tore open the bellies of some of them and placed a living cat within the belly and left them alive thus, first cutting off their hands so that they should

---

and C.E. (common era) instead of A.D. (*anno Domini*, "in the year of the Lord"). This book adopts that policy.

not be able to take the living cat out of the belly ... and there was never an unnatural death in the world that they did not inflict upon them.[6]

The *permanence* (as well as depth) of antisemitism is attested to by the obsessive attention given to the "Jewish Problem" by antisemites throughout history. *At one time or another nearly every one of the world's greatest powers that has had a large Jewish population has regarded this group, which never constituted more than a small percentage of the population, as an enemy.* To the Roman Empire in the first century, the Christian world for over fifteen centuries, the Nazi Reich, and to the Arabs, Muslims, and the Soviet Union today, the Jews have been or are regarded as an insufferable threat.

Jews have been perceived as so dangerous that even after their expulsion or destruction hatred and fear of them remain. The depiction of Jews as ritual murderers of young Christian children in Chaucer's "Prioress's Tale" in *The Canterbury Tales* one hundred years after all Jews had been expelled from England, and the characterization of Jews as usurers who wish to collect their interest in flesh in Shakespeare's *The Merchant of Venice* three hundred years after the Jewish expulsion, attest to the durability of antisemitism.[7] A contemporary example is Poland in 1968 when for months the greatest issue on Polish radio, television, and in Polish newspapers was the "Unmasking of Zionists in Poland." Of the 33 million citizens of Poland in 1968, the Jews numbered about 20,000, or less than one-fifteenth of 1 percent.[8]

How are the universality, depth, and permanence of antisemitism to be explained? Why such hatred and fear of people who never constituted more than a small minority among those who most hated and feared them? Why, nearly always and nearly everywhere, the Jews?

Many answers have been offered by scholars. These include, most commonly, economic factors, the need for scapegoats, ethnic hatred, xenophobia, resentment of Jewish affluence and professional success, and religious bigotry. But ultimately these answers do not explain antisemitism: they only explain what factors have *exacerbated* antisemitism and caused it to erupt in a given circumstance. None accounts for the universality, depth, and persistence of antisemitism. In fact, we have encountered virtually no study of antisemitism that even attempts to offer a universal explanation of Jew-hatred. Nearly every study of antisemitism consists almost solely of historical narrative, claiming implicitly that no universal reason for antisemitism exists.

We reject this approach. To ignore the question of ultimate causation, or to deny that there are ultimate causes for antisemitism, contradicts both common sense and history. Antisemitism has existed too long and in too many disparate cultures to ignore the problem of ultimate cause and/or to claim that new or indigenous factors are responsible every time it erupts. Factors specific to a given society help account for the manner or time in which antisemitism erupts, but they do not explain its genesis—why antisemitism at all? To cite but one example, the depressed economy in Germany in the 1920s and 1930s may help to explain why and when the Nazis came to power, but it does not explain why Nazis hated Jews, let alone why they wanted to murder every Jew in the world. Economic depressions do not account for gas chambers.

The very consistency of the passions Jews have aroused demands a consistent explanation. Ancient Egyptians, Greeks, and Romans, medieval and many modern Christians and Muslims, and Nazis and Communists have perhaps only one thing in common: they have all counted the Jews as their enemy, often their greatest enemy. Why?

This question has been posed only by modern Jews. From the recorded beginnings of Jewish history until the modern age, Jews never asked, "Why the Jews?" They knew exactly why. Throughout their history Jews have regarded Jew-hatred as an inevitable consequence of their Jewishness. Contrary to modern understandings of antisemitism, the age-old Jewish understanding of antisemitism does posit a universal reason for Jew-hatred: Judaism. And the historical record confirms the traditional Jewish view of antisematism that the Jews were hated because of distinctly Jewish factors. Modern attempts to dejudaize antisemitism, to attribute it to economic, social, and political reasons, and universalize it into merely another instance of bigotry are as opposed to the facts of Jewish history as they are to the historical Jewish understanding of antisemitism.

Antisemites have not opposed Jews because Jews are affluent—poor Jews have always been as hated; or strong—weak Jews have simply invited antisemitic bullies; or because Jews may have unpleasant personalities—kindly Jews have never been spared by antisemites; or because ruling classes focus worker discontent onto Jews—precapitalist and contemporary noncapitalist societies such as those of the Soviet Union and other Communist states have been considerably more antisemitic than capitalist societies. Antisemites have hated Jews because Jews are Jewish. Christian antisemites ceased hating rich Jews when they became Christians. The same has held true for virtually all other antisemites except the Nazis, whom we shall discuss later.

The ultimate cause of antisemitism is that which has made Jews Jewish—Judaism. There are four basic reasons for this and each revolves around the theme of a Jewish *challenge* to the values of non-Jews.

1. For thousands of years Judaism has consisted of three components: God, Torah, and Israel; that is, the Jewish (conception of) God, Jewish law, and Jewish nationhood. Jews' allegiance to any of these components has been a major source of antisemitism because it has rendered the Jew an outsider, and most important, it has been regarded by non-Jews (often correctly) as challenging the validity of the non-Jews' god(s), law(s), and/or national allegiance.

By affirming what they considered to be the one and only God of all mankind, thereby denying legitimacy to everyone else's gods, the Jews entered history—and have often been since—at war with other people's most cherished values. The Jews compounded this hostility by living by their own all-encompassing set of laws in addition to or even instead of the laws of their non-Jewish neighbors. And by continually asserting their own national identity in addition to or instead of the national identity of the non-Jews among whom they lived, Jews have created or intensified antisemitic passions.

2. From its earliest days the *raison d'être* of Judaism has been to change the world for the better (in the words of an ancient Jewish prayer still recited daily, "to perfect the world under the rule of God"). This attempt to change the world, to challenge the gods, religious or secular, of the societies around them, and to make moral demands upon others (even when not done expressly in the name of Judaism) has constantly been a source of tension between Jews and non-Jews.

3. As if the above were not enough, Judaism has also held from the earliest time that the Jews were chosen by God to achieve this mission of perfecting the world. This doctrine of the Jews' divine election has been a major cause of antisemitism.

4. As a result of the Jews' commitment to Judaism, they have led higher quality lives than their non-Jewish neighbors in almost every society in which they have lived. This higher quality of life has expressed itself in a variety of ways. To cite but a few examples: Jews have nearly always been better educated; Jewish family life has usually been far more stable; Jews aided one another considerably more than their non-Jewish neighbors aided each other; and Jews have been far less likely to become drunk, beat their wives, abandon their children, and the like. As a result of these factors, the quality of life of the average Jew, no matter how poor, was higher than that of a comparable non-Jew in that society.

This higher quality of life among Jews, which, as we shall show, directly results from Judaism, has challenged non-Jews and provoked profound envy and hostility. In this way, too, Judaism has been the source of antisemitism.

Once we perceive that it is Judaism which is the root cause of antisemitism, otherwise irrational and inexplicable aspects of antisemitism become rationally explicable.

We now understand why so many non-Jews have regarded the mere existence of Jews—no matter how few—as terribly threatening. The mere existence of the Jews, with their different values and allegiances, constituted a threat to the prevailing order.

Since Judaism is the root cause of antisemitism, Jews, *unlike victims of racial or ethnic prejudice*, could in every in-

stance of antisemitism, except Nazism, escape persecution.
For thousands of years and until this day, Jews who abandoned their Jewish identity and assumed the majority's religious and national identity were no longer persecuted.*

For these reasons, Jews have always seen antisemitism as
the somewhat inevitable and often quite rational, though of
course immoral, response to Judaism. Thus, Jews until the
modern era, and religious Jews to this day, would describe
every Jew murdered by an antisemite not as a victim of ethnic prejudice but as having died *al kiddush hashem*, a martyr
to the cause of Judaism, sanctifying the name of God before
the world.

Once one understands why Judaism has precipitated antisemitism, the unique universality, depth, and permanence of
Jew-hatred also become understandable. It takes infinitely
more than economic tensions or racial prejudice to create the
animosity—so often to the point of torturing children and
murdering whole communities—that Jews have created
throughout their long history. Only something representing a
threat to the core values, allegiances, and beliefs of others
could arouse such universal, deep, and lasting hatred. This
Judaism has done.

That Judaism, rather than race or economics, is at the root
of antisemitism also helps to explain why totalitarian regimes
are inevitably antisemitic. Totalitarian regimes by definition
aim to control the totality of their citizens' lives and can
therefore tolerate no uncontrolled religious or national expressions, both of which are part of Judaism.

---

* There is one apparent exception to this rule, the Marranos of Spain.
In the fourteenth and fifteenth centuries, Jews who converted to
Christianity in Spain were not easily accepted into Christian society.
But this was overwhelmingly due to the circumstances of the Jews'
conversions. The Christian hierarchy was reluctant to accept these
Jewish converts as genuine Christians because it knew that they had
converted under threats of expulsion or death, and therefore the sin-
cerity of the Jews' Christianity was questioned. But the Jews who
proved by their behavior that they had become religious Christians
were accepted. And, in fact, almost all of these tens of thousands of
Marranos who remained in Spain did assimilate into Spanish society.

Once the Jewish bases of antisemitism are recognized, the only solutions to the "Jewish Problem," as far as antisemites are concerned, are obvious. The Jews must either convert, be expelled, or be murdered. Indeed, in the 1880s, the Russian czar's procurator of the Holy Synod and architect of Russian government policy at the time, Constantine Pobedonostsev, is said to have offered precisely this advice. One-third of the Jews living in the Russian Empire, he said, should be converted to Christianity, one-third should be expelled from the empire, and one-third should be put to death.[9] In fact, for the last two thousand years, this has repeatedly been the chronological order of antisemitic acts. First, attempts would be made to convert the Jews. When the Jews refused, they were often expelled. And when even expulsion failed to solve the "Jewish Problem," there remained one "Final Solution," which is precisely the name the Nazis gave to their plan to murder all the Jews.

It is also clear that antisemitism is not ethnic or racial prejudice, though it obviously shares certain features with them. Antisemites persecuted Jews for the same reasons Romans persecuted Christians, Nazis tortured members of the Resistance, and Soviets imprison dissidents. In each instance the group is persecuted because its different beliefs represent a threat to the persecuting group. This hatred must be understood as being very different from a prejudice. Blacks in America, for example, have been discriminated against because of the physical fact of their blackness, not because of specific Black ideas or beliefs which they represent. Hatred of Blacks is racial prejudice. Blacks cannot stop being Black. But Soviet dissidents can stop being dissenters, and a Jew has always been able to, and in general still can, stop being a Jew. The single exception to this rule has been Nazi antisemitism. But even this apparent exception confirms the Jewish basis of antisemitism. The Nazis simply maintained that Jews could never really become non-Jews, that no matter how much Jews may consciously attempt to appear and behave like non-Jews, they nevertheless retain the values of Judaism. Nazi anti-Jewish "racism" emanated from a hatred of Judaism and

what Jews represent. Nazi racism is *ex post facto;* first came
the antisemitism, then came the racist doctrine to explain it.

Antisemitism is, therefore, as Jews have always regarded it:
a response to Jews and their way of life. The charges made
against Jews, that they poison wells, drink blood, plot to take
over the governments of the world, or control world finance,
are hallucinatory. But the roots of antisemitism are not. The
real reasons antisemites hate Jews and the accusations they
make against them are not necessarily the same. This is
hardly uncommon. When people harbor hatreds, individually
or communally, they rarely articulate rationally the reasons
for their hatred.

We should not be so naive as to regard all antisemitic accusations as the reasons for the antisemitism. For example,
the modern belief that economic factors cause antisemitism,
besides confusing exacerbating factors with causes of antisemitism, grants the accusations of antisemites far too much cre-
dence. It is reminiscent of some historians' preoccupation
with determining the historical accuracy of the Christian
claim that the Jews killed Jesus, because Christian antisemites
called Jews "Christ killers," as if proving one way or another
would end Christian antisemitism. The question for those
wishing to understand the roots of antisemitism is not
whether some Jews helped execute Jesus around the year 30
C.E. or how great a role Jews played in the German economy.
The question is why, to begin with, people hate Jews. The answer is Judaism, its distinctiveness and its challenge, and we
have offered four general reasons why this is so. In the pages
that follow let us pursue a more detailed analysis of these
reasons.

TWO

Antisemitism:
The Hatred of Judaism
and Its Challenge

JUDAISM CONSISTS of three components: God, Torah (laws and teachings), and Israel (Jewish nationhood). Throughout Jewish history, the Jews' affirmation of one or more of these components has challenged, often threatened, the gods, laws, and nationalism of non-Jews among whom the Jews have lived.

THE JEWS' GOD AS SOURCE OF ANTISEMITISM

Judaism's first component asserts that the God who revealed Himself to the Jews is the one God of all the world, that all other gods or anything else worshiped are false, and that this God makes moral demands upon every person and nation. These ideas, known as ethical monotheism, have generated animosity against the Jews ever since the Jews introduced them to the world.

In the ancient world, every nation but the Jews worshiped its own gods and acknowledged the legitimacy of others' gods. The Jews declared that the gods of the non-Jews were nonsense: "They have mouths but cannot speak, eyes but

27

cannot see, ears but cannot hear . . ." (*Psalms* 115:5–6). There is but one God and He had revealed Himself to mankind through the Jews. One need not be a theologian or historian to understand why these doctrines bred massive anti-Jewish resentment.

The Jews' belief in God threatened more than their neighbors' gods. It challenged all their values. "It was Judaism," wrote the Reverend Edward H. Flannery of the National Conference of Catholic Bishops, "that brought the concept of a God-given universal moral law into the world"; willingly or not "the Jew carries the burden of God in history [and] for this has never been forgiven."[1] The world to which the Jews have introduced God and His moral demands has always resented this challenge. It is little wonder why hatred of the Jew became, as Father Flannery wrote, "the greatest hatred in human history."

A basic element of antisemitism is, therefore, a rebellion against the thou shalts and thou shalt nots introduced by the Jews in the name of a supreme moral authority. One explanation for the antimonotheism roots of antisemitism is offered by the contemporary (non-Jewish) social psychologist Ernest van den Haag: "Fundamental to [antisemitism] . . . though seldom explicit and conscious, is hostility to the Jewish belief in one God, a belief to which antisemites very reluctantly converted and which they never ceased to resist. Antisemitism is one form this resistance takes. Those who originated this burdensome religion—and yet rejected the version to which the Gentiles were converted—easily became the target of the resentment. One cannot dare to be hostile to one's all-powerful God. But one can be to those who generated Him, to whom He revealed Himself and who caused others to accept Him.

"The Jewish God is invisible and unrepresentable; even unmentionable, a power beyond imagination, a law beyond scrutiny. He is universal, holding power over everybody and demanding obedience and worship from all. Nonetheless, He entered history and listened to, argued with and chose the Jews—and the Jews alone. . . . No wonder they are the target of all those who resent His domination . . . .

"Most unpleasant, their invisible God not only insisted on being the one and only and all-powerful God—creator and lord of everything and the only rightful claimant to worship—He also developed into a moral God. . . .

"The Jews have suffered from their own invention ever since; but they have never given it up, for it is, after all, what makes the Jews Jewish. . . ."[2]

From the earliest times, as van den Haag notes, the Jews have suffered for representing (even if not always embodying) obedience to God, and for denying the validity of the gods of the non-Jews. Jewish opposition to Roman gods, for example, was unique and notorious. The fourth-century Roman emperor Julian attacked the Jews for "striving to gratify their own God [while] they do not at the same time serve the others." A first-century emperor, Caligula, was outraged at the Jews because they were the only people in the Roman Empire who refused to place his statue in their Temple. When a delegation of Jews came to meet with him, Caligula complained: "So you are the enemies of the gods—the only people who refuse to recognize my divinity, and yet you worship a god whose name you dare not pronounce." When the Jewish group protested that the Jews had already brought three sacrifices on the emperor's behalf to their Temple in Jerusalem, Caligula rightly noted, "Yes, you make a sacrifice *for* me, but not *to* me."[3]

Yet it was the Jews' God, not the Romans' gods, who ultimately prevailed in Rome. In the fourth century, the Roman Empire adopted the God of the Jews as Christianity became the Roman religion. This proved to be no blessing for the Jews, however. For the Church created the most virulent form of antisemitism prior to Nazism—and the root cause, again, was the Jews' understanding of God.

Christianity adopted the Jews' God, but it also posited the divinity of a first-century Jew, Jesus of Nazareth. To the Jews, however, belief in the divinity of Jesus was contrary to monotheism. This denial alone would have sufficed to cause Christian antisemitism, just as the Jews' denial of Roman gods had provoked Roman hostility. But the Jews' denial of Jesus' divinity was far more threatening to the Church than the Jews' denial of Roman divinities was to Rome. For Jesus was a Jew, directed his message entirely to the Jews (*Matthew* 15:24), and all religious claims made for him were based completely on Jewish sources. Yet the Jews rejected the divine (and messianic) claims made for or by him.

The Jews came to constitute the one group in the Christian world to deny the fundamental tenet, the defining characteristic, of Christianity, the divinity of Jesus. The Jews' monotheism which dictated this denial has been the single most important factor in Christian antisemitism.

Belief in the God introduced by the Jews continued to spread, and in the seventh century, on the Arabian peninsula, the second offshoot of Judaism, Islam, arose. A more strictly monotheistic religion than Christianity, Islam, like Judaism, denied the divinity of Jesus, asserting the divinity of no one but Allah (Arabic for God). This rendered the Jews' situation under Islam somewhat easier, though the Jews incurred continuous Muslim hatred for denying the divine nature of Muhammad's message, particularly since Muhammad had wanted the Jews to validate his message and convert to Islam.

With the decline of religion in the West beginning in the eighteenth century, and with the rise of nationalism often in its place, the Jews remained objects of hostility—now both for their adherence to the national component of Judaism as well as for their religious beliefs.

The most virulent forms of modern antisemitism have been secular. Both Nazism and Communism have sought to destroy the God, as well as the national identity, of the Jews. The Nazis' ultimate aim was to destroy the mortal threat posed by monotheism's God-based morality to their nation-based morality. Hitler declared that his mission in life was to destroy the "tyrannical God of the Jews" and His "life-denying Ten Commandments."[4] In 1936, a Nazi official, Supreme Group Leader Schultz, speaking at a meeting of the National Socialist Confederation of Students, made this very point: "We cannot tolerate that another organization is established alongside of us that has a different spirit than ours. We must crush it. National Socialism in all earnestness says: 'I am the Lord thy God, thou shalt have no other gods before me . . .' "[5]

Because of the threatening nature of their religion, the Jews, who through Judaism and Christianity had introduced monotheism, had to be destroyed.

Communist regimes also perceive monotheism's mortal threat. Both religious individuals and party members agree that one can either be true to God or to the party, but not to both. The moment one believes in God, one has an external standard by which to judge the government. This is why a person who advocates belief in God in the Soviet Union, for example, risks incarceration.

Though affirmation of God's existence is not widespread among today's Soviet Jewish dissidents, they deny the proclaimed truths of Communism just as their ancestors challenged the deities of ancient Rome or the divinity of Jesus. The denial of the non-Jews' gods is as much an operative principle among Soviet Jewish dissidents, and a cause of antisemitism, as it was among Jews in the Hellenic, Roman and Christian worlds. In the words of one of the best known Soviet Jewish protest songs:

Nye boyusa nikavo
Krome boga odnavo

I fear no one
Except God, the only one

In sum, throughout their history, Jews have consistently denied the most revered objects of their neighbors. This alone would have sufficed to engender antisemitism. But affirmation of God and the concomitant denial of other gods is only the first of the three components of Judaism. The other two, Jewish laws and Jewish nationhood, concretized the Jews' otherness and further assured antisemitism.

JEWISH LAW AS SOURCE OF ANTISEMITISM

Had the Jews only believed differently from their non-Jewish neighbors, they would not have made as profound an impact as they have upon the non-Jewish world, and consequently would not have generated as much hostility. The component of Judaism that has concretized the Jewish challenge has been Jewish law. It put the Jews' challenging beliefs into action.

The first aim of Jewish law is to have the Jew express his affirmation of God and denial of other gods in daily actions. Much of Jewish law emanates from these two considerations. Specifically, eight Torah laws deal with the public affirmation of God's existence, and fifty-one legislate the denial of other gods. These laws compel Jews to make public their distinctive beliefs. It is not enough for a Jew to acknowledge monotheism privately; his belief in God and denial of other gods must be publicly expressed. Jewish law prevents Jews from even appearing to share their neighbor's gods while privately affirming the Jewish God. Maimonides, the preeminent codifier of Jewish law, legislated in the twelfth century that "... [Jews] are in duty bound to proclaim this true religion to the world, undeterred by fear of injury from any source. Even if a tyrant tries to compel us by force to deny Him, we must not obey, but must positively rather submit to death; and we must not even mislead the tyrant into supposing that we have denied Him while in our hearts we continue to believe in Him."[6]

But Jewish law legislates far more than monotheism. The 613 laws ascribed to the Torah and the myriad laws of the oral legal tradition legislate every aspect of the Jew's life. The laws of monotheism ensured that Jews put their different beliefs into practice. The social laws ensured that Jews put their different ethical values into practice. The final area of Jewish law, the laws of sanctity and ritual, further ensured that Jews act and even dress and eat differently from their non-Jewish neighbors. Any group acting so differently from the majority culture is bound to elicit hostility.

The best known example of Jewish laws that separated Jews from their neighbors is Kashrut, the Jewish dietary laws. By observing Kashrut a Jew could eat little at his non-Jewish neighbor's home. Kashrut, which may be characterized as Judaism's compromise with a vegetarian ideal,[7] restricted the

Jew to eating a very few species of animals. Nor could a Jew eat even the permitted meat and fowl of his non-Jewish neighbor, for meat and fowl had to be killed in a specific Jewish manner which minimized the animal's pain and ensured its quick death. This in turn meant that Jews could not hunt, always a highly popular sport and mode of obtaining food among non-Jews. Finally, Kashrut did not permit eating milk and meat products together.[8]

Observance of the many laws of the Jewish Sabbath also increased the otherness and isolation of the Jews. One day every week, the Jews would retreat further from their non-Jewish neighbors and act even more differently from them. They refused to work, travel, cook, play musical instruments, plant, engage in business, or even touch money or attend public events.[9] Instead, Jews would spend the day with their families and with fellow Jews in prayer, study, song, and conversation. On the Sabbath, even more than on other days, the Jews would appear to live in their own world.

But the Jews have not lived in their own world. They have not physically removed themselves from society as have, for example, the Amish in America. On the contrary, Jews have tended to immerse themselves in society while maintaining their way of life. Had the Jews removed themselves from society, or been social failures, while adhering to their distinctiveness, they would have provoked far less hostility. Precisely because they have lived among non-Jews, and often prospered while maintaining their separateness, have the Jews and their practices provoked such antipathy.

From the time of their earliest writings Jews have understood the challenging nature of their laws and the resentment they can engender. In the *Book of Esther,* the Persian king plans to destroy the Jews because they are "... dispersed among the peoples in all provinces of [the] kingdom, *and their laws are different from those of everybody else (Esther* 3:8; emphasis ours).

In the Christian world, Jewish law, along with the Jews' rejection of Jesus, was the major source of contention between the nascent Christianity and its mother religion. Judaism holds that one is put right with God through performing the good deeds of the law. But in the view of Paul, the foremost Christian figure after Jesus, this belief is irreconcilable with Christian salvation.[10] "For if a person could achieve salvation through good works [the law], then Christ would have died in vain" (*Galatians* 2:21). Therefore, according to Paul and the New Testament, "... we conclude that a man is put right with God only through faith and not by doing what the law commands" (*Romans* 3:28), and furthermore "Christ redeemed us from the curse of the law" (*Galatians* 3:10).

The Jews' insistence on the continuing validity of Jewish law was consequently seen by many Christians as a denial of salvation through Christ, and it was often attacked in Christian literature. The contemporary Catholic theologian Rosemary Ruether writes of the centuries of hostile writings by influential Christians against Jewish law. A typical example appears in the medieval Church document *Epistle of Diognetus:* "... But now, as to certain ridiculous matters that call for no discussion—such as their scruples in regard to meat, their observance of the Sabbath days, their vain boasting about circumcision, and the hypocrisy connected with fasting and the feasts of the new moon—I don't suppose you need any instruction from me. For how can it be other than irreligious to accept some of the things God has created for man's use and to reject others, as though some were created for a good purpose and others were useless and superfluous? ... And is it not ridiculous to boast of a mutilation of the flesh as a sign of a chosen people, as though on account of this they were particularly loved by God? ... Who would look on all this as evidence of religion, and not, rather, as a sign of folly?"[11]

Until the modern era, Jews observed Jewish laws, and throughout that time it differentiated them from their non-Jewish neighbors and engendered anti-Jewish sentiments. Even today when most Jews have ceased strictly observing Jewish law, however, thousands of years of observance continue to influence their behavior. The generally higher quality of Jews' lives, as exemplified by the stability of the family life, significantly lower rates of intoxication and wife beating, higher education, greater professional success, much less violent crime, and greater communal solidarity, has been due solely to millennia of adherence to Jewish law, and has provoked profoundly ambivalent reactions from non-Jews.

JEWISH NATIONHOOD AS SOURCE OF ANTISEMITISM

The third component of Judaism is Israel, the biblical and historical name of the Jewish nation, and the name of the modern Jewish state.[12] Between 70 and 1948, Israel the nation existed while Israel the state did not exist. To non-Jews and even to many Jews, the nationhood of the Jews is usually the most perplexing aspect of Judaism.

This confusion about Jewish nationhood is understandable. For one thing, one normally associates a national group with a land and a state, and for nearly two thousand years the Jews have lived without their state and almost all Jews lived in exile from their land. A second source of confusion is that the Jews constitute the only group in the modern world that is both a religion and a nation. For both these reasons they are unique, a uniqueness which of itself often renders the Jews suspect in the eyes of others.

But as perplexing, unique, and even discomfiting as it may be, the Jew is a member of both the Jewish nation and Jewish religion, and this has been so since the beginning of Jewish history. To deny that nationhood is a component of Judaism is as untenable as to deny that God or Torah are components of Judaism. This is particularly evident today, since Jewish nationhood is the one component of Judaism with which both religious and secular Jews identify.

There was one attempt by a group of Jews to eliminate the national component of Judaism. During the nineteenth and early twentieth centuries, Reform Jews in Germany and the United States, fearing that any mention by the Jews of their peoplehood would offend non-Jews, called for the elimination of the national component of Judaism.[13] But even these radical Reformers never denied that nationhood had always been a part of Judaism; they simply wanted it removed. The attempt failed. Judaism cannot survive without nationhood, since without this component it is by definition not Judaism but a new religion.

On the other hand, Jewish nationhood cannot survive the elimination of the religious components of Judaism. For the Jewish nation is defined by the Jewish religion. The only way a non-Jew can become a member of the Jewish nation is by converting to Judaism. The Jews are, therefore, the only nation that an outsider can join irrespective of geographical considerations (for example, to become a Canadian, one must first live in Canada). As a consequence, the Jews are the only transnational nation, and this has been and continues to be a major source of antisemitism.[14]

For most of the Jews' history, their commitment to monotheism, Jewish law, and their doctrine of chosenness (discussed in the next chapter), and the resultant distinctive quality of Jews' lives, have been the primary reasons for antisemitism. These factors, which may be characterized as religious, have been the primary causes of antisemitism in religious societies. In the modern age, however, when nationhood has become a supreme value, the Jews' nationhood and since 1948 the Jews' state have become added causes and the primary targets of antisemitism.

Jewish nationhood became an additional target of non-Jews' animosity the moment the modern age of nationalism began. Immediately following the French Revolution, in December 1789, during a discussion in the French National Assembly on granting French Jews equal rights, Count Stanislas de Clermont-Tonnerre declared: "The Jews should be denied everything as a nation, but granted everything as individuals. . . . There cannot be one nation within another nation."[15]

These were fateful and prophetic words. They foretold much of the modern world's attitude toward the Jews. To be equal to non-Jews, the Jews must abandon their Jewish national identity. This is the price of emancipation.

In 1789, French Jews were told what virtually all European Jews would eventually hear: the price of individual emancipation is national extinction. In 1807, Napoleon convened a Sanhedrin (the name of the Jewish high court in ancient Jerusalem) of seventy-one leading rabbis and lay Jews.

They were to disavow any commitment to Jewish nationhood and declare that the only national identity of the Jews of France is French. Having little choice, they acceded to all of Napoleon's demands, except the sanctioning of intermarriage. (This, too, was most prophetic. To this day many Jews adopt virtually every characteristic of the non-Jews among whom they live but oppose their children marrying a non-Jew.)

In the age of religion, the Jews were offered equality on the condition that they abandon their religion and convert to the majority religion. In the new age of nationalism, the Jews were offered equality on the condition that they abandon their national identity and adopt the majority's national identity only. In both ages opponents of the Jews have delivered the same message: cease being Jews.

Today, as in 1789, the refrain of opponents of the Jews is "The Jews should be denied everything as a nation, but granted everything as individuals." The Soviets say this. The Muslims and Arabs say this. The United Nations in delegitimizing Zionism says this. They all deny opposing Jews as individuals; they wish only to destroy Jewish nationhood. This is why they do not call themselves antisemites but rather "anti-Zionists."

But the major difference between antisemites throughout Jewish history and today's anti-Zionists is only which component of Judaism each has found most intolerable. For example, medieval Christian antisemites found the Jews' religious beliefs intolerable, and today's anti-Zionists loathe the Jews' national commitment.

Among the most ardent enemies of Judaism today is the Left. Marxists, for example, are theoretically opposed to all religions. But from Marxism's earliest days its adherents have tended to be particularly anti-Jewish. Among other reasons, Judaism, unlike other religions, incorporates nationhood, and basic to Marxist theory is the tearing down of national as well as religious allegiances. In practice, however, Marxist parties have been intensely nationalistic wherever they have attained power, and the combination of chauvinistic nationalism with Marxist theory produces a particularly dangerous strain of antisemitism. Neither can tolerate the Jews. Thus, for example,

Soviet Jews who are committed to the God and Torah components of Judaism provoke antisemitism for Marxist reasons
(quite aside from traditional Russian Orthodox antisemitism),
and those who affirm the national component of Judaism provoke Jew-hatred for Soviet nationalist as well as Marxist reasons. Soviet antisemitism is a reaction against every component of Judaism.

This same intensity of Jew-hatred also holds true for any
country that combines religious fundamentalism, nationalist
chauvinism, and Marxist rhetoric. Each alone is antisemitic.
Together they are lethal to Jews. Recent examples of such
combinations have been Qaddafi's Libya, and Muslim radicals
in Lebanon and Iran.

For these reasons (developed further in chaps. 9 and 11),
the world's centers of antisemitism today are in Islam and the
Left. With few exceptions, they have supplanted the Right
and Christendom, the former perhaps only temporarily, the
latter (except for its extreme Rightist and Leftist elements)
perhaps permanently. And for both Islam and the Left it is
Judaism's third component, nationhood, as embodied in the
state of Israel and Zionism, which elicits the greatest hostility.

Nationalism and Communism, two of the most potent
ideologies born after the French Revolution, have been antisemitic from their births primarily because of the national
component of Judaism. This was true before the modern
Zionist movement was born, and it has been true ever since.

Concerning the subject of the national component of Judaism, it would be valuable to discuss briefly the oft-raised
issue of Jewish "dual loyalty." Does the fact of Jewish nationhood mean that Jews outside of Israel have more than one
loyalty?

The answer is possible once we define the question. If we
are asking whether Jews outside Israel are loyal to two governments, the government of the country in which they reside
and the government of Israel, the answer is no. Jews who affirm the national component of Judaism, both in fact and Jewish legal obligation (*dina dimalkhuta dina*, the law of the land

is the law according to the Talmud), live as every other good citizen in accordance with the constitution and laws of the country in which they reside, presuming, of course, that the government is not a dictatorship and does not pass immoral laws.

But, it is often asked, what should happen if a war were to arise between the United States and Israel?

In view of the fact that two democracies have never before been at war against one another, the only foreseeable way in which the United States and Israel could fight is if either country abandons its democratic and/or other moral principles. In such an event, as with any war, the individual would have to follow the dictates of morality, which are higher than all governments.

If, however, "loyal to America" or "loyal to Israel" means supporting the country's policies whether morally right or wrong, then one would hope that all American and Israeli citizens would reject such a code. Both Christians and Jews are obligated to a moral law higher than any state and any individual.

Finally, does not the fact of Jewish nationhood still mean that Jews are members of two nations—the Jewish nation and the nation among whom they reside? The answer should by now be clear. Yes, and in this respect Jews are unique; but so long as moral rather than national values are held supreme, this should trouble no one. And if this fact in and of itself should provoke certain individuals to antisemitism, that, as we have repeatedly seen, is the price a Jew pays when nationalism becomes a god.

THREE

The Chosen People Idea
as a Cause
of Antisemitism

THE JEWS' AFFIRMATION of any one of Judaism's components, God, law, or nationhood, would have provoked antisemitism; their affirmation of all three has rendered Jew-hatred even more intense. Yet another Jewish belief has further inflamed antisemitic passions throughout Jewish history, that the Jews are the Chosen People—that of all the nations of the world God has chosen them to be His messengers to mankind.

Since non-Jews first became aware of this doctrine, that is, from the time the Bible became known to non-Jews, chosenness has evoked jealousy and hostility. The Jews' belief in chosenness did not necessarily have to evoke such hostile reactions in non-Jews. But due to the Jews' distinctive religion and particularly because of their generally higher quality of life, their doctrine of chosenness was never dismissed as an innocuous belief of an innocuous people. The Jews' profound influence on others and the quality of their lives have caused non-Jews to take Jewish claims of chosenness most seriously.

So seriously was the Jews' chosenness taken by Christians, for example, that among the first beliefs adopted by them was that the Church had taken over divine election from the Jews. The Church leaders did not deny Jewish chosenness; rather they so believed in it that they sought to appropriate it to themselves. Islam did the same thing. Muhammad did not deny the chosenness of Abraham; he simply called Abraham a Muslim. Christianity and Islam have had a love-hate relationship with the Jews' idea of chosenness. They loved and believed in the idea and hated the Jews for continuing to claim it for themselves.

Surprisingly, however, antagonism toward the Jews for considering themselves chosen has continued to the present day despite two facts which should have greatly reduced antagonism toward the belief: the general decline in religious beliefs among non-Jews (who presumably should regard this belief at worst as a pompous anachronism), and, at least as important, the decline of belief in chosenness among many modern Jews and the lack of reference to it among modern Jews who do believe it.

Antisemites continue to base many of their attacks on the Jews on this issue. Contemporary Soviet and Arab antisemitism, for example, constantly harps on Jewish chosenness in their anti-Jewish writings and speeches. A typical example is the 1973 statement of the Soviet ambassador to the United Nations, Yakov Malik, with which he initiated a United Nations debate on the subject of Jewish chosenness: "Racism and Zionism are racist creeds. The Zionists have come forward with the theory of the chosen people, an absurd ideology. That is religious racism."[1] Malik then challenged the Israeli ambassador to "prove to the world" that Jews are the chosen people (October 21, 1973).

A recent American study of "potentially negative" beliefs about Jews disclosed that of eighteen such beliefs the one with the widest acceptance among American non-Jews is that "Jews still think of themselves as God's chosen people." According to this University of California Five-Year Study of Antisemitism in the United States, 59 percent of the American public agrees with this statement, five times as many as those who believe that the "Jews have too much power in the United States," three times as many as those who hold that

"Jews are trying to push in where they are not wanted," and more than twice as many as those who hold that "Jews don't care what happens to anyone but their own kind." The study concludes that the widespread association of the Jews with the claim to chosenness evokes considerable antagonism toward Jews in America.[2]

This is not surprising. Antisemites have long attempted to portray the chosen people belief as a Jewish claim to innate national superiority. Some have contended the Jews' belief in their chosenness lies at the heart of their attempt to take over the world. *The Protocols of the Elders of Zion*, perhaps the most widely distributed forgery in history, and the best known modern work of antisemitism, was based on this portrayal of chosenness.[3]

But one need not be an antisemite to misinterpret the Chosen People concept and thus find it offensive. In the mid-1930s, at the very same time the Nazis were passing antisemitic laws against the Jews of Germany, George Bernard Shaw, the most noted playwright of the twentieth century, said that the Nazis, with their doctrines of racial superiority, were merely imitating the Jews' doctrine of chosenness.[4]

Attacks on Jewish chosenness continue to the present day. In 1971, *Religion in Life,* a liberal Methodist journal, wrote "it is not surprising that Hitler retaliated against the chosen race by decreeing that it was not the Jewish but the Aryan race that was chosen."[5]

Reactions to the Jewish belief in chosenness have been often so negative that some Jews have actually called for elimination of this belief from Judaism, in much the same way as early Reform Jews called for elimination of the nationhood component of Judaism because of the hostility it aroused. The most noted attempt at removing chosenness from Judaism was undertaken by Mordecai Kaplan, the founder of the small but influential Reconstructionist movement of Judaism. In 1945, Kaplan's movement published its first prayer book which noted: "Modern minded Jews can no longer believe that the Jews constitute a divinely chosen people."[6] Kaplan explained that his movement's abandonment of this belief was "the best way . . . to answer the charge that the chosen people doctrine has been the model for theories of national and racial superiority."[7]

Given, then, that chosenness is an integral belief of Judaism, and that so many Jews react to it defensively, it is important that the chosen people concept be explained. For while a proper understanding of the doctrine will still elicit antisemitic reactions from some non-Jews, the moral onus will then be clearly on those who attack it rather than on the Jews who hold it.

Jewish chosenness has always meant that Jews have believed themselves chosen by God to spread ethical monotheism to the world and to live as a moral "light unto the nations" (*Isaiah* 49:6). *All other meanings imputed to Jewish chosenness are non-Jewish.*[8]

The Hebrew Bible, where the concept originates in its entirety, neither states nor implies that chosenness means Jewish superiority or privilege. The Bible repeatedly goes out of its way to declare that the Jews were not chosen because of any intrinsically positive qualities. Every nation is equal before God—"Are you not as the children of Ethiopia to me, children of Israel?" states the prophet Amos (9:7). God chose the Jews, "not because you are big, indeed you are of the smallest nations" (*Deuteronomy* 7:7), but simply because they are the offspring of the first ethical monotheist, Abraham (*Genesis* 18:19). That is their single merit.

The Jews' chosenness confers neither privilege nor superiority, only obligation and suffering—"Since I have known only you of all the peoples of the earth, I will visit upon you all your sins" (*Amos* 3:2). The Jews are chosen only to complete a task. This people either chose itself, or as the believing Jew holds, were chosen by God, to make humanity aware of the Supreme Moral Being. This is in fact what the Jews, often despite themselves, have done. Louis Jacobs discusses this in *A Jewish Theology:* "It becomes obvious that [regarding Jewish chosenness] we are not discussing a dogma incapable of verification but the recognition of sober historical fact. The world owes Israel the idea of the one God of righteousness and holiness. This is how God became known to mankind."[9]

Another reason why Jewish chosenness could never be understood as a doctrine of racial superiority is that by no accepted definition of either Jew or race, are the Jews a race. The Jewish people is composed of members of every race. It is a nation defined by its religion, not by its race. Hence anyone, of any race or nationality, can become a Jew *and thereby chosen.* Whoever assumes the Jewish task becomes a member of the chosen people. Since everyone can become chosen, chosenness cannot be racial. One might just as well speak of a race of ethical monotheists, or a Christian race. Jews are descendants of Abraham, a Mesopotamian. What rendered him a Jew were his beliefs, not his blood.

On innumerable occasions, Jewish literature, from the Bible to the Talmud to the most recent rabbinic writings, has emphasized that chosenness is a matter of values rather than of race. Jewish sources repeatedly portray Jews in negative ways (hardly the characteristic of people who consider themselves racially superior), and go out of their way to depict righteous non-Jews. To cite one dramatic instance, the first two chapters of the *Book of Exodus* imply that it was a *Jew* who reported Moses' killing of an Egyptian slave-master to the Pharaoh, and states that it was an *Egyptian,* Pharaoh's daughter, who saved Moses' life when he was an infant.

The incorporation of the *Book of Ruth* into the Bible demonstrates how unethnic Judaism and chosenness are. Ruth, born a pagan, chose to become a Jew, and is so highly regarded that the Jewish tradition has awarded her the distinction of having the future Messiah come from her family. That Ruth belonged to a different people has been as irrelevant to the Jewish people as the color of her hair. The rabbis of the Talmud likewise delighted in tracing the ancestry of some of their most illustrious teachers to non-Jews. They claimed, for example, that Rabbi Akiva, one of the greatest figures of the Talmud and the most famous martyr in Jewish history, was a descendant of converts, and that one of his ancestors was Sisera, the great military enemy of the Jews (as described in *Judges,* chap. 4).

Almost every nation sees itself as special in some sense—from the Chinese whose word for China is "center of the earth" to the Americans and their belief in "manifest destiny." Christians have believed that only Christians go to heaven, and Muslims see themselves as God's messengers. Yet of all the world's peoples it is the Jews whose doctrine of chosenness is the one that elicits the sharpest attacks. That is yet another unique aspect of the unique phenomenon known as Jew-hatred.

FOUR

The Higher Quality
of Jewish Life
as a Cause of Antisemitism

IN NEARLY EVERY SOCIETY in which the Jews have lived
for the past two thousand years, they have been better educated, more sober, more charitable with one another, committed far fewer violent crimes, and had a considerably more
stable family life than their non-Jewish neighbors. *These characteristics of Jewish life have been completely independent of
Jews' affluence or poverty.* As the noted Black economist
Thomas Sowell has concluded: "Even when the Jews lived in
slums, they were slums with a difference—lower alcoholism,
homicide, accidental death rates than other slums, or even
the city as a whole. Their children had lower truancy rates,
lower juvenile delinquency rates, and (by the 1930s) higher
IQs than other children. . . . There was also more voting for
congressmen by low income Jews than even by higher income
Protestants or Catholics. . . . Despite a voluminous literature
claiming that slums shape people's values, the Jews had their
own values, and they took those values into and out of the
slums."[1]

It is, of course, impossible to measure precisely to what extent the higher quality of Jews' lives has been a major cause of
antisemitism. Few antisemites list the Jews' good qualities as

46

reasons for attacking them. But it is human nature for individuals and groups who are perceived as better, however that may be understood, to elicit jealousy and resentment.

There are, as we shall see, specific reasons for believing that Jews generally have led higher quality lives (quite aside from questions of economic status), and that Judaism is responsible for that high level. In exploring that claim, we shall also see the role of Judaism in causing antisemitism.

JEWISH EDUCATIONAL AND PROFESSIONAL SUCCESS

The high level of Jewish intellectual and professional achievement in the Western world is the most obvious example of Jews successfully applying to the secular world a value they acquired from Judaism. Since its inception, Judaism has made study a *religious obligation* for its members. Unlike Christianity, for example, which required only its clergy to study,[2] among the Jews study was not only a commandment, but, along with charity, the supreme commandment. The biblical injunction "you shall teach your children" (*Deuteronomy* 6:7) was translated two thousand years ago into a system of universal education.[3] The Talmud legislated that every city was required to have schools and that no teacher could be assigned more than twenty-five students. The poor were to be taught free of charge. Parents were forbidden to live in a city without a school system, and if they spent time in such a place, the father bore full responsibility for his children's education.

The purpose of all this education was not to achieve professional and financial success (though in the contemporary world such commitment has brought Jews such rewards). Its purposes were religious and moral, to understand what God demanded of man. Thus, study was obligatory even when it was financially disadvantageous. In his code of Jewish law, Moses Maimonides ruled: "Every Jew is under an obligation to study Torah, whether he is poor or rich, in sound health or ailing, in the vigor of youth or very old and feeble. *Even a man so poor that he is maintained by charity or goes begging from door to door,* as also a man with a wife and children to support, are *under the obligation to set aside a definite period during the day and night for the study of the Torah.* . . . Until what period in life ought one to study Torah? Until the day of one's death. . . ."[4]

At a time when nearly all Christian and Muslim men, and certainly women, were illiterate, nearly all Jewish men and women could read and write, and many of them achieved high levels of knowledge. A twelfth-century monk who was a student of the great Catholic theologian, Abelard, reported that "A Jew, however poor, if he has ten sons, would put them all to letters, not for gain, as the Christians do, but for the understanding of God's Law, and not only his sons but his daughters."[5]

A letter, written in the same century in Egypt by a Jewish woman on her deathbed, exemplifies Abelard's description: "I tell you my sister . . . that I have fallen into a grievous disease and there is little possibility of recovering from it. . . . If the Lord on High should decree my death, my greatest wish is that you should take care of my little daughter and make an effort for her to study. Indeed I know that I am imposing a heavy burden on you. For we do not have the wherewithal for her upkeep, let alone the cost of tuition. But we have an example from our mother and teacher, the servant of the Lord."[6] The historian of medieval Jewry, Haim Hillel Ben-Sasson, has concluded: "Here is an instance of a Jewish family that was certainly not well-to-do in which the women of two generations were educated and saw to the education of their daughters."[7]

Because they believed that study was sacred, Jews made every effort to prolong their children's education. Whereas most of their poor non-Jewish neighbors put young children to work, Jewish parents, even when poor, strove to keep their children in school at least until Bar Mitzvah, thirteen. And once the children started working, no matter what their work, their education was expected to continue. The Jewish theologian Abraham Joshua Heschel quotes a Christian scholar who visited Warsaw during the First World War:

"Once I noticed a great many coaches on a parking place but with no drivers in sight. In my own country I would have known where to look for them. A young Jewish boy showed me the way; in a courtyard on the second floor was the *shtibl* [combination of synagogue and study hall] of the Jewish drivers. It consisted of two rooms, one filled with Talmud volumes, the other a room for prayer. All the drivers were engaged in fervent study and religious discussions. . . . It was then that I found out . . . that all professions, the bakers, the butchers, the shoemakers, etc., have their own *shtibl* in the Jewish district; and every free moment which can be taken off from work is given to the study of Torah."[8]

An old book saved from the millions of Jewish books burned by the Nazis, and now at the YIVO library in New York, bears the stamp THE SOCIETY OF WOODCHOPPERS FOR THE STUDY OF MISHNAH [the earliest part of the Talmud] IN BERDICHEV. That the men who chopped wood, an arduous job with low social status, met regularly to study Jewish law demonstrates the pervasiveness of study in the Jewish community.

In the modern world in which general education became widely available and the key to professional advancement, Jews, thanks to Judaism's tradition of intellectual achievement, were in a very advantageous position.

The secularization of this commitment to study among American Jews has produced remarkable results. It is not surprising that the American grandchildren of Jews such as the woodchoppers of Berdichev, though numbering less than 3 percent of the American population, have won 27 percent of the Nobel Prizes awarded American scientists, that Jews are overrepresented in medicine by 231 percent in proportion to the general population, in psychiatry by 478 percent, in dentistry by 299 percent, in law by 265 percent, and in mathematics by 238 percent,[9] that American Jews are twice as likely as non-Jews to go to college,[10] and that they are represented in Ivy League schools over five times their percentage in the population.[11] This Jewish passion for study in turn helps to explain why Jews have the highest income of any ethnic group in the United States, earning 72 percent more than the national average, and 40 percent more than the Japanese, the second highest earning ethnic group.[12]

This unique intellectual achievement is not due, as is sometimes alleged, to some innately superior intelligence among Jews, but solely and directly to Judaism. Though many Jews have ceased to keep the laws of Judaism, the belief in the need for education has remained a value to almost all Jews.

JEWS AND ALCOHOLISM

That Jews have a low rate of alcoholism has long been a part of both Jewish and non-Jewish folk wisdom. A well-known Yiddish folk song bears the title "A Drunkard Is a Non-Jew."

Is this perception of Jews and sobriety based on fact? At least until the recent past, yes. In 1925, separate studies were conducted in Warsaw and New York, comparing alcoholism among Jews and non-Jews. The Warsaw study revealed that non-Jews were 68.6 times as likely as Jews to be alcoholics, and in New York non-Jews were 59 times more likely than Jews to be admitted to hospitals for treatment of alcoholism.[13] Even more remarkable, the Jews achieved this phenomenally higher level of sobriety despite the fact that 87 percent of Jews drink liquor, whereas a 1950s study indicated that only 79 percent of Catholics and 59 percent of Protestants drink.[14]

How is this low level of alcoholism among Jews to be explained? The evidence again points to Judaism. Certainly no one can contend that there exists some genetic predisposition to sobriety on the part of Jews.

Judaism made drinking a *mitzvah* (religious obligation) and sanctified it (the *kiddush*), while drunkenness was deemed a sin. Jewish law thus encouraged and even commanded moderate drinking. The Psalmist's praise "Wine makes glad the heart of man" (104:15), along with the Talmudic dictum "There is no [meal of] joy except with wine," became popular adages in Jewish life. The Sabbath meals commence with the *kiddush* prayer over wine, in which even children participate. At the Passover Seder it is a *mitzvah* for each participant to drink *four* cups of wine.

On the other hand, in the words of the third-century Rabbi Yohanan, "A Jew should never have a passion for wine" (*Genesis Rabbah* 36:4). The Hebrew Bible and Judaism generally repeatedly warn against drunkenness. The story of Noah's drunkenness and its tragic results (*Genesis* 9:18–28) is read to the Jews at least once a year in synagogue. The prophets Hosea and Isaiah condemned drunkenness, and the biblical *Book of Proverbs* cataloged a variety of results from inebriety,[15] "including foolishness, poverty, woes, ravings, wounds, confusion and in the case of kings and princes perversions of justice."[16] Later the Talmud ruled that "A drunken person is forbidden to say the prayers. One who recites the prayers while drunk is like one who serves idols" (*Berakhot* 31B).

Anthropologist Raphael Patai concluded: "Since until the Enlightenment the Bible and Talmud were by far the most potent formative influences upon Jewish thinking, attitudes and values, one need not wonder that these sources acted as effective deterrents against inebriety. . . . Thus . . . deterrents on the negative side combined with traditional approval of moderate drinking, and the frequent ritual use of wine on the positive side, made wine a regular part of the God centered life of the traditional Jew and effectively removed it from the realm of dangerous excess or frenzy. One may say that the ritual use of wine immunized the Jews against drinking to the point of intoxication and thus against alcoholism."

That Jews' sobriety is a function of Judaism is attested to further by the enormous rise in alcoholism among Jews which has accompanied the corresponding decline in Jews' religiosity in recent years. Patai summarizes the various studies with the observation that "the traditional Jewish resistance to alcoholism is weakened to the extent to which Jews become assimilated to their Gentile environment." A comprehensive study of drinking patterns among students in New Haven, Connecticut, showed that as Jewish religious observance went from Orthodox to Conservative to Reform and then to secular and unaffiliated the pattern of drunkenness went from negligible to a percentage that was identical to the Protestant students.[17] In March 1976, Patai reports, Commissioner Jerome Hornblass of the New York City Addiction Services Agency called attention to data which showed that Jews with a strong commitment to Judaism or to the Jewish national causes had very low rates of alcoholism. However, among assimilated Jews rates of alcoholism had become virtually the same as among non-Jews.

When Jews dropped the *kiddush,* they dropped their model for moderate drinking.

JEWS AND CHARITY

Jews give a higher percentage of their income to charities and public causes, both Jewish and non-Jewish, than do non-Jews with comparable earnings.[18] Though Jews in the United States constitute only 2.6 percent of the American population, the United Jewish Appeal alone annually raises $300 million, making it one of the largest charities in the United States. This is remarkable considering that many charities appeal to a constituency almost forty times larger than does the UJA.

This disproportionate Jewish philanthropy is neither unique to American Jewry nor to the present time. Jewish communities have always been extraordinarily charitable. This is why Jews have always been less likely than non-Jews to be in need of food or clothing. For example, among the few thousand Jews living in seventeenth-century Rome seven charitable societies provided clothes, shoes, linens, and beds for the poor. Two other societies provided trousseaus for poor brides, another aided families struck by a sudden death, and yet another was responsible for visiting the sick. One special society collected charity for Jews in Israel, and another eleven groups raised money for Jewish educational and religious institutions.[19] One particularly dramatic, though not atypical, example of Jewish charitableness was in London in the early 1800s where about half of the Jewish community was supported by the contributions of the other half.[20]

This Jewish giving has not always made a favorable impression on non-Jews. While some have seen Jewish philanthropy as a model to emulate, many non-Jews have concluded that Jews must all have money, since extreme Jewish poverty is rarely encountered. In a seventeenth-century account of the Jews of North Africa, Christian observer Lancelot Addison warned against the erroneous belief that "Jews had no beggars." He attributed this misconception to the "regular and commendable way" in which the Jews supplied the needs of their poor and thus "concealed their poverty."[21]

The Talmudic declaration that "Charity is as important as all the other commandments together" (*Bava Bathra* 9A) indicates the importance of charity in Jewish life. Charity in Hebrew is *tzedaka,* meaning "justice." *Tzedaka* is a duty, an act of justice, and withholding *tzedaka* is not simply uncharitable, it is an injustice.

The Torah legislated that the poor be given a minimum of 10 percent of one's income, and in general it seems that Jews came close to observing this law. By the second century C.E. every Jewish community had a charity box, supervised by three trustees. Two respected members of the community went door to door each week to collect the 10 percent of each family's income. Those whom the Jewish court determined were not tithing were compelled to pay. In addition to cash, food and clothing were collected and distributed by special committees.[22]

Tzedaka laws also helped to reduce the number of Jews needing public funds. First, they obligated Jews to accept *tzedaka* only as a last resort—"Better [to earn money by] skinning an animal's carcass than by taking charity" was the Talmudic admonition (based on *Pesachim* 113A). Second, the highest form of *tzedaka* was to start a poor person in a business or profession so that he never again needs *tzedaka.* Finally, virtually every Jewish community has had a *gemilut hesed* society to provide interest-free loans—again to avoid poverty and the need for *tzedaka.*

As noted, many non-Jews have erroneously believed that all Jews have had money. But Jews have simply aided their needy more than other groups have aided theirs. This pattern continues. To cite one large-scale example, between 1948 and 1951, Israel almost doubled its population by absorbing 500,-000 penniless Jewish refugees who had fled the Arab world. The 600,000 Jews of Israel, with help from Jews elsewhere, housed, clothed, fed, educated, and provided a livelihood for these Jews. In contrast, at the very same time, an equal number of Palestinian refugees was left to virtual starvation by all the Arab states. *Non-Arabs* provided the large majority of the Arab refugees' aid.

Jewish aid to other Jews has led to the often heard attack "Jews only care for their own." Aside from being untrue, that is not the point. Those who make this charge are not so much complaining that "Jews only care for their own" as that "only Jews care for their own."

The Jewish Family

Judaism's insistence on the sanctity of the nuclear family differentiated the Jews from non-Jews more in ancient times than today. Even the Greeks, who had a more advanced culture than other ancient peoples, differed markedly from the Jews. Plato, in his *Republic* (Book V) and his *Laws* (Book V), on the basis of the Greek proverb "Friends have all things in common," advocated that everyone be friends without the need for nuclear families as we know them today. Lycurgus, credited as the formulator of Sparta's constitution, decreed that Spartans should give "their wives to those whom they should think fit, so that they might have children by them," and thereby produce strong soldiers for Sparta.[23] Similar ideas were offered by two other leading Greek philosophers, Zeno (late fourth and early third century B.C.E.), who founded the Stoic school in Athens, and Diogenes the Cynic.[24] The first-century writings of the leading scholars of Rome, Seneca, Juvenal, and Tacitus, portray a society filled with heterosexual and homosexual promiscuity. The Reform Jewish leader

Rabbi Abba Hillel Silver noted that study of Greek and Roman writings on the family "helps us to realize the violent contrast between the standards of [their] society and the Jewish standards of sexual decency, the sanctity of marriage and of family life."[25]

While Christianity profoundly and positively helped alter the ancient world's negativism toward the family, it, too, idealized nonfamily life, but in a very different way. Paul saw marriage as a concession to human weakness: "It is well for a man not to touch a woman. But because of the temptation to immorality, each man should have his own wife and each woman her own husband. . . . I say this by way of concession, not of command. I wish that all were as I myself am [unmarried]."[26] Two hundred years later, Origen, one of Christianity's most influential theologians, wrote that three sacrifices are pleasing to God: a martyr's death, voluntary celibacy, and abstinence from sexual intercourse on the part of married persons.[27]

At the same time, the rabbis of the Talmud were formulating an entirely different set of values for Jews. According to the Talmud, "Did you fulfill your duty with regard to establishing a family?" is among the first questions a Jew will be asked on his Day of Judgment. Basing themselves on the verse "Be fruitful and multiply" (*Genesis* 1:28), the rabbis declared that it was a Jew's obligation to have at least two children. A man could not be a high priest unless he was married, nor a member of the Jewish high court unless he had children, it being Judaism's belief that raising children humbled, humanized, and increased the wisdom of a judge.[28] Even among the Jewish mystics asceticism was never a value (as it was among Christian and Eastern mystics). The foremost scholar of Jewish mysticism, Gershom Scholem, has concluded: "At no time was sexual asceticism accorded the dignity of a religious value, and the mystics made no exception."[29]

The family was strengthened by other Jewish laws as well. The Jewish Sabbath, for example, is observed more in the home than in the synagogue. Its central religious rituals are fulfilled in the house: the Sabbath candles, the parental blessing of the children, the *kiddush* over the wine, the lengthy meal and concluding grace, and the custom that a husband and wife have sexual relations on Friday night.[30]

Judaism's effects on the Jewish family have been powerful. Sociologists have long noted that fewer Jewish families break up than do non-Jewish ones,[31] and that among families that stay intact, the members of Jewish families generally remain closer than do members of non-Jewish families.[32]

That Judaism has been the source of Jewish family values has been reconfirmed of late by the rates of divorce and spouse desertion among secular Jews, which are approximately the same as for the non-Jewish society.[33]

CONCLUSION

The higher quality of Jewish life is objectively verifiable. That it has provoked anti-Jewish sentiments especially, though not only, when accompanied by the Jews' commitments to God, law, nationhood, and chosenness, is not as easily proven. People rarely admit to envy as the cause of their resentment. Nevertheless, the link here is undeniable. Had the Jews been committed to being different and been social failures, few people would have bothered to hate them. It has been the Jews' very success that has made their being Jews so challenging. To put it another way, the Jews' belief in Jewish chosenness has provoked hostility because the quality of Jewish life has made Jews seem as if they really were chosen.

The higher quality of Jewish life has clearly provoked hostility. But it has done more: it has also made otherwise irrational charges against Jews sound plausible. It has rendered believable antisemitic accusations that Jews dominate the intellectual, economic, and political life of nations where they compose less than 5 percent of the population (usually much less—in pre-1933 Germany, for example, Jews constituted 1 percent of the population). As recently as 1975, the highest ranking military figure in the United States, General George Brown, Chairman of the Joint Chiefs of Staff, accused Jews of dominating American society through their ownership of the banking industry and the press. Brown's statements are factually false, but the nature of the false accusation he made is very revealing. Had Brown wanted to attack Blacks rather than Jews, it is unlikely that he would have leveled a similar charge, and equally doubtful that he would have been taken seriously. Yet such a charge when made against the Jews, though false, is not obviously false. Jews, after all, do have the highest earnings of any ethnic group in the United States, and they are greatly overrepresented in the most prestigious and well-paying professions.

Perhaps the best way to understand the admiration and resentment that the quality of Jewish life has elicited is to compare the reactions of the world to the higher quality of life in the United States. No country in the world has so many people seeking to live in it. At the same time, no country, *with the exception of Israel,* is the target of so many hateful and false attacks.

The United States, by its success and its ideals, challenges nearly all other countries. How did America, a nation composed largely of those rejected by other societies ("The wretched refuse of your teeming shore" declare the words at the base of the Statue of Liberty), become the most affluent and arguably the freest and most democratic society in the world? American historians generally attribute this success to the idealism and hard work of the country's founders and subsequent waves of immigrants. Enemies of America attribute it to the country's natural resources, just as many people attribute Jewish success to their unfair natural resource, alleged greater innate intelligence; or they claim that through capitalist exploitation America cheated poorer countries, paralleling charges that Jewish success has been attained through economic bloodsucking; or they invent an imperialist version of America's history and present, paralleling the anti-Jewish charge of a world Jewish conspiracy.*

But the United States is hardly the only society with great natural resources, and it has been perhaps the least imperialistic of the world's powers. Americans and their values, not

* This paralleling of America-hatred and Jew-hatred is not the authors' invention but that of America-haters throughout the world who constantly link "American imperialism and Zionism."

unfair resource distribution or world exploitation, have made
America better, just as Judaism and its values, not genetic ad-
vantage or economic conspiracies, account for the quality of
life led by Jews. And this quality of life of the two peoples has
provoked similar reactions—admiration by many, resentment
and hatred by more.

FIVE

Non-Jewish Jews
and Antisemitism

THROUGHOUT JEWISH HISTORY Jews have identified
with one or more of Judaism's components or converted to
another religion. Beginning in the nineteenth century and
through the present day, however, we encounter an entirely
new group of Jews. These people do not feel rooted in anything Jewish, religious or national; their Jewish identity consists of little more than having been born Jews, and they affirm none of Judaism's components. They remain Jews by
virtue of having not converted to another religion. These
people are non-Jewish Jews.[1]

Among non-Jewish Jews there have been some who, in addition to their alienation from Jewish roots, have not felt
rooted in the non-Jewish society in which they lived and who
in the course of the last century have helped to cause intense
Jew-hatred. These are radical and revolutionary Jews. It must
be understood that the reasons for the antisemitism they engender are unique. First, their challenges to non-Jews do not
come from within Judaism. Second, they not only challenge
the non-Jews' *values*, but the non-Jews' national and religious

59

identity as well. Third, they are as opposed to Jews' values and identity as to non-Jews'. Nevertheless, and unfortunately for other Jews, the behavior of these radical non-Jewish Jews is identified as Jewish behavior.

The association of Jews with revolutionary doctrines and ideological social upheaval has not, unfortunately, been the product of antisemites' imaginations. The names Marx,[2] Trotsky, Kamenev, Zinoviev, Luxemburg, Béla Kun, Mark Rudd, Abbie Hoffman, Jerry Rubin, Noam Chomsky, and others come immediately to mind. The phenomenon of the utterly disproportionate role played by Jews in Leftist revolutionary causes has often been commented upon. As Ernest van den Haag noted, "although very few Jews are radicals, very many radicals are Jews: out of one hundred Jews five may be radicals, but out of ten radicals five are likely to be Jewish. Thus it is incorrect to say that a very great number of Jews are radicals but quite correct to say that a disproportionate number of radicals are Jews. This was so in the past, and it has not changed."[3]

How are these Jewish radicals made and why do they cause antisemitism?

The making of a Jewish radical is a complex social and psychological process but its essential elements can be discerned. First, these Jews have inherited a tradition of thousands of years of Jews challenging others' values—though of course in the name of Judaism and ethical monotheism rather than radical secular ideologies. Of course, non-Jewish Jews do not base their radical doctrines on the Jewish tradition, indeed they usually denigrate it, but the tradition's impact could not be avoided, only transformed.[4]

Second, and most important, radical non-Jewish Jews are rootless. They do not feel rooted in either the Gentiles' religion or nation or the Jews' religion or nation, and they may very well have become revolutionaries in many instances precisely in order to overcome this rootlessness or alienation. Since they refuse to become like the non-Jews through identification with their traditional religious or national values, they seek to have the non-Jews become like them, alienated from traditional religious and national values. Only then will these revolutionaries cease to feel alienated.* These reflections on why non-Jewish Jews have flocked to the radical left have been made before. One of the leading sociologists in the United States, Stanford's Seymour Martin Lipset, writing in the late 1960s, when a disproportionate number of those active in the New Left were Jews—6o percent of the leadership of the Students for a Democratic Society, for example[5]— noted that "participation in the Socialist and Communist world meant for many Jews a way of escaping their Judaism, of assimilating into a universalistic non-Jewish world."[6]

A European historian, Peter Pulzer, has likewise noted the need for European Jews who had abandoned their Jewish roots to adopt the universalist, non-nationally rooted idea of socialism. Pulzer writes that it is mainly "those Jews who attempted to cut themselves most completely from their Jewish environment who became the Socialist leaders, such as Adler and Bauer in Austria, Singer and Kurt Eisner in Germany, Rosa Luxemburg in Poland and Germany, and Trotsky and Zinoviev in Russia."[7]

As a consequence of their lack of rootedness many non-Jewish Jews have felt it necessary to turn radical and work to tear down traditional and national values and institutions in the name of "universalism." Feeling no kinship, hence no responsibility, to any nation (only to "mankind"), they have not felt concerned with the consequences of such destructiveness. Neither the demoralization of the non-Jewish nation nor the resultant non-Jewish antipathy to Jews concerns these people. They feel part of neither community, only the "community of man."[8] Leon Trotsky, when asked whether he consid-

---

* There is a related problem of Jews who do feel Jewish but who are rootless in terms of religion. These secular Jews, like non-Jewish Jews, feel much more secure, much more rooted, when non-Jews become like them, secular. This is one major reason (the other is traditional Jewish fear of Christianity) why secular Jews have been in the vanguard of contemporary movements to secularize America. Religious Jews, on the other hand (despite the same fear of Christianity), tend to support more religious expression in the United States.

ered himself a Russian or a Jew, responded, "No, you are mistaken. I am a social-democrat. That's all."[9] Fifty years later, Jerry Rubin referred to himself and other American Jewish radicals as "ex-Amerikan [sic] ex-Jews."[10]

These Jews have been active in societies as diverse as the despotic and antisemitic Russia of the czars and the democracies of Weimar Germany and the United States. In Russia, non-Jewish Jews were so disproportionately represented in the less radical Menshevik wing of the Communist party that Stalin is reported to have said that with one large pogrom there would no longer be a Menshevik movement. Among the Bolsheviks there were fewer Jews than among the Mensheviks, though by 1922 they constituted 15 percent to 20 percent of the Bolshevik leadership.[11] After Lenin's death in 1924, the battle to succeed him took place among five men, Stalin, Bukharin, Trotsky, Kamenev, and Zinoviev. The latter three were non-Jewish Jews.

Certainly the Russian populace identified Marxism with Jews, and since a vast number of Russians and Ukrainians did not support Communism, popular identification of Jews with Communism terribly exacerbated already deep antisemitism among those two peoples. During the 1918–20 civil war that followed the Bolshevik Revolution, the anti-Communist Ukrainian fighters murdered 50,000 innocent Ukrainian Jews. Their anti-Jewish passions were raised by General Petlura who constantly referred to the Bolshevik armies under the leadership of "the Jew Trotsky."

Russian and Ukrainian Jews found themselves in an oft-repeated modern Jewish horror story: the Jews were hated by both sides. Had the Whites won the civil war, the Jews would have suffered terribly as a result of age-old Ukrainian and Russian antisemitism as well as the new popular association of Communism with Jews. The Communists emerged victorious, and under their rule the Jews have suffered terribly, since in addition to traditional Russian (and Ukrainian, and Lithuanian, and other) antisemitism, it has been a basic tenet of Marxism and Leninism that the Jewish nation should disappear through assimilation (see chap. 11). Thus the Russian

Jewish revolutionaries helped increase antisemitism both among Communists and among anti-Communists: among Communists by their advocacy of the disappearance of the Jewish nation, and among anti-Communists by the Jew-hatred which the Jewish Communists aroused. The only Jews who did not suffer from antisemitism, at least not immediately, were the Jewish Bolsheviks. As Moscow's Chief Rabbi Mazeh is reported to have said to Trotsky in 1920 after the latter refused to help Jews suffering from the civil war pogroms, "The Trotskys make the revolutions and the Bronsteins pay the price" (Trotsky's original name was Bronstein).

A related but almost forgotten chapter of Jewish revolutionary activity is the Soviet-inspired Hungarian revolution of 1919. Béla Kun, a Jew, established the short-lived Hungarian Soviet Republic in March 1919. Of the 48 people's commissars in his government, thirty were Jewish, as were 161 of its 202 highest officials.[12]

In Germany, until 1933 when Hitler came to power, the predominance of Jews on the revolutionary Left was as dramatic as in Russia. Unlike the radicals in Russia, however, in Germany the Left did not attain power.

But there is much to be learned from studying the German Jews of the Left prior to 1933, for while Nazi and German antisemitism was caused by factors far older and deeper than German Jewish radicalism, the radical non-Jewish Jews of the Weimar Republic greatly exacerbated German antisemitism and along with radical non-Jews helped to demoralize the Weimar democracy.

These Jewish radicals wielded a major influence over the cultural and intellectual life of Weimar Germany, an influence utterly disproportionate to their numbers. Among them were brilliant and successful satirists, writers, playwrights, artists, and orators, whose influence was seen by many Germans as destructive of German tradition, good and bad, and this perception (which is borne out in objective perspective) was a major component of Weimar German antisemitism. The great majority of German Jews voted for center parties in the Weimar Republic, but these Jews were not in the limelight; the non-Jewish Jews of the Left were, and they stood out as destroyers of everything German.

Foremost among those radicals who wielded such immense power over the intellectual and cultural life of Weimar Germany were those who convened around and published in the Berlin weekly *Die Weltbühne*. Of the *Weltbühne*'s sixty-eight writers whose religious origins could be established, forty-two were Jews. These were of course non-Jewish Jews, so non-Jewish that "only a few of the *Weltbühne* circle openly acknowledged that they were Jews."[13]

A sample of *Die Weltbühne* statements about Germany illustrates why German Jewish radicals helped to increase German antisemitism. The magazine utilized its prestige and the abundant talent of its writers and editors to *indiscriminately* attack German culture and national life. They were motivated not by an urge for reform; rather, they were attacking the very *idea* of the German nation itself.[14] The following statements were written by its most famous satirist and critic, its onetime editor, Kurt Tucholsky, a Jew:

> This country which I am allegedly betraying is not my country; this state is not my state; this legal system is not my legal system. Its different banners are to me as meaningless as are its provincial ideals. . . .
>
> We are traitor. But we betray a state that we disavow in favor of a land that we love, for peace and for our true fatherland: Europe.[15]

As Weimar historian Istvan Deak notes, "Tucholsky abominated the majority of his fellow citizens. Princes, barons, Junkers, officers, policemen, judges, officials, clergymen, academicians, teachers, capitalists, *Bürger*, university students, peasants and all Bavarians he condemned collectively."[16] According to Tucholsky the only thing in Germany worth loving was the countryside.

While some of the left-wing intellectuals' criticisms were specific, pointing to genuine weaknesses, their overall attacks were perceived by the overwhelming majority of Germans, including anti-Nazis, as purely destructive. And today, when one reads excerpts from old issues of *Die Weltbühne*, it is difficult not to share the same reactions. "The left-wing intellectuals opposed the Weimar Republic all along the line," writes George Mosse, one of the foremost historians of modern Germany, "without providing what might prove to be a viable alternative method of change. Thus they tended to become critics rather than builders and in that process alienated, almost masochistically, large parts of the intellectual community from a state which, for all its injustices, provided an almost unprecedented freedom of expression and political action."[17]

Indeed possibly the only nationalism that these non-Jewish Jews hated as much as the Germans' was the Jews'. As late as 1932, *Die Weltbühne* published an article entitled "Hitler in Jerusalem," which likened Zionism to Nazism.[18] As Mosse explains, these non-Jewish Jews "wanted to be not Jews, but part of the progressive brotherhood of all humanity. . . . [this] made them impassioned enemies of Zionism."[19]

Tucholsky later fled to Sweden where during the war he committed suicide. But his ideological heirs live on in the United States where, again, non-Jewish Jews have played a dominant role in attacking American (and Jewish) nationalism.

While it has long been a tradition in America, as it was in Europe, for intellectuals to assume an adversary role in relation to established institutions, perhaps nowhere has the adversary role been so outspoken as among the intellectuals of the Left—as strident and garrulous a group as one could imagine. And since few of these have seemed as shrill as the Jewish intellectuals of the radical Left, it was perhaps inevitable that many of them would be received by the general public as unequivocably hostile to everything American. Since the 1930s a highly visible percentage of people on what has been perceived by many as the American-hating Left has been Jewish. While the overwhelming majority of American Jews identify themselves as politically moderate, some Jews have been as identified with destructive attacks on America as were radical Jews in Weimar Germany. And like their

German and Russian predecessors, these Jews have nearly always been non-Jewish Jews, equally hostile to Jewish and American rootedness.*

In the 1930s and 1940s non-Jewish Jews were among the leading pro-Soviet and anti-American agitators. During these two decades Jews constituted half of the membership of the American Communist party.† Two alienated Jews, Julius and Ethel Rosenberg, were convicted of playing key roles in smuggling America's atom bomb technology to Stalin. Since the 1960s non-Jewish Jews have been among the leading radical opponents of virtually everything American. In 1970, a Harris study showed that 23 percent of Jewish college students termed themselves "far Left" versus 4 percent of Protestants and 2 percent of Catholics. A national survey sponsored by the American Council of Education in 1966–67 revealed that the "best single predictor of campus protest was the presence of a substantial number of students from Jewish families." A study by Joseph Adelson in the early 1960s of politics and personality at the University of Michigan revealed that 90 percent of the radical students came from Jewish backgrounds.[20]

Their similarity to the non-Jewish Jews who attacked Weimar Germany is remarkable. For example, just as the only thing about democratic Germany that Kurt Tucholsky could admit to liking was its scenery, so, too, leftist philosopher Herbert Marcuse (who declared the United States to be Fascist) could find only one beautiful thing about America: its scenery. A 1971 article in *The New York Times Book Review*,

---

* A recent study of radical students revealed that among Jewish radicals 92 percent termed themselves either hostile or indifferent toward Judaism. See Stanley Rothman and S. Robert Lichter, *Roots of Radicalism: Jews, Christians and the New Left*, p. 410.

† Nathan Glazer, *The Social Basis of American Communism*, chap. 4. Glazer and Daniel Patrick Moynihan also point out, however, that the Jews were the dominant group among the Socialists who opposed the Communists and among the intellectual opposition to the Communists. "When the Cold War broke out, they inevitably supplied a good number of the experts—who else had spent their college (and even high school) years fighting the Stalinists?" (*Beyond the Melting Pot*, p. lx.)

reported this in an interview with Marcuse: "When Professor Marcuse, who had insisted that he loved and understood America, was pressed to specify which aspects of American life he found attractive, he fumbled for an answer, said he loved the hippies, with their long hair, and after some more fumbling, mentioned the beautiful American scenery, threatened by pollution. Despite an obvious effort, he could think of no other items."[21]

A reader of Noam Chomsky's political writings might very well conclude that the most evil nations are the United States and Israel. They are the target of nearly all his invective, and in his most recent book he denies that Israel is a democracy or that it could even become one.[22] Every chapter in this book concerns American or Israeli evils. Typical of his statements about the evil nature of America was his statement in *The New York Review of Books* during the war in Vietnam that the U.S. Defense Department is "the most hideous institution on earth."[23] As regards the Jews and Zionism, Chomsky has become so hostile that in 1980 he defended the publication of a book written by a French neo-Nazi professor who claimed that the Holocaust was a fiction made up by Zionists. Chomsky's defense was subsequently published as the introduction to the book. Chomsky claims that he was merely defending the French professor's academic freedom. But when Herbert Mitgang of *The New York Times* asked Chomsky to comment on the professor's views, Chomsky noted that he had no views he wished to state. As Martin Peretz, editor of *The New Republic,* has noted: "On the question, that is, as to whether or not six million Jews were murdered, Noam Chomsky apparently is an agnostic."[24]

In the 1960s and early 1970s *The New York Review of Books* could be labeled an American *Die Weltbühne*. It was and still is edited by Robert B. Silvers and Barbara Epstein, most of its political writers were Jews, and its tone, in the words of Irving Howe, a Democratic Socialist and identifying Jew, was a "snappish crude anti-Americanism."[25] Journalist Richard Rovere summarized the *Review*'s attitude toward America: ". . . their American politics are Stone's and Chomsky's."[26]

The Stone mentioned in Rovere's assessment is I. F. Stone (Isidor Feinstein Stone), contributing editor of *The New York Review of Books,* and for half a century a major American journalist. Stone has to this day devoted his considerable journalistic talents to attacking American policies, and, since 1967, Zionism and Israel. Stone's negative view of America is made evident by the overwhelming proportion of his essays that attack American policies, by the few that ever defend or praise anything American, and by the few that criticize America's adversaries. In his book *Hidden History of the Korean War,* Stone accuses the United States of equal responsibility with China for starting that war. As regards Israel, since 1967 Stone has announced that "I feel honor-bound to report the Arab side, especially since the U.S. press is so overwhelmingly pro-Zionist."[27] This implication that Jews (or Zionists) dominate and prejudice the American press has, of course, long been a theme of antisemitism. As for Stone's honor-bound obligation to report the Arab side, Martin Peretz has written: "One would think that a writer's compulsion would be to tell the truth, regardless of whether it has been aired or not."[28] It is worth noting that as the Arab position increasingly became the only position heard on the Left, Stone did not experience an honor-bound obligation to report the Israeli side. During the 1970s and 1980s he increased his anti-Israel rhetoric.

Jason Epstein of the *Review*'s governing board echoed the *Weltbühne*'s view of the Weimar Republic, the German people, and its culture, in his description of the American Republic and its people and culture. Epstein found America a sick civilization. Each morning on his way to work he was oppressed by the sight, as he put it, of "so much dead culture . . . where, in the deepest winter . . . lines of New Jerseyites and others—thousands of them—stand in rows, uncomfortable, patient, grinning."[29] So worthless is American life in Epstein's view that he sympathetically portrayed the mind-set of the terrorist Weathermen. Epstein wrote that the Weathermen have been suppressed by an American "culture that has perverted and collectivized their energies and converted them to purposes of mass killing, leaving its individual members psychologically feeble and thus unable to confront their brutal culture with sufficient force."[30]

A similar if not quite as extreme view of American culture is noted, by Ben Stein in *The View from Sunset Boulevard,* among the people who write and produce American television programs and their attitudes toward America: "A distinct majority [of the producers and writers] is Jewish. . . . TV writers and producers do not hold criminals responsible for crimes but rather place the blame on [American] society. . . . Middle-class people appear generally as either heavies or fools. . . ." These producers and writers hold that "religion is trivial and unimportant" and when depicted as significant "we see religion as sinister . . ." And echoing Tucholsky's descriptions of Weimar's respected groups, "the sum of it is that groups that have leadership or power roles—businessmen, bankers, government leaders, military men, religious figures—are treated as bad or irrelevant."[31]

No hater of Weimar Germany described that society in more destructive terms than Norman Mailer has described America: "We kill the spirit here [in America]. . . . We use psychic bullets and kill each other cell by cell. . . . We have a tyranny here. . . . We have been fighting with sick dead hearts against the cold insidious cancer of the power that governs us. . . . our police, our secret police, our corporations, our empty politicians, our clergymen, our editors and cold frightened bullies who govern a machine made out of people they no longer understand."[32]

There are innumerable other examples of radical non-Jewish Jews in America, particularly among journalists, writers, and professors whose basic attitude toward American society is one of hostility.[*]

---

[*] Two Jewish political scientists, Stanley Rothman of Smith College and S. Robert Lichter of George Washington University, who have recently published a major study of American radicalism, *Roots of Radicalism: Jews, Christians and the New Left,* write: "The basic thrust [of a radical] is to undermine all aspects of the *culture* which contribute to his or her marginality. Thus Jews in the United States and Europe have been in the forefront of not only political radicalism but also various forms of cultural 'subversion.' The *Weltbuhne* circle

This problem of a small number of non-Jewish Jews destroying their own and the non-Jews' roots has been recently commented upon by others. This destructive phenomenon was most clearly described by the prominent modern historian Walter Laqueur in an essay entitled "The Tucholsky Complaint."[33] It has also been commented upon by the distinguished political scientist Leonard Schapiro: "Why were there so many Jews among the intellectuals searching for utopia in Russia, China, or Cuba, *and motivated in their search by hatred of the United States?* Perhaps simply because the proportion of Jews among all intellectuals is generally high? Or is there some more profound reason?"[34]

The problem of radical non-Jewish Jews is a painful and obvious one to Jews, so obvious that most of the writings about their harmful roles come from other Jews—Walter Laqueur, Leonard Schapiro, Nathan Glazer, Ben Stein, Stanley Rothman, and S. Robert Lichter, to cite only those people quoted in this chapter. There is, however, one other group concerned with the writings of radical non-Jewish Jews—antisemites, who attribute the destructive words and actions of these Jews to all Jews.

---

played this role in the Weimar Republic. In America there was a tradition of literary criticism. Nevertheless, in the 1960s deracinated Jewish authors such as E. L. Doctorow, Joseph Heller, and Norman Mailer were disproportionately represented among those whose critical efforts, even when not overtly political, were designed to demonstrate the 'sickness' of the society. . . . Often such subversion involves an attack upon genuine inequities or irrationalities. Since all societies abound in both, there is never an absence of targets. However, the attack is generally not directed at the particular inequity or irrationality per se. Rather such inequities or irrationalities are used as a means for achieving a larger purpose: the general weakening of the social order itself" (p. 130).

Other Theories
of Antisemitism

FOR NEARLY ALL of Jewish history people recognized that antisemitism was a reaction to the Jews and Judaism. But today Jew-hatred is generally attributed to factors having little to do with Jews and Judaism. The causes of antisemitism are generally held to be economics, political use of the Jews as scapegoats, general ethnic prejudice, the psychopathology of hate, and human irrationality—all of which dejudaize Jew-hatred.

Among those most committed to these dejudaizing interpretations of Jew-hatred are secular and non-Jewish Jews who are committed to the notion that Jews are not essentially different from all other people. Accordingly, they want to believe that antisemitism is but another form of bigotry, that it is not permanent, that in the secular world it will die out, that there are no rational reasons for Jew-hatred, and/or that antisemitism is a sickness. Another reason why many modern Jews believe in these explanations for Jew-hatred, rather than in the one held by Jews for thousands of years, is simply that the dejudaizing explanations are more or less the only ones offered. Modern scholars tend to seek and to teach secular and universalist explanations for nearly all human problems, including, of course, antisemitism; and the traditional Jewish understanding of antisemitism has been the opposite—religious and particularist.

Among modern scholars there is a high number of Jews whose universalist world views make them particularly averse to the Jewish explanation of Jew-hatred. Indeed they oppose any thesis, about anything, not only antisemitism, that depicts the Jews as distinctive, let alone unique. Accordingly, they have expended great efforts to prove that the Jews are not different from anyone else.[1]

The dejudaization of antisemitism reached its nadir in the rewriting of the most famous document of the Holocaust, *The Diary of Anne Frank*. As an adolescent in Amsterdam Anne Frank and her family spent more than two years hiding before being captured by the Nazis. During this time Anne Frank kept a diary which was found and published after the war.

Though raised in a secular and assimilationist home, Anne came to feel during her years in hiding that there were specific Jewish reasons for the suffering she and other Jews were undergoing. On April 11, 1944, she wrote: "Who has inflicted this upon us? Who has made us Jews different from all other people? Who has allowed us to suffer so terribly up till now? It is God who has made us as we are, but it will be God, too, who will raise us up again. If we bear all this suffering and if there are still Jews left, when it is over, then Jews, instead of being doomed, will be held up as an example. Who knows, it might even be our religion from which the world and all peoples learn good, and for that reason and that reason only do we now suffer. We can never become just Netherlanders, or just English, or representatives of any country for that matter. We will always remain Jews, but we want to, too." Anne Frank's thesis that Judaism was at the root of Jew-hatred and that the Jews were different was eliminated in the Broadway version of *The Diary of Anne Frank*, written by Alfred and Francis Hackett with the advice of the radical Jewish playwright Lillian Hellman. They simply deleted Anne's statement which had been central to Anne's thinking and to

Meyer Levin's original version of the play, and instead put into her mouth words she had never said but which reflected their own universalist views: "We are not the only people that have had to suffer . . . sometimes one race sometimes another."

The Hacketts thus presented their dejudaized interpretation of antisemitism in place of the Jewish interpretation offered by Anne Frank that the Jews are hated precisely because of Judaism.

JEWS AS SCAPEGOATS

The universalization of antisemitism into one more example of ethnic hatred is only one of several dejudaizing explanations for antisemitism.

Perhaps the most widely held interpretation of antisemitism, the scapegoat theory, thoroughly dejudaizes antisemitism; it posits that Jews are merely convenient targets for a society in trouble. Antisemitism is orchestrated by the society's leaders in order to direct popular discontent away from themselves. For example, the pogroms against Jews in late-nineteenth- and early-twentieth-century Russia were often fomented by the czar and his ministers in order to divert oppressed Russians' resentment from them. The Nazis, too, are believed by many to have used Jew-hatred as a tactical device to achieve power.

The major fallacy of the scapegoat theory is not that Jews have not been used as scapegoats. They have. The problem with the scapegoat thesis is that it does not explain antisemitism. It only explains why, when, or how people *use* antisemitism—not why they are antisemitic. It does not even purport to answer the question, why the Jews—why, to begin with, do people hate Jews? What is it about this small group that enables so many people to believe the most horrible accusations leveled against them?[2]

The authors have asked many Jews how they understand Nazi antisemitism and the Holocaust. Overwhelmingly the responders cite the scapegoat theory: the Nazis blamed Germany's problems on the Jews and used antisemitism to gain power.

The widespread belief in the scapegoat theory to help explain the Holocaust is remarkable because Nazi Jew-hatred was an end, not a means. Hitler was so preoccupied with Jews that he withdrew troops and vehicles from the war fronts so that the killing of European Jewry would not slacken. The killing itself proves that Hitler did not view the Jews as scapegoats. If the Jews had been only scapegoats, then why murder them? Why not, let us say, compel them to do forced labor? Instead, Hitler ordered the overwhelming majority of Jews to be immediately murdered, and those who were used as slave labor by the Nazis were treated so abominably that most died within a few months. Antisemitism was not a vehicle for the Nazis; Nazism was a vehicle for antisemitism.

The real question to be asked is why the Jews? And this question is untouched by the scapegoat thesis.

ECONOMIC EXPLANATIONS

Among the theories of antisemitism are various economic explanations. Jew-hatred in medieval Europe, for example, is said to have been a reaction to the Jews having been usurious moneylenders. Elsewhere Jews evoked Jew-hatred because they collected taxes from poor peasants on behalf of corrupt landowners. The Jews' identification with capitalism in Europe is cited as yet another economic cause of antisemitism. And in the modern period, the Jews' disproportionate wealth and concentration in business and professions is said to provoke anti-Jewish hostility.

Of course, the purest version of economic theories of antisemitism is Marxist. While it has variations, the Marxist theme is that capitalist society inevitably causes Jew-hatred. The ruling classes direct worker discontent onto the Jews, and since many Jews are visible capitalists they will in any case elicit worker hostility.

Now it is undeniable that economic factors can and often do exacerbate antisemitism, and that they often create crises in which antisemites may flourish. After all, economic factors impinge on virtually all aspects of society, and when an economic crisis occurs, the resultant social crisis may unleash many of the worst aspects of a society. Among these is Jew-hatred. But economic factors do not create Jew-hatred. *They provide opportunities for it to be expressed.* And under certain circumstances the economic position of Jews will exacerbate the Jew-hatred. But economic factors do not *cause* Jew-hatred.

For one thing, there is little, if any, correlation between Jews' wealth and antisemitism. Jews have often suffered the worst antisemitism when they were poor, as was true of the overwhelming majority of Jews in nineteenth- and twentieth-century Poland and Russia, and have encountered the least amount of antisemitism when affluent, as in the United States and Canada today.

As regards attributing medieval antisemitism to the Jews' role as moneylenders, we have here a classic example of putting the cart before the horse. In medieval Europe, as a result of Christian antisemitism, Jews were often denied the right to practice professions other than moneylending. *Jews were not hated because they lent money; they lent money because they were hated.* Obviously, once Jews became moneylenders Jew-hatred was exacerbated.

Nor was that the only time when the Jews' economic status exacerbated antisemitism. In many societies Jews, because of antisemitism, have played economic roles which could only intensify hostility to them. But Jew-hatred preceded these economic factors and it is so much deeper than any economic factors that to ascribe antisemitism to economics is a materialist reduction of theology, human passions, moral values, nationalism, and whatever else animates human beings. Antisemites have equally hated poor Jews and rich Jews, and they ceased hating rich Jews not when they became poor Jews, but when they became rich members of the antisemites' religion or cause.

As regards the Marxist notions that antisemitism is caused

by capitalism and that socialism will eliminate antisemitism, suffice it to say that both socialist theory and socialist countries have fostered terrible Jew-hatred.

In all our research we could find no major instance of a society's antisemitism created by economic factors. In each case, pagan, Christian, Muslim, Enlightenment, Nazi, Communist, and contemporary anti-Zionist antisemitism, factors unrelated to economics have been at the root of Jew-hatred. In every one of these instances, two groups would have found absurd the attribution of antisemitism to economics: the antisemites and their Jewish victims.[3]

HANNAH ARENDT'S ECONOMIC EXPLANATION

In the 1950s political scientist and philosopher Hannah Arendt offered a novel economic interpretation of modern antisemitism. In her classic *The Origins of Totalitarianism* she argued that modern antisemitism was something new, basically unrelated to pre-nineteenth-century Jew-hatred. As Europe's nation-states developed in the nineteenth century, national leaders found that they could dispense with the court Jews and wealthy Jewish bankers who had been so important until then. In the modern era, the Jews no longer filled their previous economic functions and became superfluous. In Arendt's words: "Wealth without visible function is much more intolerable because nobody can understand why it should be tolerated. Antisemitism reached its peak when Jews had similarly lost their public functions and their influence and were left with nothing but their wealth."[4] Thus the Jews and their functionless wealth bred the antisemitism which culminated in the Holocaust.

Even if Arendt were entirely correct, her analysis only applies to late-nineteenth- and early-twentieth-century antisemitism in Europe. It in no way explains 2,000 years of Jew-hatred throughout the world. As Columbia University historian Arthur Hertzberg writes, "Hannah Arendt was eager to avoid the notion of an eternal anti-Semitism."[5] And was Auschwitz really the result of superfluous Jewish wealth in modern Europe? Or, as Hertzberg puts it, "is it conceivable that the enormous power of this hatred was bred in a few short years and decades? Did the new antisemitism of the nineteenth century really arise essentially out of the contemporary historical situation?"[6]

PSYCHOLOGICAL EXPLANATIONS

Psychological explanations of antisemitism have become very popular in the recent past. Given the widespread belief that psychology can ultimately account for nearly all human behavior, this is to be expected. But there are additional reasons why psychological explanations of antisemitism are so attractive, especially to Jews. Most important, they give cause for optimism. By describing Jew-hatred as a psychological abnormality and labeling antisemites sick, psychology renders antisemitism curable, and it enables Jews to feel comfortable with their neighbors. If antisemites are sick people, then Jews have nothing to fear from the normal men and women among whom they live. An additional comfort to many is that psychological explanations universalize and thus dejudaize Jew-hatred. They place it under the general heading "prejudice," and they make the abnormality of the antisemites rather than the Jewishness of the Jews the cause of Jew-hatred.

The most widely acclaimed psychological explanation of antisemitism is to be found in a multivolume work on prejudice commissioned by the American Jewish Committee. The preface to the study's major volume, *The Authoritarian Personality*,[7] summarizes the study's thesis: "The central theme of the work is a relatively new concept—the rise of an 'anthropological' species we call the authoritarian type of man.... He seems to combine the ideas and skills ... of a highly industrialized society with irrational or anti-rational beliefs.... This book approaches the problem with the means of socio-psychological research."[8]

The entire study revolves around this theme, that prejudiced people are sick and irrational. And, of course, antisemitism is regarded throughout as another form of prejudice, though perhaps a more virulent one than others. This is reflected in the title of and contents of another volume in this work, *Anti-Semites and Emotional Disorders*. A third volume, *Dynamics of Prejudice* by Bettelheim and Janowitz, analyzes the connection between personality traits and prejudice; and a fourth volume, *Prophets of Deceit*, attempts to "expose the psychological tricks" used by demagogues to attain power.

In 1954, four years after the publication of the American Jewish Committee's study of prejudice, the most widely acclaimed book ever on that subject was published, *The Nature of Prejudice*, by Harvard psychologist Gordon Allport. The essential thesis of his work, which includes substantial discussions of antisemitism, is that prejudiced people are psychologically abnormal. In the preface to his work, Allport refers to the long and tragic history of group hatreds, but he concludes: "Yet the situation is not without its hopeful features. Chief among them is the simple fact that human nature seems, on the whole, to prefer the sight of kindness and friendliness to the sight of cruelty. Normal men everywhere reject, in principle and by preference, the path of war and destruction. They like to live in peace and friendship with their neighbors."[9]

Thus, ten years after the Holocaust, antisemitism was declared a prejudice and Jew-haters were pronounced sick by a preeminent organization of American Jewry and a preeminent psychologist of Harvard University.

This explanation of Jew-hatred generally and of the Holocaust specifically must have come as welcome news to Jewry after Auschwitz. The Nazis were sick, as are all deeply prejudiced people. That was the lesson to be learned. There was one other lesson for American Jews which the authors of *The Authoritarian Personality* noted, "The major concern [is] with the potentially fascistic individual...."[10] Antisemitism is a function of Fascism, and the danger to Jews is on the Right. Hitler was a Fascist, therefore the Right is the threat to Jews. But this single-minded concern with Fascist individuals has been misplaced. Why not equal concern with Communist antisemites? The lesson which those authors, like so many contemporary Jews, have drawn from the Holocaust is that six million Jews were murdered because their murderers were sick and Fascist—not because the six million were Jews.

While there is little doubt that Adolf Hitler and many of his associates were psychologically disturbed, this fact did not cause antisemitism, let alone the Holocaust. Were the tens of millions of Germans and other Europeans who supported Nazi antisemitism also sick? Did tens of millions of Christians in medieval Europe hate Jews because they were sick? Is Soviet antisemitism a function of some psychosis? Is the Muslim world psychopathological because it wants the Jewish state destroyed? And have Egyptians since signing a peace treaty with the Jewish state been psychologically transformed?

We do not hold that antisemites are models of psychological health. But until we recognize that it is possible to be psychologically unhealthy and not be an antisemite, and that to be antisemitic does not necessarily imply psychopathology, we will never be able to combat antisemitism. Antisemitism is evil, and evil is not necessarily sick. Unfortunately.

SARTRE'S EXPLANATION

All the attempts to dejudaize Jew-hatred reach their climax in what may be the most widely read modern explanation of antisemitism, Jean-Paul Sartre's *Anti-Semite and Jew.*[11] In this work, the Nobel Prize–winning French philosopher offers all the major dejudaizing explanations for antisemitism cited in this chapter: the use of Jews as scapegoats, typical ethnic prejudice, economic (especially capitalist) reasons, and the psychological problems of antisemites. "The Jew," he writes, "only serves [the antisemite] as a pretext; elsewhere his counterpart will make use of the Negro or the man of yellow skin."[12] Elsewhere he labels antisemitism a capitalist problem: "What is there to say except that the socialist revolution is necessary and *sufficient* for the suppression of the anti-Semite?" (our emphasis). But Sartre goes beyond all others in dejudaizing Jew-hatred. Not only does he hold that the Jews are not the *cause* of Jew-hatred, he holds that the

Jews are not even the *object* of Jew-hatred. As he writes: "the anti-Semite . . . is a man who [is] afraid. Not of the Jews to be sure, but of himself, of his own consciousness, of his liberty . . . of everything except the Jews."[13]

Sartre then goes even further, taking his complete dejudaization of Jew-hatred to its logical conclusion: the dejudaization of the Jew. Jews, being neither the cause nor even the object of Jew-hatred, do not really exist. They are made to feel as Jews by Jew-haters (who, of course, do not hate Jews but themselves). "The Jew," writes Sartre, "is one whom other men consider a Jew. . . . It is the anti-Semite who makes the Jew. . . . It is neither their past, their religion, nor their soil, that unites the sons of Israel. . . . The sole tie that binds them is the hostility and disdain of the societies which surround them."[14]

With Sartre's thesis, then, modern interpretations of antisemitism, all of which seek to deny anything specifically Jewish to Jew-hatred, reach their incredible conclusion: Jews do not cause antisemitism, Jews are not hated by antisemites, Jews do not actually have their own existence; Jew-haters have invented them.

For well over two thousand years people have hated a group which does not really exist outside of the haters' minds. "We [non-Jews] have created this variety of men who have no meaning [except as scapegoats)."[15] Thus concludes Jean-Paul Sartre, one of the esteemed minds of the twentieth century.

When you ask the wrong questions, you get wrong answers. That is what happens when you ask for an explanation of Jew-hatred that starts with the belief that it is not a response to Jews and Judaism.

PART TWO

The Historical Evidence

The purpose of part two is to document the thesis—the traditional Jewish view—that Judaism, with its distinctiveness and moral challenge, is at the root of Jew-hatred. It is not intended to imply that all Christians, Muslims, pagans, or men of the Enlightenment (as opposed to Nazis or contemporary "anti-Zionists") were enemies of the Jews, but only to explain the anti-semitism of those who were.

SEVEN

Antisemitism in the Ancient World

PHILOSTRATUS, A THIRD-CENTURY TEACHER and resident of Athens and Rome, summarized the pagan world's perception of the Jews: "For the Jews have long been in revolt not only against the Romans, but against humanity; and a race that has made its own life apart and irreconcilable, that cannot share with the rest of mankind in the pleasures of the table nor join in their libations or prayers or sacrifices, are separated from ourselves by a greater gulf than divides us from Sura or Bactra of the more distant Indies."[1]

In the pagan world, the Jews' God and laws were clearly the causes of Jew-hatred. Pagans generally tolerated different peoples and different gods, but the Jews and "their" God did not merely differ, they threatened. The Jews' God alone was God, and He was the God everywhere—which meant, of course, that all gods of the pagans were false. Understandably, this infuriated the Jews' neighbors. No nation or religion had ever made such audacious claims. As the historian of the classical world, Yitzhak Heinemann, has described it: "no other nation at that time denied the gods of its neighbors. . . . None of the peoples refrained from partaking of the sacrifices offered to the gods, except the Jews. None of the peoples refused to send gifts to its neighbors' temples, except the Jews."[2] As the first-century Greek writer, Apion, protested: "Why, if they [the Jews] are citizens, do they not worship the same gods. . . ?"[3]

The Jews' laws, too, angered their neighbors. For example, the Jewish dietary laws restricted what and where Jews ate, and many non-Jews interpreted the Jewish refusal to eat with them as motivated by hostility. So, too, they interpreted Judaism's ban on intermarriage as hostile.

The Jews of the pre-Christian world were hated because they were Jews, not because they were rich, or successful, or for any other reason not directly related to their Judaism. If a Jew ceased practicing Judaism and adopted the majority culture's religion, he was not persecuted. A Jew who was willing to give up Judaism to worship and respect his neighbor's gods, to eat his neighbor's food, to marry his neighbor's child, and, in short, to cease challenging the non-Jews' values was accepted by the surrounding pagan society. Jews were rejected and characterized as haters of mankind because they practiced Judaism.

The Hellenic World

The first non-Jewish record of antisemitism dates from Alexandria, Egypt, where in the third-century B.C.E., many Greeks and Jews had migrated as a result of Alexander's conquest of Egypt.

Given the human propensity to resent strangers, it is not surprising that the indigenous Egyptian population came to resent the Jewish immigrants. What is noteworthy, however, is that the Egyptians bore much greater animosity toward the Jews than toward the other foreigners, the Greeks. Apparently, the Egyptians' dislike of the Jews was deeper than the usual hostility toward foreigners.

The Egyptians found the Jews' religious culture and traditions offensive. One prominent example was the Egyptian priest, Manetho, who, annoyed by the Jews' liturgy and Bible (which had just been translated into Greek) with their depictions of the Jews' exodus from Egypt, decided to rewrite that event. According to Manetho, the Jews did not flee Egypt, but were expelled because they were lepers.*

In succeeding generations, the Alexandrians developed other antisemitic themes. In addition to spreading leprosy, the Jews were accused of hating all other people, a charge that became one of the most often repeated in Jewish history. The Jews were also accused of being atheists because they worshiped a God that no one, themselves included, had ever seen, while dismissing all visible gods as false.

Lysimachus, an Egyptian historian of the second or first century B.C.E., summarized the perceptions held about the Jews. "Moses exhorted them to show kindliness to no one, to follow only the worst advice, and overthrow all the sanctuaries and altars of the gods they might come upon."[4]

In 167 B.C.E., the first recorded antisemitic persecution in the postbiblical period took place. The Hellenic ruler of Syria and Palestine, Antiochus Epiphanes, incited in part by certain assimilated Jews, attempted to destroy Judaism, which he correctly perceived as the basis of the Jewish opposition to his leadership. Owing to their religious beliefs, the Jews rejected Antiochus' claim to being the "god manifest" ("Epiphanes" in Greek). Consequently, according to the biblical Apocrypha, Antiochus sent an emissary to Judea "in order to force the Jews to transgress the laws of their fathers and not to live according to God's commandments" (*Maccabees II* 6:11). He renamed the Holy Temple in Jerusalem after Zeus Olympus, prohibited the observance of the Sabbath and circumcision, and forced the Jews to participate in the festival procession in honor of Dionysus.[5]

Antiochus' action was virtually without precedent for a

---

* The absence of any historical basis for Manetho's statements did not deter later anti-Jewish writers from repeating this accusation. In the first century, the leading historian of Rome, Tacitus, recorded that the Jews had apparently been expelled from Egypt as lepers (*The Histories*, 5:3). Two thousand years after Manetho, the eighteenth-century leader of the Enlightenment, Voltaire, repeated the same slander. A century later, the libel was repeated in a letter of Karl Marx (see p. 139).

Hellenic ruler, for the Greeks rarely attempted to destroy a religion or philosophy. Only when it was deemed a serious challenge to the legitimacy of the Greek gods, and capable of undermining the state, was a religion suppressed or a philosopher put to death. The most famous challenger was Socrates who was charged with bringing new gods into Athens and corrupting the youth.[6] But Judaism was far more dangerous than any other ideology to the Hellenic leaders. *Jews constituted the one instance when not one or two philosophers, but an entire nation, held values in opposition to Hellenic society.*

Hellenic antisemitism increased accordingly. Even the accusation of ritual murder, associated almost exclusively with Christian antisemitism, was first made by a Greek. Apion, the noted Homeric scholar, charged the Jews with slaughtering and eating non-Jews in religious rituals. In his *History of Egypt*, Apion wrote that when Antiochus invaded the Jewish Temple he found a Greek prisoner inside who recounted to Antiochus "the unutterable law of the Jews. . . . They would kidnap a Greek foreigner, fatten him up for a year, and then convey him to a wood, where they slew him, sacrificed his body with their customary ritual, partook of his flesh, and, while immolating the Greek, swore an oath of hostility to the Greeks."[7]

ROME

By the time the Romans assumed control over Judea in 63 B.C.E., antisemitism was already deeply rooted in the classical world. Though the Roman rulers recognized Judaism as a licit religion, they soon found reason to water those anti-Jewish roots. The Jews' insistence on denying Roman gods, living by different values and rules, and leading their own national life was regarded by the Romans, particularly the intellectuals, as proof of the Jews' hatred for others. In the words of the greatest Roman historian, Tacitus, writing in the first century, the Jews "reveal a stubborn attachment to one another . . . which contrasts with their implacable hatred for the rest of mankind."[8]

Tacitus regarded the Jews' attachment to their own God, laws, and peoplehood as a challenge to Rome's highest values: "The Jews regard as profane all that which we hold sacred: on the other hand, they permit all that we abhor." Another of Tacitus' attacks on the Jews demonstrates how central the conflict of moral values was to Roman antisemitism: "The Jews," he wrote, "regard it as a crime to kill any newborn infant." The Romans, as the Greeks before them, killed mentally and physically handicapped infants. To the Roman and Greek mind keeping such children alive was pointless and unaesthetic.

That the Jews refusal to acknowledge the divinity of the Roman gods and emperors caused Roman antisemitism is well illustrated by the meeting in 39 C.E. between a Jewish delegation and the emperor Caligula (see p. 29). The emperor was furious over the Jews' refusal to place his statue in their Temple. Only his sudden death saved the Jews of Palestine from a massacre.[9]

While the attitude toward Judaism was almost uniformly negative among Rome's politicians and intellectuals, many other Romans, disenchanted with Roman paganism's immorality and vacuity, and repulsed by such horrors as the gladiator fights, were attracted to the ethical monotheism and spirituality of the Jews. By the middle of the first century, between 7 and 10 percent of the people living in the Roman Empire, as many as seven million out of seventy million, were Jews, many of them converts.[10] To the leadership of Rome this was distressing, for as Seneca, the first-century Stoic philosopher and adviser to Emperor Nero, put it, "the conquered have given their laws to the conquerors."[11]

Throughout the first century the Jews found themselves under continuous attack from Romans of all ranks. For example, Josephus, the first-century Jewish historian, reported that Roman soldiers in Jerusalem publicly demonstrated their contempt for Judaism, one going so far as to expose his backside in the Temple court during Passover, while another destroyed a Torah scroll before the eyes of the Jews.[12]

As a result of Roman provocations, the Jews of Palestine rebelled twice, each time failing to overthrow Roman rule.

With the second failure in 135 C.E., the Jews lost for over eighteen hundred years whatever sovereignty they had managed to maintain in their homeland.

CONCLUSION

There was one basic reason for pagan antisemitism and one recurring theme to it. The reason was hostility to Judaism, which the pagan world found threatening to many of its most cherished values. Pagan antisemitism was therefore directed only against Jews who upheld Judaism. Jews who were willing to disavow Judaism were accepted into pagan society. For example, one of the Roman appointed procurators in Judea, Tiberius Alexander, was a convert from Judaism. Only those Jews who insisted on observing Judaism with its monotheistic rejection of pagan gods and its general opposition to the pagan way of life were subjected to literary and physical attacks.

Consequently, the recurring theme of pagan antisemitism was that the Jews are haters of mankind. To pagans, the Jews' hostility, or at least indifference, to the values and life-style of the non-Jews could only be attributed to a Jewish sense of superiority and contempt for humanity (exacerbated by the Jewish belief in chosenness—see pp. 40–45). As Tacitus wrote: ". . . toward every other people they feel only hate and enmity, they sit apart at meals and they sleep apart, and although as a race they are prone to lust, they abstain from intercourse with foreign women."[13]

That the Jews regarded their values as so important that they were willing to die for them only reinforced the conviction that they must hate their neighbors, for they preferred to die than to live like them.

Though antisemitism reached a new and far more intense phase when Rome became Christian, hatred of the Jews obviously preceded Christianity. Salo Baron, the great Jewish historian, has noted that "almost every note in the cacophony of medieval and modern antisemitism was sounded by the chorus of ancient writers."[14] And this antipathy, as Catholic theologian and historian Rosemary Ruether has shown,[15] was "a reaction caused by the special social consequences of Jewish religious law. ... This reaction was not racial, since it would disappear as soon as a Jew gave up ... Jewish law."[16]

Nearly all the causes and themes of subsequent antisemitism were present in the pagan world. But the rise of Judaism's first daughter religion, Christianity, gave birth to new and ever more frightening expressions of Jew-hatred.

EIGHT

Christian Antisemitism

IN THE FOURTH CENTURY, the Roman Empire substituted a monotheistic faith for paganism. That faith should logically have been Judaism. It was Judaism that introduced God to the Roman world, it was Judaism alone that had opposed paganism for over a thousand years, and it was Judaism that by the first century of the Common Era counted one out of every ten citizens of the Roman Empire as an adherent.

Yet it was not Judaism but Christianity, the creation of a handful of Jews, that became the religion of the Roman Empire. Christianity, and not Judaism, the religion from which Christianity took its God, its Bible, its Messiah, its apostles, and its founders, became the religion of the empire. Why?

Some reasons for the amazingly rapid spread of Judaism's daughter religion, rather than of Judaism itself, are clear. Christianity was in many ways considerably more accessible to the pagan. Christianity offered the pagan not only the universal God of the Jews, but also a son of God, a god in human form who died and was resurrected as many pagan gods had been. In addition, it announced the good news that the Messiah had come, whereas the Jews were still waiting for him.

Christianity also dropped Jewish law, which had been another factor standing in the way of many prospective converts. The Church adopted Paul's position, as articulated in *Romans* 3:28, that now that Christ had come all God demanded was the proper faith, and this faith ensured eternal salvation. Judaism, on the other hand, continued to demand adherence to its laws, and it focused much more on this world than on eternity.

Christianity was also easier to convert to. Whereas conversion to Judaism meant not only adoption of the Jewish religion but also membership in the Jewish nation, conversion to Christianity implied no breaking of, or adding to, previous national ties. Moreover, Christianity made the process of conversion painless by dropping the requirement of male circumcision.

The Jews rejected the Christians' changes in the nature of God, the messianic and divine claims made for Jesus and their elimination of law and peoplehood. But Church leaders could not ignore the Jews' denial of the validity of Christianity. The Jews were not merely another group of non-Christian pagans. If it were not for the Jews, there would be no Christianity. Jesus was an observant Jew.[1] All his apostles were Jews. The Jewish Bible was the entire basis for the messianic claims made for Jesus. The Jews were God's chosen people, and the people to whom Jesus addressed his words "I am sent only to the lost sheep of the house of Israel" (*Matthew* 15:24).

Yet it was the Jews who rejected Jesus' claims. The people to whom Jesus belonged and addressed his message, and therefore the one people able to validate his message, rejected all the Christian claims made for Jesus.

The founders of Christianity were confronted with the terrible fact that the Jews, *merely by continuing to be Jews*, threatened the very legitimacy of the Church. If Judaism remained valid, then Christianity was invalid. Therein lie the origins of Christian hatred of the Jews, the most enduring Jew-hatred in history.

The Church Fathers had to deal with this Jewish challenge, and they did so in a most logical manner. Since the existence of the Jews and Judaism challenged the legitimacy of the Church, the Church had to deny the legitimacy of the Jews and Judaism. The Church was now Israel; the other Israel had to be discredited.

To that end the founders of Christianity promulgated a number of doctrines to theologically invalidate the Jews' continuing existence. These doctrines were given the greatest possible significance, divine authentication, by being placed in the Christian Bible and by often being attributed to Jesus himself. In this way the New Testament canonized antisemitism.

Thus, the editors of the New Testament did not content themselves with a simple historical narration of the Crucifixion or of the Jews' opposition to Jesus. It would not suffice to depict the Crucifixion as the Roman execution it was, or merely to discredit the Jews' theological arguments against the divine claims made for Jesus. The Jews, not their arguments, had to be permanently discredited. Thus, for example, the New Testament depicted the Jews not as merely having rejected Jesus' claims, but as having him murdered. Moreover, the New Testament added, it was not one group of Jews that was guilty of murdering God, but *all* Jews then and forever: the New Testament put into the mouths of Jews present at the Crucifixion, "let his blood be on our heads and the heads of our children" (*Matthew* 27:25).

Thus, the New Testament created the most often repeated Christian accusation against the Jews, and the greatest source of Christian Jew-hatred: the Jew, every Jew, in every age is a "Christ-killer." It has been this New Testament assertion that ultimately legitimized the torture and murder of Jews in Christendom for nearly two thousand years. For this charge that the Jews committed deicide, destructive enough in itself, gave birth to other equally destructive anti-Jewish libels in the New Testament.

For example, only one explanation could account for the Jews' rejection of God's son, and for their murder of him. The Jews were obviously incarnations of the Devil, for who else could murder God?

This identification of the Jews with the Devil originates in the Gospel of John, written about 100 C.E. A particularly anti-Jewish work, John explained the Jews' rejection and kill-ing of Jesus by formulating the "Jews as Devils" theory, and he endows it with divine credibility by having Jesus mouth it (the three other Gospels, each written in closer proximity to Jesus' life, attribute no such statement to him). In chapter 8:43–44, 47, John reports that Jesus said to the Jews,[2] "Why do you not understand what I say? It is because you cannot bear to hear my word? You are of your father, the Devil, and your will is to do your father's desire. . . . The reason why you do not hear [the words of God revealed in Jesus] is because you are not of God."[*]

With these charges of deicide and collusion with the Devil, the early Church put the Jew, rather than itself, on the theo-logical, not to mention moral and ultimately physical, defen-sive. It established the logic of the oft-repeated Christian doctrine that merely by being Jews, Jews in effect murder Jesus anew in every generation.

THE CHURCH FATHERS

The antisemitic themes of the New Testament were ex-panded and spread throughout the Roman Empire by the early Church leaders. Among these were John Chrysostom and Bishop Ambrose, both made saints by the Roman Catho-lic Church. Living during the formative century when the Roman Empire became Christian, they were able to perma-nently influence Christian attitudes and policies toward the Jews.

---

[*] Many Christian apologetics attempt to defend this passage by not-ing that only the Jews who refused to accept Jesus were called chil-dren of the Devil. This is sophistry, however. A Jew who accepts Jesus as the Messiah and as divine is no longer a Jew, but a Christian. The New Testament passage, therefore, refers to all Jews as children of the Devil.

St. John Chrysostom of Antioch, Archbishop of Constantinople

Among the most admired and beloved figures in Church history is St. John Chrysostom, whose Greek name translates as St. John the Golden Mouthed. The nineteenth-century Protestant cleric R. S. Storrs called him "one of the most eloquent preachers who ever since apostolic times have brought to men the divine tidings of truth and love." Storrs's contemporary, the great Catholic theologian, John Henry Cardinal Newman, described Chrysostom as a "bright, cheerful, gentle soul, a sensitive heart . . . all this elevated, refined, transformed by the touch of heaven—such was St. John Chrysostom."[3]

St. John Chrysostom's warmth did not extend to the Jews: "They know only one thing," wrote St. John Chrysostom, "to satisfy their stomachs, to get drunk, to kill."[4]

"The synagogue," he wrote, "is worse than a brothel. . . . It is the den of scoundrels and the repair of wild beasts . . . the temple of demons devoted to idolatrous cults . . . the cavern of devils . . . a criminal assembly of Jews . . . a place of meetings for the assassins of Christ . . . the refuge of devils." When some Christians responded that synagogues were entitled to a degree of respect if only because they contain the writings of Moses and the Prophets, St. John Chrysostom objected. The fact that synagogues contain holy books, he noted, is simply one more reason to despise the Jews; they recognize the holy books, but obstinately refuse to accept or understand their true Christian meaning. Clearly, then, they are of the Devil as the Gospel of John declares.

When St. John Chrysostom learned that some Christians in Antioch were continuing to maintain cordial relations with Jews, he denounced them: "The Jews have assassinated the Son of God! How dare you . . . associate with this nation of assassins and hangmen!"

Perhaps St. John Chrysostom's most significant contribution to antisemitism was his theological justification of Christian violence against Jews. He argued that when Christians beat and murder Jews, it is the Jews who are to blame, not the Christians: "It was men, say the Jews, who brought these misfortunes upon us, not God. On the contrary, it was in fact God who brought them about. If you attribute them to men, reflect again that, even supposing men had dared, they would not have had the power to accomplish them, unless it had been God's will." Concerning such justifications of Jewish suffering at the hands of Christian antisemites, the Catholic historian Malcolm Hay noted: "Such logic would justify the German race murderers. St. John Chrysostom could have preached a powerful sermon beside the mass grave at Dubno [Poland]. He could have explained that a revengeful God had chastised the little Jewish boy who had tried to keep back his tears so that the Germans would not see that he was afraid; and the little baby, and the Jewish family who all went down into the pit. . . . [Chrysostom's thinking] would have been useful to the defense at Nuremberg."[5]

St. Ambrose of Milan

At about the time St. John Chrysostom was reviling the Jews of Antioch, St. Ambrose, to this day revered as among the most noble of the Church Fathers, was bishop of Milan. During his term as bishop, in 388, a bishop in Mesopotamia encouraged the burning of a synagogue. The Roman emperor, Theodosius the Great, who reigned 379–395, ordered the bishop to pay for the rebuilding of the synagogue. Upon learning of this, St. Ambrose wrote a letter of protest to Theodosius, but the emperor ignored the protest.

A short time later, the emperor attended a church service officiated by Ambrose. The bishop refused to administer the Mass unless the emperor assured him that the order to rebuild the synagogue would be rescinded. "There is no adequate cause for such a commotion," Ambrose told the emperor, "that the people should be so severely punished for the burning of a building; and much less since it is the burning of a synagogue, a home of unbelief, a house of impiety, a receptacle of folly, which God Himself has condemned."[6] This time, Ambrose's protest was successful, and a precedent sought by this fourth-century Church Father was established: if Christians destroy a synagogue, the Jews are to pay for it to be re-built.

THE CRUSADES

By the eleventh century, the Church had converted vir-tually all the inhabitants of Europe, except the Jews. Until then, the situation of the Jews was tenuous but tolerable. With the First Crusade, in 1096, however, the status and se-curity of European Jewry declined precipitously.

In 1095, at the Council of Clermont-Ferrand, Pope Urban II called for a Crusade to regain Palestine from the Muslims. Tens of thousands of Christians then embarked for the Holy Land. But the Muslims were not the Crusaders' only enemies. As historian Leon Poliakov noted, the Crusaders "were God's avengers, appointed to punish all infidels, whoever they might be . . . What could be more natural than to take re-venge along the way upon the various infidels living in Chris-tian territories?"[7]

A contemporary chronicler, Guibert de Nogent, quoted the Crusaders of Rouen: "We desire to go and fight God's ene-mies in the East; but we have before our eyes certain Jews, a race more inimical to God than any other."

Wherever Crusaders found Jews they offered them the choice of Christianity or death. The experience of the Jews of Worms, Germany, is typical of what happened to French and German Jews during this period. In May 1096, upon learning of the Crusaders' murder of the Jews of Speyer, the Jews of Worms sought assistance. Some Jews sought refuge in the pal-ace of Bishop Adalbert, while others, having been promised help by the local burghers, remained in their homes. Those Jews who remained in their homes were immediately mur-dered, while those in the palace, after refusing Bishop Adal-bert's offer to save them from the Christian mobs if they con-verted, were murdered under the bishop's orders. Eight hundred Jews were murdered in two days. A Christian chronicler, Albert of Aix, wrote: "Only a small number of Jews escaped this cruel massacre, and a few accepted baptism, much more out of the fear of death than from love of the Christian faith."[8]

In many places bishops and counts tried to protect the Jews from the Christian masses and offered the Jews the choice of baptism or death only when pressured by the Christian mobs. But the Jews had little reason to trust in the goodwill of the Church hierarchy. When the few Jews who chose baptism over death wished to return to Judaism after the Crusaders passed their city, it was prohibited. This prohibition was formalized in a bull issued by Pope Innocent III in September 1201: ". . . he who is led to Christianity by violence, by fear and by torture, and who received the sacrament of baptism to avoid harm (even as he who comes falsely to baptism) receives indeed the stamp of Christianity. . . . They [the forced converts] themselves having been anointed with the holy oil and having participated in the body of the Lord, must be duly constrained to abide by the faith they had accepted by force." The only option, according to the pope, was for a person to "object expressly" to baptism, and to refuse to undergo the ceremony. As Poliakov notes, "Since those who 'objected expressly' to a forced baptism were generally executed on the spot, all cases of baptism became valid in practical terms."[9]

The Second Crusade, begun in 1147, accelerated the decline of the Jews' status among Christians. Christian clerics stirred Christian masses to anti-Jewish frenzy. In France, the Abbé Pierre of Cluny challenged his parishioners: "What is the good of going to the end of the world, at great loss of men and money, to fight the Saracens, when we permit among us other infidels a thousand times more guilty towards Christ than the Mohammedans."[10]

During the decades following the Crusades new anti-Jewish libels helped lead to the murders of hundreds of thousands of more Jews.

THREE MEDIEVAL LIBELS

Throughout the Middle Ages, Christians repeated the accusation in the Gospel of John that the Jews are the Devil's children. Millions of Christians came to believe that the Jews were not actually human beings, but creatures of the Devil, allies of Satan, and personifications of the Antichrist. This diabolical dehumanization of the Jews rendered plausible every accusation against them. *I was not taught this*

Such was the case regarding the three anti-Jewish libels that were most widely circulated by the medieval clergy and believed by nearly every Christian: Jews murder Christians and drink their blood for ritual purposes; Jews poison Christians; and Jews kidnap the wafer that is transubstantiated into the body of Jesus and torture it by sticking needles into it, thus torturing Jesus.

Each of these three charges was made and believed despite the nonexistence of *any* supporting evidence except for confessions extracted under torture.[11] But the absence of any evidence fooled few Christians—agents of the Devil are notoriously tricky.[12]

Ritual Murder

The first accusation of ritual murder was made in 1144 in England. According to a contemporary Christian document: "The Jews of Norwich brought a child before Easter, and tortured him with all the tortures wherewith our Lord was tortured, and on Long Friday hanged him on a rod in hatred of our Lord, and afterwards buried him." A Christian convert from Judaism, Theobold of Cambridge, testified that Jews were required to sacrifice a Christian child annually, the choice of place being made at an annual conference of rabbis.[13] This first accusation of ritual murder had no immediate consequences. As no evidence was ever produced that a murder had been committed, let alone a Jewish ritual murder, no Jew was tried for the alleged crime.

But the long-term effects of this accusation were to be devastating. Between the twelfth and the twentieth centuries, Jews and often entire Jewish communities were put on trial on over 150 occasions for engaging in ritual murder. In almost every instance Jews were tortured and put to death.

The case of Hugh of Lincoln provides a typical example. In

1255, many Jews visited Lincoln, England, to attend the wedding of a prominent Jew's daughter. The day after the wedding, the body of a Christian boy, Hugh of Lincoln, missing for over three weeks, was found in a cesspool into which he had accidentally fallen. Matthew Paris, a contemporary Christian chronicler, wrote what he and other Christians believed to have really occurred: "The child was first fattened for ten days with white bread and milk, and then . . . almost all the Jews of England were invited to the crucifixion."[14] Subsequently, a Jew named Copin was arrested, and under torture confessed "that the Jews had crucified the boy in the manner that the Jews had once crucified Jesus." One hundred Jews were arrested, and nineteen, including Copin, were hanged without trial.

The case of Hugh of Lincoln had a profound impact on the popular image of Jews in England and throughout the Western world. A century later Geoffrey Chaucer wrote of the Jews' murder of Hugh in "The Prioress's Tale" in his classic *The Canterbury Tales*. In the nineteenth century, one of the leading essayists in England, Charles Lamb, wrote: "I confess that I have not the nerve to enter their synagogues. Old prejudices cling about me. I cannot shake off the story of Hugh of Lincoln."[15] Dozens of ballads were inspired by Hugh's death. The two authors, on a visit to the Ozark Mountains of Arkansas, purchased a book of Ozark Mountain folk songs, printed in 1973, which included a ballad inspired by the "Jewish ritual murder" of Hugh of Lincoln.[16] In it, a Jewish woman is described as inviting a young Christian boy into her house, whereupon:

> *She pinned a napkin o'er his face*
> *And pinned it with gold pin*
> *Then called for a vessel of gold*
> *To catch his heart blood in,*
> *In, in,*
> *To catch his heart blood in.*

The Jews' allegiance to their understanding of God, with its denial of the Christian trinity, was always at the heart of the ritual murder charge. A sixteenth-century document explains that the murder of Christian children and the distribution of their blood among Jews is "a token of their eternal enmity towards Christendom," for "if they had Christ today they would crucify Him as their fathers did, but since they do not have Christ, they martyr in His stead an innocent Christian child."

By the fourteenth century the ritual murder charge had become associated with the Jewish holiday of Passover, attesting to the antisemitism which the Jews' adherence to their laws, as well as to their understanding of God, aroused among Christians. Christians accused Jews of using Christian blood in their unleavened bread (matzoh) and in their wine. In Savoy, in 1329, Christians claimed that the Jews "compound out of the entrails of murdered Christian children a salve of food called aharance [haroseth], which they eat every Passover in place of a sacrifice; they prepare this food at least every sixth year because they believe they are saved thereby."[17]

The accusations of ritual murder followed the Jews throughout Europe. Historian Haim Hillel Ben-Sasson wrote that "Generation after generation of Jews in Europe was tortured and Jewish communities were massacred or dispersed and broken up because of this libel."[18] The blood libel has, in fact, persisted into the twentieth century. The Protestant historian James Parkes reported that "In Central Eastern Europe, among both Roman Catholics and Eastern Orthodox Christians . . . there are almost more examples of the accusation in the years between 1880 and 1945 than in the whole of the Middle Ages."[19]

In the 1930s the Nazis renewed the libel. The entire May 1, 1934, issue of the Nazi newspaper *Der Stürmer* was devoted to Jewish ritual murder, and the regular weekly edition of the paper routinely carried illustrations of rabbis sucking the blood of German children.

In the 1960s and the 1970s the blood libel was spread by the leading financial figure in the Arab world, the late King Faisal of Saudi Arabia. On a number of occasions Faisal in-

formed newspaper interviewers that the Jews annually celebrated Passover by murdering a non-Jew and consuming his
blood.[20]

As a postscript to this discussion of the ritual murder
charge, two ironic points are worthy of note. First, the blood
libel was directed against the first nation in history to outlaw
human sacrifice (*Genesis* 22, *Deuteronomy* 18:10) and the
only nation in the ancient Near East to prohibit the consumption of *any* blood (*Leviticus* 3:17; 7:26; 17:10–14; *Deuteronomy* 12:15–16; 12:23–25).[21]

That so many medieval Christians believed and spread this
lie about the Jews led to a second irony. The early Zionist
thinker Ahad Ha-Am contended that the blood libel was actually of some psychological benefit to the Jews in that it enabled them to resist internalizing the world's negative portrayal of them. "This accusation is the solitary case in which
the general acceptance of an idea about ourselves does not
make us doubt whether all the world can be wrong, and we
right, because it is based on an absolute lie. Every Jew who
has been brought up among Jews knows as an indisputable
fact that throughout the length and breadth of Jewry there is
not a single individual who drinks human blood for religious
purposes. . . . 'But,' you ask, 'is it possible that everybody can
be wrong, and the Jews right?' Yes, it is possible: the blood
accusation proves it possible."[22]

Plots to Poison Christians

"If a king had a Jewish physician," notes James Parkes,
"and did not actually perish on the battlefield, cloven in two
by the battle-axe of the enemy, there is nothing surprising in
his unfortunate doctor being accused of poisoning him."[23]
Parkes cites several instances of Jewish royal physicians being
executed after a king's death.

In actuality almost every medieval Jewish doctor was en-
dangered. In 1161, in Bohemia, eighty-six Jews were burned
as punishment for an alleged plot of Jewish physicians to poison the populace."[24] Such accusations were endorsed by
leading intellectual circles in European society. In 1610, the

medical faculty of the University of Vienna declared that Jewish physicians were bound by Jewish law to kill every tenth Christian through the use of drugs.[25]

Martin Luther said that "if they [the Jews] could kill us all, they would gladly do so, aye, and often do it, especially those who profess to be physicians. They know all that is known about medicine in Germany; they can give poison to a man of which he will die in an hour, or in ten or twenty years; they thoroughly understand this art."[26]

The libels that the Jews were plotting to poison the Christian world had particularly tragic results during the Black Death of 1348–49. This plague, which killed about one-third of Europe's population, was blamed on the Jews despite the fact that the plague also killed Jews. A Christian physician, Konrad of Regensburg, in his *Buch der Natur*, was one of the few Christians to recognize the irrationality of blaming the Jew: "But I know that there were more Jews in Vienna than in any other German city familiar to me, and so many of them died of the plague that they were obliged to enlarge their cemetery. To have brought this on themselves would have been folly on their part." But the doctor's reasoning had no impact.

Jews were first tortured to confess to spreading the Black Death in September 1348 in Switzerland. According to the "confession," a rabbi had instructed the Jews: "See, I give you a little package, which contains a preparation of poison and venom. . . . This you are to distribute among the wells, the cisterns and the springs . . . to poison the people who use the water." In October 1348, the verdict was announced: ". . . all Jews from the age of seven, cannot excuse themselves from this crime, since all of them in their totality were cognizant and are guilty of the above actions. Jewish children under the age of seven were then baptized and reared as Christians after their families were murdered."[27]

Antisemitic libels die hard. In 1953, Joseph Stalin accused a group of doctors, most of them Jews, of a plot to poison the Communist leadership of the Soviet Union. Stalin died three days before their trial was to begin, but we now know that Stalin intended to use the "doctors' plot" to arouse the Russian public against the Jews, and in the ensuing crisis, exile Russia's Jews to Siberia.

Desecration of the Host

In 1215, the Fourth Lateran Council accepted the doctrine of transubstantiation as official Church dogma. This dogma asserted that the wafer used at the Mass was miraculously transformed into the body of Jesus. The wafer was to be regarded not as a symbolic representation of Jesus, but as his actual body. Just how literally Christians accepted this teaching is exemplified in writings of a leading preacher of the thirteenth century, Berthold of Regensburg. He explained that Christ, though present in the wafer, does not allow himself to be seen in it for "who would like to bite off the little head, or the little hands, or the little feet of a little child?"[28]

Christian belief in the doctrine of transubstantiation led to the torture and murder of thousands of Jews. Since Jesus is brought to life through the wafer, would not the Jews who had once crucified him wish to torture and kill him again? In 1243, only twenty-eight years after the Fourth Lateran Council, the first accusation of "host desecration" occurred in Berlitz, near Berlin. The city's entire Jewish community was burned alive for allegedly torturing a wafer. Charges of "host desecration" spread throughout Europe. In Prague, in 1389, the Jewish community was collectively accused of attacking a monk carrying a wafer. Large mobs of Christians surrounded the Jewish neighborhood and offered the Jews the choice of baptism or death. Refusing to be baptized, three thousand Jews were murdered. In Berlin, in 1510, twenty-six Jews were burned and two beheaded for reportedly "desecrating the host." A charge of host desecration was reported as late as 1836 in Romania.

The "host desecration" libel is among the clearest examples of the Christian perception of the Jews as devils. Clearly, no one, not even a Jew, tortures cookies. If a person does torture one, it could mean only one thing: he, too, recognizes that it is the body of Jesus, and wishes to make him suffer. Who but the people of the Devil recognize the divinity of Jesus but wish to destroy him?

CHRISTIAN ROOTS OF THE HOLOCAUST

Sixteen hundred years of such hatred of Jews culminated in
the Holocaust. Christianity did not create the Holocaust; indeed Nazism was anti-Christian, but it made it possible.
Without Christian antisemitism, the Holocaust would have
been inconceivable.

Nazi antisemitism differed from Christian antisemitism,
however, in at least two important ways. It did not allow the
Jews the choice of conversion or death, as medieval Christian
antisemites had, but only death. And it called for the murder
of all Jews, rather than, as the medieval Christian world had
called for, the suffering of all Jews and the random murders of
many. In virtually every other way, Nazism depended upon
Christian antisemitic ideas, libels, policies, and legislation.

Hitler and the Nazis found in medieval Catholic anti-Jewish legislation a model for their own, and they read and reprinted Martin Luther's virulently antisemitic writings. It is
instructive that the Holocaust was unleashed by the only
major country in Europe having approximately equal numbers of Catholics and Protestants. Both traditions were saturated with Jew-hatred.

CATHOLICISM

When the Church was Europe's most powerful force, from
the fourth until the eighteenth century, its laws, many of
which were directed against Jews, were Europe's laws. Concerning Church anti-Jewish legislation the Holocaust historian, Raul Hilberg, has noted: ". . . in reviewing the documen-
tary record of the destruction of the Jews, one is almost
immediately impressed with the fact that the German admin-
istration knew what it was doing. . . . The German bureau-
cracy could draw upon . . . precedents and follow . . . a guide,
for the German bureaucrats could dip into a vast reservoir of

administrative experience, a reservoir which church and state had filled in fifteen hundred years of destructive activity."[29] In *The Destruction of the European Jews,* Hilberg constructed a chart substantiating his thesis.[30]

CHURCH LAW	NAZI LAW
Jews and Christians not permitted to eat together, Synod of Elvira, 306.	Jews barred from dining cars (Transport Minister to Interior Minister), Dec. 30, 1939.
Jews not allowed to hold public office, Synod of Clermont, 535.	Law for the Re-establishment of the Professional Civil Service, April 7, 1933.
Jews not allowed to show themselves in the street during Passion Week, Third Synod of Orleans, 538.	Decree authorizing local authorities to bar Jews from the street on certain Nazi holidays, Dec. 3, 1938.
Burning of the Talmud and other Jewish books, 12th Synod of Toledo, 681.	Book burnings in Nazi Germany.
Christians not permitted to patronize Jewish doctors, Trulanic Synod, 692.	Decree of July 25, 1938.
Jews obliged to pay taxes for the support of the Church to the same extent as Christians, Synod of Gerona, 1078.	The "Sozialaugleichsabgabe" which provided that Jews pay a special income tax in lieu of donation for party purposes imposed on Nazis, Dec. 24, 1940.
The marking of Jewish clothes with a badge, Fourth Lateran Council, Canon 68 (copied from Islamic legislation which had decreed that Christians wear blue belts and Jews, yellow belts).	Decree of Sept. 1, 1941, authorizing that Jews are required to wear yellow star.
Christians not permitted to attend Jewish ceremonies, Synod of Vienna, 1267.	Friendly relations with Jews prohibited, Oct. 24, 1941.
Jews not permitted to dispute with simple Christian people about the tenets of the Catholic religion, Synod of Vienna, 1267.	

Compulsory ghettos, Synod of Breslau, 1267.	Order by Heydrich for ghettoization of Jews, Sept. 21, 1939.
Christians not permitted to sell or rent real estate to Jews, Synod of Ofen, 1279.	Decree providing for compulsory sale of Jewish real estate, Dec. 3, 1938.
Jews not permitted to obtain academic degrees, Council of Basel, Sessio XIX.	Law against Overcrowding of German Schools and Universities, April 25, 1933.

Even more obvious than the Nazi copying of old Christian antisemitic legislation was the Nazi use of centuries-old Christian antisemitic libels. All the negative images created by Catholics in the early and late Middle Ages were echoed by the Nazis. Though anti-Christian (in large part because of Christianity's Jewish roots and values), the Nazis filled their speeches and journals with stories of Jews murdering non-Jews to drink their blood, and of Jews poisoning Germany's water systems. Julius Streicher, the chief Nazi antisemitic ideologist, hanged at Nuremberg for his war crimes, often appealed to the Christian instincts of his fellow Germans by describing the Jews as the "people of whom Christ said its father was the devil."[31]

PROTESTANTISM

The centuries-old Catholic antisemitism in Germany was more than matched by the virulence of the newer Protestant antisemitism.

Martin Luther (1483–1546), who was one of history's most vehement Jew-haters, was both the founder of Protestantism and the father of German nationalism. Accordingly, his antisemitic statements profoundly influenced the attitudes of nearly all Germans, not only Protestants.

In his early days, Luther was critical of Church anti-Jewish policies because he believed that such policies prevented the Jews from converting to Christianity. When Luther later realized that his approach did not prompt Jews to cease being Jews, he turned furiously against them. His later writings against the Jews were so venomous that the Nazis often cited them. Indeed, Julius Streicher argued in his defense at the Nuremberg trials that he had never said anything about the Jews that Martin Luther had not said four hundred years earlier.[32]

Streicher was largely correct. There was a genuine similarity of themes between Luther and the Nazis, and Hitler was quite familiar with and admired the writings of Luther. In *Mein Kampf* Hitler called Luther one of the three great figures of Germany along with Frederick the Great and Richard Wagner;[33] and in conversations as early as 1918, he said: "Luther was a great man, a giant. With one blow he heralded the new dawn. . . . He saw the Jew as we are only beginning to see him today." When, on November 9, 1938, the Nazis carried out their first large-scale pogrom in which they destroyed almost all of Germany's synagogues and murdered thirty-five Jews, they announced that the pogrom was in honor of the anniversary of Martin Luther's birthday.[34]

Just as Catholic legislation anticipated virtually every Nazi anti-Jewish decree with the exception of genocide, so, too, Martin Luther had anticipated most Nazi actions against the Jews. In a pamphlet published toward the end of his life, *Concerning the Jews and Their Lies*, Luther outlined eight actions to be taken against the Jews:

Burn all synagogues.
Destroy Jewish dwellings.
Confiscate the Jews' holy books.
Forbid rabbis to teach.
Forbid Jews to travel.
Forbid Jews to charge interest on loans to non-Jews and confiscate Jewish property.
Force Jews to do physical labor.
Expel the Jews from provinces where Christians live.[35]

It is fair to say that insofar as Luther's anti-Jewish writings are concerned, the Nazis saw themselves as followers of Martin Luther. The Nazi depiction of the Jews as vermin to be exterminated echoed Luther's depiction of the Jews as "a plague, pestilence, pure misfortune in our country."[36] Owing to the towering role he played in German national and religious thought, Luther constituted an important ally for the Nazis in the carrying out of the "Final Solution."

CONCLUSION

For nearly two thousand years Christian antisemitism was a reaction to Judaism. Indeed the mere act of remaining a Jew constituted, in the eyes of millions of Christians, living refutation of Christianity. Consequently, the Christian world relentlessly dehumanized the Jew, enabling the Holocaust, the ultimate consequence of this dehumanization, to take place. While it is true that many Nazis were anti-Christian (and that Nazism itself was anti-Christian), they were all, as the Jewish philosopher Eliezer Berkovits has pointed out, the children of Christians.[37] The Holocaust took place in Christian Europe. Christians must confront these facts if Christianity is to remain credible after Auschwitz, and if the Christian world is to establish a positive relationship with the Jewish people.

At the same time, however, Jews' assessments of the Christian world must adapt to the contemporary reality. While never forgetting the past, Jews must recognize that major changes have taken place, both within Protestantism and Catholicism. While there are still Jew-haters in both branches of Christianity, particularly among the extreme Right and extreme Left in Europe and South America, there are now also many Jew-lovers. Jews must recognize that in the contemporary world Christianity is often an ally rather than an oppressor of Jews. In this century, Nazism, and today Islam and the Left, have replaced Christianity as the world's foremost purveyors of antisemitism. Moreover, the ideals of both religions demand that Jews and Christians forge an alliance to "perfect the world under the rule of God." Of course, such an alliance will not develop easily. Many Jews, knowledgeable of Christianity's past, will be reluctant to believe that Christians have really changed. And many Christians will suspect that the Jews are a theological anomaly awaiting conversion to the "New Israel." But the time has come for Jews to recognize that there have been major changes in contemporary Christianity, that there are forces, particularly in the United States and Western Europe, that are very open to the Jews. Christians, for their part, must acknowledge the horrors of Christian antisemitism and the latent antisemitic as well as blatant antisemitic elements that still live on in Christendom. They must also understand that the Jews retain their place in God's scheme despite their rejection of Christian claims for Jesus. One Christian who did was Pope John XXIII. Shortly before his death he composed this prayer: "We realize now that many, many centuries of blindness have dimmed our eyes, so that we no longer see the beauty of Thy Chosen People and no longer recognize in their faces the features of our firstborn brother. We realize that our brows are branded with the mark of Cain. Centuries long has Abel lain in blood and tears, because we had forgotten Thy love. Forgive us the curse which we unjustly laid on the name of the Jews. Forgive us that, with our curse, we crucified Thee a second time."[38]

NINE

Islamic Antisemitism

ISLAM WAS THE SECOND RELIGION to emanate from Judaism, but as its founder was not a Jew and as it was not originally a Jewish sect, Islam's encounter with Judaism was significantly less bitter than Christianity's. As Salo Baron notes: "It was, therefore, from the beginning, a struggle between strangers, rather than an internecine strife among brethren."[1] Largely because of this factor, Jews in the Islamic world were rarely persecuted as violently as their brethren in the Christian world. S. D. Goitein, the leading historian of Jewish life in the Arab world, concludes: ". . . when the known facts are weighed, I believe it correct to say that as a whole the position of the non-Muslims [Christians and Jews under medieval Islamic rule] was far better than that of the Jews in medieval Christian Europe."[2]

Goitein's assessment is valid, but it tells us far more about the Jews' condition under Christians than about their treatment by Muslims. For while the Jews of the Muslim world may have rarely experienced the tortures, pogroms, and expulsions that typified Jewish life under medieval Christian rule, their life under Islam was at most times a life of degradation and insecurity. At the whim of a Muslim leader, a synagogue would be destroyed, Jewish orphans would be forcibly converted to Islam, or Jews would be forced to pay even more excessive taxes than usual.

MUHAMMAD AND THE JEWS

Like Christianity, Islam's anti-Judaism is deeply rooted. Islam, too, was born from the womb of Judaism; it, too, was rejected by the Jews whose validation was sought; and it, too, suffered an identity crisis vis-à-vis Judaism.

When Islam was born in the seventh century, there was a substantial Jewish population in Medina where the first Muslim community arose. The Jews of pre-Islamic Arabia were active advocates of their religion—to the extent that several kings of Himyar, now Yemen, had converted to Judaism. Contemporary inscriptions described Dhu Nuwas As'ar, the last Jewish king of Himyar, as a believer in one deity whom the king called Rahman, the Merciful One, as God was called in Judaism and later in Islam.

During his early years, Muhammad related well to the Jews of Arabia, and their religious practices and ideas deeply influenced him. As Goitein indicated: "The intrinsic values of the belief in one God, the creator of the world, the God of justice and mercy, before whom everyone high and low bears personal responsibility came to Muhammad, as he never ceased to emphasize, from Israel."[3]

The profound influence of the Jews, their Bible, and their laws on Muhammad is clearly expressed in the Quran, the Muslim bible, and in Muhammad's early religious legislation. Indeed Muhammad saw himself as another Moses. In the Quran, he writes of his message (Sura 46, verse 12) that "Before it the Book of Moses was revealed. . . . This Book confirms it. It is revealed in the Arabic tongue. . . ."[4] Moses is mentioned in the Quran over one hundred times, and is, in fact, the predominant figure in it.

The Jewish doctrine which most deeply influenced Muhammad was monotheism: "There is no God but God." Indeed, Muhammad's monotheism was so attuned to the un-

compromising nature of Judaism's monotheism that though
he had also been influenced by Christian teachers, he rejected
the Christian trinity and the divinity of Jesus as not monotheistic: "Unbelievers are those that say: 'Allah is the Messiah,
the son of Mary' . . . Unbelievers are those that say, 'Allah is
one of three.' There is but one God. If they do not desist from
so saying, those of them that disbelieve shall be sternly punished" (5:71–73).

Jewish law also deeply influenced Muhammad. In the early
days of Islam, Muslims prayed in the direction of the Jews'
holy city, Jerusalem, and observed the most solemn Jewish
holiday, Yom Kippur, the Day of Atonement. Only later,
when Muhammad reluctantly concluded that the Jews would
not embrace him as their prophet and convert to Islam, did
he substitute Mecca for Jerusalem, and the fast of Ramadan
for Yom Kippur. Similarly, Muhammad based Muslim dietary
laws upon Judaism's laws of Kashrut: "You are forbidden car-
rion, blood, and the flesh of swine; also any flesh . . . of animals sacrificed to idols" (5:3). The five daily prayers of Islam
are likewise modeled on the thrice daily service of the Jews.

Second in importance only to his adoption of the Jews' God
was Muhammad's adoption of the Jews' founding father,
Abraham, as Islam's founder. In Sura 2, verse 125, Muhammad writes how Abraham and his son Ishmael converted the
Ka'ba, the holy rock of Arabian paganism, into the holy
shrine of Islam.

Believing himself to be the final and greatest prophet of
Mosaic monotheism, and having adopted so much of Jewish
thought and practice, Muhammad appealed to the Jews of
Arabia to recognize his role and to adopt Islam as the culmi-
nation of Judaism. "Even Luther," Princeton's renowned philosopher Walter Kaufmann wrote, "expected the Jews to be
converted by his version of Christianity, although he placed
faith in Christ at the center of his teaching and firmly believed in the trinity. If even Luther . . . could expect that,
how much more Muhammad whose early revelations were so
much closer to Judaism?"[5] Muhammad's deep desire for Jewish recognition reflected similar needs of Jesus and his followers. No group could validate his religious claims as could the

Jews. No group could so seriously threaten to undermine them as could the Jews.

The Jews rejected Muhammad's claims as they had Jesus', holding in both cases that what was true in their messages was not new, and that what was new was not true. Islam may have served as a religious advance for Arabian pagans, but for the Jews it was merely another offshoot of Judaism.

One major factor that rendered Muhammad's prophetic claims untenable to Jews was his ignorance of the Bible. In large part because Muhammad never read the Bible, but only heard Bible stories, his references to the Bible were often erroneous. In Sura 28:38, for instance, he has Pharaoh (from *Exodus*) ask Haman (of the *Book of Esther*) to erect the Tower of Babel (which appears at the beginning of *Genesis*).

Another obstacle to Jewish acceptance of Muhammad was the moral quality of some of his teachings. These did not strike the Jews, or the Arabian Christians, as equaling, let alone superseding, the prophetic teachings of Judaism and Christianity. In 33:50, for example, Muhammad exempts himself from his own law limiting a man to four wives, and in 4:34 he instructs men to beat disobedient wives. Walter Kaufmann notes that "there is much more like this, especially in the 33rd Sura," and that "it must have struck the Jews as being a far cry from Amos and Jeremiah, and the Christians as rendering absurd the prophet's claim that he was superseding Jesus."[6]

Finally, Muhammad's suspension of many Torah laws invalidated him in the Jews' eyes.

For these and other reasons, the Jews rejected Muhammad's prophetic claims and refused to become Muslims. This alone infuriated Muhammad. But even more angering, the Jews publicly noted the errors in Muhammad's biblical teachings and may have even ridiculed his claims to prophecy. Thus, Goitein writes, ". . . it is only natural that Muhammad could not tolerate as a neighbor a large monotheistic community which categorically denied his claim as a prophet, and probably also ridiculed his inevitable blunders. . . ."[7]

As a result Muhammad turned against the Jews and their

religion, and he never forgave them. And just as early Christian hostility to the Jews was canonized in the New Testament to provide divine delegitimization of the Jews and Judaism, so Muhammad's angry reactions to the Jews were recorded in the Quran, giving millions of Muslims throughout history divinely based antipathy to the Jews.

In the Quran, Muhammad attacked the Jews and attempted to invalidate Judaism in several ways. First, and most significantly, he changed Abraham from a Jew to a Muslim: "Abraham was neither Jew nor Christian. [He] surrendered himself to Allah. . . . Surely the men who are nearest to Abraham are those who follow him, this Prophet . . ." (3:67–68).

Second, he condemned the Jews and delegitimized their law by advancing a thesis similar to Paul's, that the many Torah laws had been given to the Jews as punishment for their sins: "Because of their iniquity we forbade the Jews good things which were formerly allowed them" (4:160).

Third, Muhammad charged the Jews with falsifying their Bible by deliberately omitting prophecies of his coming.[8] For example, in the Quran (2:129), Muhammad has Abraham mouth a prophecy of his (Muhammad's) coming. Muhammad charged that the Jews "extinguish the light of Allah" (9:32) by having removed such prophecies from their Bible.

Fourth, Muhammad asserted that Jews, like Christians, were not true monotheists, a charge he substantiated by claiming that the Jews believed the prophet Ezra to be the Son of God. "And the Jews say: Ezra is the son of Allah . . . Allah fights against them. How perverse are they . . ." (9:30).

These anti-Jewish fabrications, articulated by Muhammad as reactions to the Jews' rejection of him, have ever since been regarded by Muslims as God's word. As such they have formed the basis of Muslim antisemitism until the present day. Though originally directed against specific Jews of a specific time, these statements often have been understood by succeeding generations as referring to all Jews at all times. One common example is 2:61: ". . . And humiliation and wretchedness were stamped upon them and they were visited with wrath from Allah. That was because they disbelieved in

Allah's revelations and slew the prophets wrongfully. That was for their disobedience and transgression." This Quranic description of the Jews of seventh-century Arabia has often been cited by Muslims to describe Jews to this day.*

Muhammad and the Quran thus laid the basis for subsequent antisemitism just as the Church Fathers and the New Testament had—and for basically the same reason. By the Jews remaining Jews they constituted a living refutation. Thus under Islam, just as under Christianity, Jew-hatred was ultimately Judaism-hatred. Any Jew who converted to Islam was accepted as an equal.

Christians under Muslim rule fared little better. Muslims and their laws generally dealt harshly with both Christians and Jews.

As we cite examples of Muslim anti-Jewish legislation, then, it is necessary to recall that so long as Christian communities survived in the Muslim world, such legislation applied to them as well. However, whereas Jewish communities often flourished in Jewish terms, Christian communities for the most part did not even survive the intense Muslim hostility. Under the yoke of Muslim laws against Jews and Christians some of the oldest and strongest Christian communities in the world converted to Islam.

No fact better underscores the intensity of Muslim persecution of *dhimmis* (non-Muslim monotheists) than this disappearance of so many Christian communities under Islam. The fact that under similar conditions many Jewish communities flourished bears witness to the Jews' tenacious commitment to Judaism, not to any Muslim benevolence toward Jews. This

---

* In a speech before Egyptian army officers on April 25, 1972, the late Egyptian President Anwar el-Sadat cited this Quranic verse: "The most splendid thing our prophet Muhammad, God's peace and blessing on him, did was to evict them [the Jews] from the entire Arabian peninsula . . . I pledge to you that we will celebrate on the next anniversary, God willing and in this place with God's help, not only the liberation of our land but also the defeat of the Israeli conceit and arrogance so that they must once again return to the condition decreed in our holy book: 'humiliation and wretchedness were stamped upon them' . . . We will not renounce this."

is often lost sight of when favorably comparing Muslim anti-semitism with Christian antisemitism. Yet the conversion to Islam of nearly every pre-Islamic Christian community in the Muslim world (the Copts of Egypt constituting the most notable exception) eloquently testifies to what Jews had to endure in their long sojourn through the Muslim world.

ATTITUDES AND ACTIONS OF ISLAM'S LEADERS TOWARD THE JEWS FROM MUHAMMAD'S DEATH UNTIL THE MODERN PERIOD

The two guiding principles of Islam's treatment of Jews and Christians are that Islam dominates and is not dominated, and that these groups are to be degraded.[9] Non-monotheists were given the choice of conversion to Islam or death.

The Muslim legal code which prescribed the treatment of Jews and Christians, or *dhimmis* as they both are referred to in Islam, was the Pact of Umar, attributed to Muhammad's second successor, but assumed to date from about 720.[10] Its key characteristic was the requirement that *dhimmis* always acknowledge their subservient position to Muslims. Jews and Christians had to pledge, for example, that "We shall not manifest our religion publicly nor convert anyone to it. We shall not prevent any of our kin from entering Islam if they wish it." The subservience that *dhimmis* were required to show publicly to Muslims is analogous to the behavior once expected of Blacks in the American South: "We shall show respect . . . and we shall rise from our seats when they [Muslims] wish to sit." They also had to pledge "not to mount saddles," since riding a horse, or, according to some Muslims, any animal, was considered incompatible with the low status of a *dhimmi*.[11] The *dhimmis* also had to vow that "We shall not display our crosses or our books in the roads or markets of the Muslims nor shall we raise our voices when following our dead."[12]

Anti-*dhimmi* legislation did not end with the Pact of Umar. In the Quran, Muhammad had urged Muslims to "Fight

against such of those who have been given the Scripture . . .
and follow not the religion of truth, until they pay the tribute
readily, being brought low" (9:29). Accordingly, Muslim officials often insisted that when paying tribute, *dhimmis* must
be "brought low," that is, humiliated. An early Muslim regulation precisely prescribed how to humiliate Jews and Christians when they pay tribute: "The *dhimmi*, Christian or Jew,
goes on a fixed day in person to the emir, appointed to receive
the poll tax, who occupies a high throne-like seat. The
dhimmi stands before him, offering the poll tax on his open
palm. The emir takes it so that his hand is on top and the
dhimmi's underneath. Then the emir gives him a blow on the
neck, and a guard, standing upright before the emir, drives
him roughly away. The same procedure is followed with the
second, third and the following taxpayers. The public is admitted to enjoy this show." The public was not merely "admitted" to this humiliating spectacle, but as Baron observes,
"Public participation was, indeed, essential for the purpose of
demonstrating, according to the Shafi'ite school, the political
superiority of Islam."[13]

In the course of time Muslim rulers developed additional
ways to humiliate *dhimmis*. Baron describes one of them:
"Equally vexatious was the tax receipt, which in accordance
with an old Babylonian custom, was sometimes stamped upon
the neck of the 'unbelieving' taxpayer. This ancient mark of
slavery . . . expressly prohibited in the Talmud under the
sanction of the slave's forcible emancipation, occasionally
reappeared here as a degrading stamp of 'infidelity.' "[14]

These humiliating and painful procedures had a terrible
effect on the Jews: "An Arab poet rightly spoke of entering
the door with bent heads 'as if we were Jews.' "[15]

Another law designed to humiliate *dhimmis* required them
to wear different clothing. The purposes of this law were to
enable Muslims to recognize Jews and Christians at all times,
and to make them appear foolish. In 807, the Abbasside caliph, Haroun al-Raschid, legislated that Jews must wear a
yellow belt and a tall conical cap.[16] This Muslim decree provided the model for the yellow badge associated with the deg-

radation of Jews in Christian Europe and most recently utilized by the Nazis.[17]

A Jew living in Baghdad in the days of Al-Muqtadir
(1075–1096) described additional measures passed by the vi-
zier, Abu Shuja, to humiliate Jews: ". . . each Jew had to have
a stamp of lead . . . hang from his neck, on which the word
dhimmi was inscribed. On women he likewise imposed two
distinguishing marks: the shoes worn by each woman had to
be one red and one black. She also had to carry on her neck or
attached to her shoe a small brass bell. . . . And the Gentiles
used to ridicule Jews, the mob and children often assaulting
Jews in all the streets of Baghdad."[18]

During the same century in Egypt, the Fatimid Caliph
Hakim ordered Christians to wear a cross with arms two feet
long, while Jews were ordered to wear around their necks
balls weighing five pounds, to commemorate the calf's head
which their ancestors had once worshiped.[19]

These clothing regulations were not only enforced in the
Middle Ages. Until their departure from Yemen in 1948, all
Jews, men and women alike, were compelled to dress like
beggars.* In fact, Yemen offers us a unique opportunity to

---

* In addition to living under these laws of humiliation, Jews constantly lived with the fear that some new interpretation of Muslim
sources would lead to greater oppression. The worst instance took
place under the Almohades. "At the beginning of the twelfth century,
a Muslim jurist in Cordova [Spain] claimed to have found . . . a tradition, soon widely accepted in Morocco and Spain, that Muhammad's
original decree of toleration of Jews had been limited to a period of
five hundred years from the hegira [Muhammad's flight from Mecca].
If by that time the expected Jewish Messiah were not to arrive, the
Jews were supposed to give up their religion and join the ranks of
Islam. The time limit expired, of course, in 1107" (Salo Baron, *A Social and Religious History of the Jews*, 3:124.) On the basis of this new
doctrine, in 1146, Abd al-Mu'min, the builder of the Almohade empire in North Africa and Spain, gave the Jews the choice of Islam or
death. When nearly all of them refused to convert, nearly every Jew
in Fez, the capital of Morocco, was murdered. As for those who converted, the Almohades put them under constant surveillance, and
those whose conversions seemed insincere were executed, had their
property confiscated, and their wives given to Muslims. Goitein

understand Muslim attitudes toward the Jews. For Yemen
was the one Muslim country with a non-Muslim minority
(Jews) that was never ruled by a European power. It was
therefore able to treat its Jews in the "purest" Muslim manner, uninfluenced by non-Muslim domination.

In 1679, Jews in most of Yemen were expelled from their
cities and villages. When recalled a year later, they were not
allowed to return to their homes, but were forced to settle in
Jewish ghettos outside the cities. During their expulsion the
synagogue of San'a, the capital, was converted into a mosque
which still exists under the name Masjid al-Jala (the Mosque
of the Expulsion).

Among the many indignities to which the Jews of Yemen
were constantly subjected was the throwing of stones at them
by Muslim children, a practice which was religiously sanc-
tioned. When Turkish officials (the Turks occupied Yemen in
1872) asked an assembly of Muslim leaders to see that this
practice be stopped, an elderly Muslim scholar responded
that throwing rocks at Jews was an old religious custom, *Ada*,
and it was therefore unlawful to forbid it.

The greatest suffering which Yemenite Jews constantly experienced was the forced conversion to Islam of Jewish children whose fathers had died. This was practiced until the
Jews fled Yemen in 1948, and was also based upon Islamic
doctrine. Muhammad was believed to have said, "Everyone is
born in a state of natural religion [Islam]. It is only his parents
who make a Jew or Christian out of him." Accordingly, a
person should grow up in "the natural religion" of Islam.
When a Jewish father died there was often a race between
the Jewish community which sought to place his children
with Jewish parents and the Muslim authorities who wanted
to convert the children to Islam and place them in a Muslim
home. The Jews often lost. Goitein reports that "many families arrived in Israel with one or more of their children lost to

---

notes: "All the horrors of the Spanish Inquisition were anticipated
under Almohade rule" (Goitein, *Jews and Arabs: Their Contact
Through the Ages,* 3d ed., p. 80).

them, and I have heard of some widows who have been be-
reaved in this way of all their offspring."

Yet, as persecuted as the Yemenite Jews were, they were
also denied the right to leave the country.[20]

THE MODERN ERA

By the nineteenth century, the Jews' situation under Islam
went from degradation to being recurrent victims of violence
as these examples from Jewish life in Egypt, Syria, and Palestine illustrate.

Egypt

In his authoritative book *An Account of the Manners and
Customs of the Modern Egyptians,* Edward Lane wrote that
at the time of his study, 1833–35, the Jews were living "under
a less oppressive government in Egypt than in any other
country of the Turkish Empire. . . ." but "they are held in the
utmost contempt and abhorrence by the Muslims in general."
Lane explained: "Not long ago, they used often to be jostled
in the streets of Cairo, and sometimes beaten merely for passing on the right hand of a Muslim. At present, they are less
oppressed; but still they scarcely ever dare to utter a word of
abuse when reviled or beaten unjustly by the meanest Arab or
Turk; for many a Jew has been put to death upon a false and
malicious accusation of uttering disrespectful words against
the Kur-an [sic] or the Prophet. It is common to hear an Arab
abuse his jaded ass, and after applying to him various oppro-
brious epithets, end by calling the beast a Jew."[21]

That this was the Jewish situation in Egypt, "a less oppressive government" than elsewhere in the Muslim Arab
world, tells us a great deal about Muslim antisemitism in the
nineteenth century—prior to the Zionist movement.

Syria

In 1840, some Christians introduced the blood libel into
the Arab world. After a Capuchin monk in Damascus van-

ished, fellow monks spread a rumor that he had been murdered by Damascus Jews who needed his blood for a religious
ritual. Several Damascus Jews were then arrested, and under
torture one of them "confessed" that leaders of the Jewish
community had planned the monk's murder. Many other
Jews were then arrested, and under torture more such confessions were obtained. Only after an international protest organized by Jewish communities throughout the world were
the Jews who survived their tortures released.[22]

The blood libel immediately became popular among Mus-
lims. Muslims attacked Jews as drinkers of Muslim blood in
Aleppo, Syria, in 1853, Damascus again in 1848 and 1890,
Cairo in 1844 and 1901–2, and Alexandria in 1870 and 1881.[23]

The blood libel played a decisive role in unsettling the lives
of nineteenth-century Syrian Jews, and since then it has been
repeatedly utilized in Arab anti-Jewish writings.

Palestine

Jews have lived continuously as a community in Palestine
since approximately 1200 B.C.E. The only independent states
ever to exist in Palestine have been Jewish. After the destruction of the second Jewish state in 70 C.E., Jews always maintained a presence in Palestine, awaiting the reestablishment
of the Jewish state. But these Jews often had to live under degrading conditions.

In nineteenth-century Palestine, under Ottoman Muslim
rule, Jews had to walk past Muslims on their left, as the left is
identified with Satan, and they always had to yield the right
of way to a Muslim, "step into the street and letting him
pass." Failure to abide by these degrading customs often provoked a violent response. In Palestine as elsewhere, Jews had
to avoid anything that could remind Arabs of Judaism: therefore, synagogues could only be located in hidden, remote
areas, and Jews could pray only in muted voice. In addition,
despite the widespread poverty among Palestinian Jews, they
had to pay a host of special protection taxes. As examples,
they paid 100 pounds a year to the Muslim villagers of Siloam
(just outside Jerusalem) not to disturb the graves at the Jewish
cemetery on the Mount of Olives, 50 pounds a year to the

Ta'amra Arabs not to deface the Tomb of Rachel on the road to Bethlehem, and 10 pounds annually to Sheik Abu Gosh not to molest Jewish travelers on the road to Jerusalem, even though the Turkish authorities were already paying him to maintain order on that road.[24] These anti-Jewish laws and taxes had a rather intimidating effect on the Jews. The British consul, James Finn, who lived in Jerusalem in the 1850s, described in his book *Stirring Times* how "Arab merchants would dump their unsold wares on their Jewish neighbors and bill them, safe in the knowledge that the Jews so feared them that they would not dare return the items or deny their purchase."[25]

THE TWENTIETH CENTURY

Muslim antisemitism continued to be brutally expressed through the twentieth century. Albert Memmi, the noted French Jewish novelist who grew up in North Africa, cites a few examples.

In Morocco in 1907, a huge massacre of Jews took place in Casablanca, along with the usual embellishments—rape, women carried away into the mountains, hundreds of homes and shops burned, etc. . . . In 1912 a big massacre in Fez. . . . In Algeria in 1934, massacre in Constantine, twenty-four people killed, dozens and dozens of others seriously wounded. . . . In Aden in 1946 . . . over one hundred people dead and seventy-six wounded, and two thirds of the stores had been sacked and burned. . . . In June, 1941, in Iraq, six hundred people killed, one thousand seriously wounded, looting, rapes, arson, one thousand houses destroyed, six hundred stores looted. . . . [In Libya]: November 4th and 5th, 1945, massacre in Tripoli; November 6th and 7th in Zanzour, Zaouia, Foussaber, Ziltain, etc. girls and women raped in front of their families, the stomachs of pregnant women slashed open, the infants ripped out of them, children smashed with crowbars. . . . All this can be found in the newspapers of the time, including the local Arab papers.[26]

Memmi summarizes the Jewish status under Islam in the century as "Roughly speaking and in the best of cases, the Jew is protected like a dog which is part of man's property, but if he raises his head or acts like a man, then he must be beaten so that he will always remember his status."[27]

MUSLIM HATRED OF ISRAEL

It is the Jews' refusal to accept this subordination that is at the heart of the Arab-Muslim hatred for Israel.* As Yehoshafat Harkabi, a leading scholar of the contemporary Arab world, has put it: "The existence of the Jews was not a provocation to Islam . . . as long as Jews were subordinate or degraded. But a Jewish state is incompatible with the view of Jews as humiliated or wretched.[28] The call for a Palestinian Arab state in place of Israel is for a state in which once again 'Islam dominates and is not dominated.'

This hatred of Jewish nationalism has been so intense that many Arab leaders have embraced Nazi antisemitism. During World War II most Arab leaders were pro-Nazi. Among them was the head of the Muslims in Palestine, the mufti Haj Amin el-Husseini, who in 1929 helped to organize the large-scale murders of the ultra-Orthodox *non-Zionist* Jews of Hebron. A friend of Hitler who spent much of the war in Nazi Germany, the mufti, on November 2, 1943, delivered this speech: "The overwhelming egoism which lies in the character of Jews, their unworthy belief that they are God's chosen nation and their assertion that all was created for them and that other peoples are animals . . . [makes them] incapable of being trusted. They cannot mix with any other nation but live as parasites among the nations, suck out their blood, embezzle their property, corrupt their morals. . . . The divine anger

---

* It was this, not the Palestinian refugee issue, which lay at the heart of Muslim anti-Zionism. Without minimizing their personal misfortune, as regards the Palestinians Albert Memmi has noted: "The Palestinian Arabs' misfortune is having been moved about thirty miles within one vast Arab nation." *Jews and Arabs*, p. 35.

and curse that the Holy Quran mentions with reference to the Jews is because of this unique character of the Jews."[29]

Though many Arab nations formally declared war against Germany in 1945 (when the German defeat was imminent) in order to be eligible for entry into the United Nations, extensive Arab sympathy with the Nazis continued after Germany's surrender. The Egyptians and Syrians long welcomed Nazis to their countries, offering them the opportunity to further implement the "Final Solution."[30]

Among many Arabs the Holocaust has come to be regarded with nostalgia. On August 17, 1956, the French newspaper *Le Monde* quoted the government-controlled Damascus daily *Al-Manar* as having written, "One should not forget that, in contrast to Europe, Hitler occupied an honored place in the Arab world. . . . [Journalists] are mistaken if they think that by calling Nasser Hitler they are hurting us. On the contrary, his name makes us proud. Long live Hitler, the Nazi who struck at the heart of our enemies. Long live the Hitler of the Arab world."[31] On June 9, 1960, after Israeli agents captured Adolf Eichmann, the Nazi who had supervised the murder of the six million Jews, the Beirut daily, *Al-Anwar*, carried a cartoon depicting Eichmann speaking with Israeli prime minister David Ben-Gurion. Said Ben-Gurion: "You deserve the death penalty because you killed six million Jews." Responded Eichmann: "There are many who say I deserve the death penalty because I didn't manage to kill the rest."

On April 24, 1961, the Jordanian English-language daily *Jerusalem Times* published an "Open Letter to Eichmann" which concluded, "But be brave, Eichmann, find solace in the fact that this trial will one day culminate in the liquidation of the remaining six million to avenge your blood."[32]

Arab Jew-hatred has also resurrected the blood libel. In 1962, the Egyptian Ministry of Education published *Talmudic Sacrifices* by Habib Faris, a book which had originally been published in Cairo in 1890. In the introduction, the editor notes that the book constitutes "an explicit documentation of indictment, based upon clear-cut evidence that the Jewish people permitted the shedding of blood as religious duty enjoined in the Talmud."[33] On April 24, 1970, Fatah radio broadcast that "Reports from the captured homeland tell that the Zionist enemy has begun to kidnap small children from the streets. Afterwards the occupying forces take the blood of the children and throw away their empty bodies. The inhabitants of Gaza have seen this with their own eyes."[34] In November 1973, the late King Faisal of Saudi Arabia said that it was necessary to understand the Jewish religious obligation to obtain non-Jewish blood in order to comprehend the crimes of Zionism.[35]

The Arab Muslims have also reached back to classical themes of Islamic antisemitism to attack the Jews and Israel. Many Arab speakers and publications echo Muhammad's charge in the Quran (5:82) that the Jews are the greatest enemies of mankind. For example, an Egyptian textbook, published in 1966 for use in teachers' seminars, teaches that Jews (not only Israelis) are "monsters of mankind [and] a nation of beasts. . . ."[36]

Among the favorite antisemitic publications of the Arabs today is *The Protocols of the Elders of Zion.* In an interview with the editor of the Indian magazine *Blitz,* on October 4, 1958, President Gamal Abdel Nasser of Egypt praised the *Protocols:* "I wonder if you have read a book called 'Protocols of the Learned Elders of Zion.' It is very important that you should read it. I will give you an English copy. It proves clearly, to quote from the Protocols, that 'three hundred Zionists, each of whom knows all the others, govern the fate of the European continents and they elect their successors from their entourage.'"[37] The late King Faisal of Saudi Arabia gave copies of the *Protocols* to the guests of his regime. When he presented the *Protocols,* along with an anthology of antisemitic writings, to French journalists who accompanied French Foreign Minister Michel Jobert on his visit to Saudi Arabia in January 1974, "Saudi officials noted that these were the king's favorite books."[38]

The Islamic world today has combined antisemitic motifs from Nazism and medieval Christendom, as well as from its own tradition. This potent combination has made the Arabs the major source of antisemitic literature in the world today. And as in other forms of antisemitism, in the words of Yehoshafat Harkabi, "the evil in the Jews is ascribed [by Arab Muslim antisemites] not to race or blood, but to their spiritual character and religion."[39]

CONCLUSION

Only through an understanding of the deep theological roots of Muslim antisemitism and an awareness of the continuous history of Muslim antisemitism can present-day Muslim hatred of Israel be understood. Only then does one recognize how false are the claims of Israel's enemies that prior to Zionism Jews and Muslims lived in harmony and that neither Islam nor Muslims have ever harbored Jew-hatred. The creation of the Jewish state in no way created Muslim Jew-hatred; it merely intensified it and gave it a new focus.

So long as the Jews acknowledged their inferior status among Muslims, they were humiliated but allowed to exist. But once the Jews decided to reject their inferior status, to become sovereign after centuries of servitude, and worst of all, to now govern some Muslims where they had so long been governed, the Jews' existence was no longer tolerable. Hence the passionate Muslim hatred of Israel and Zionism, a hatred that entirely transcends political antagonisms. Hence the Muslims call not for a defeat of Israel, but for its annihilation. As so often in Jewish history it is the Jewish nation's *existence* that arouses hatred and needs to be ended. Though there is some hope for peace as a result of the Egypt-Israel peace treaty, for most Muslims the source of their hatred remains the Jewish state's existence, not its policies, nor even its borders. The Muslim and Arab claim that the issue is anti-Zionism rather than antisemitism really means that so long as the Jews adhere to their *dhimmi* status in Arab Muslim nations, and do not express the national component of Judaism, their existence as individuals is acceptable. But for a Jew to aspire to equality among Muslims, for a Jew to aspire to a status higher than "humiliation and wretchedness," is to aspire too high.

TEN

Enlightenment Antisemitism

TOWARD THE END of the eighteenth century, Christianity's domination of European life and thought was increasingly challenged. Its chief opponents, the men of the Enlightenment, challenged biblical beliefs as well as Christian political power.

Not surprisingly, many Jews welcomed the Enlightenment with open arms. Having so long suffered religious antisemitism, the Jews expected the secularization of Europe to lead to a dramatic improvement in their status. The calls for universal equality and fraternity so eloquently made by leaders of the Enlightenment were welcomed by no one more than the Jews.

The Jews' hopes were not fully realized, however, for this equality was offered to them more as individuals than as Jews. Their emancipation was made conditional upon their ceasing to identify as a distinct people. The Jews quickly learned that the Enlightenment did not end Jew-hatred; it only changed its target from the God and law (religious) components of Judaism, to the national component of Judaism.

Jews to this day have found Enlightenment antisemitism

127

the most incomprehensible expression of Jew-hatred. Most modern Jews, themselves secular, have believed that the demise of religion would lead to the demise of antisemitism. Yet the twentieth century, the most secular century in history, has been the most antisemitic. A dispassionate look into the roots of modern antisemitism shows them to be as secular as they are religious, and to have been planted in large part by the leaders of the Enlightenment.

FRANCE

In the most universalist hearts of the men of the Enlightenment there was often a hostile spot for the Jews. The most significant example was Voltaire, the father of the Enlightenment. This man, whose thinking had such a profound impact on eighteenth- and nineteenth-century Europe that the eighteenth century came to be known as the "century of Voltaire," was an antisemite.

Though the Jews numbered less than 1 percent of France's population in the second half of the eighteenth century, Voltaire was obsessed with them. In his most important work, *Dictionnaire Philosophique,* 30 of his 118 articles dealt with the Jews, and described them in consistently negative ways.[1] As examples, in an article on Abraham, he describes the Jews as "our masters and our enemies . . . whom we detest," and under the entry "Anthrouphagi," Voltaire defines Jews as "the most abominable people in the world." The article *Jew,* the longest in the *Dictionnaire,* contains this characteristic assessment: ". . . In short they are a totally ignorant nation who, for many years, have combined contemptible miserliness and the most revolting superstition with a violent hatred of all those nations that have tolerated them. Nevertheless, they should not be burned at the stake."[2] In 1770 Voltaire appended to his entry on Jews that the Jews engage in ritual murder: "your priests have always sacrificed human victims with their sacred hands."

Historian Leon Poliakov pointed out that "during Hitler's domination of Europe, a history teacher, Henri Labrou, had no difficulty in compiling a 250-page book of Voltaire's anti-Jewish writings."[3]

Contemporary scholars, heirs to many Enlightenment values, have been perplexed by Voltaire's extraordinary hatred of the Jews. How could the rational and tolerant Voltaire be so irrational and illiberal when it came to the Jews? The best known contemporary authority on the Enlightenment, Peter Gay, himself a Jew, while not denying Voltaire's hostility toward the Jews, has offered two mitigating explanations for it.[4] First, Voltaire's attacks on the Bible and the Jews were really only his way of attacking Christianity: "Voltaire struck at the Jews to strike at Christianity."[5] Second, Voltaire's antisemitism derived from some negative personal experiences with Jews.

These attempts of Professor Gay to explain Voltaire's antisemitism do not, however, stand up before the facts.

The first explanation is demonstrably untrue. Its validity rests entirely upon the proposition that for whatever reasons, perhaps censorship or fear of persecution, Voltaire found it impossible to attack Christianity directly, and therefore attacked Judaism. Although it is true that fears of the censor caused Voltaire often to disguise his anti-Christian critiques by attributing them to others, he nonetheless made his negative attitudes toward Christianity very clear. Evidence for this is amply supplied in Gay's own work which cites numerous anti-Christian themes developed by Voltaire in the *Dictionnaire*:

The Church has consistently been the implacable enemy of progress, decency, humanity, and rationality.

It has been in the interests of Church officials everywhere to keep people as ignorant and submissive as children.

It is in the interest of Church officials to burn heretics, and to stamp out rational dissent.

It is in the clergy's interest to quibble about meaningless philosophical constructions and waste the time of educated men on ridiculous theological controversies (for example, in "Catechisme du Japonaise" Voltaire ridicules the theological controversies among Christian denominations by portraying schools of cooks disputing over recipes).

For the first time in history, a happy society, based on power over nature, was within human grasp, but Christians were exerting all their efforts to obstruct its realization.[6]

If despite censorship, Voltaire could express such strongly anti-Christian sentiments, why would he need to rely on attacks on Judaism in order to attack Christianity? One might respond that Voltaire aimed to disprove Christianity by disproving Judaism since Christianity is based on Judaism. But as true as this may be, it is irrelevant to the issue of Voltaire's antisemitism, since Voltaire did not confine his anti-Jewish attacks to those aspects of Judaism upon which Christianity was based. He repeatedly made it clear that he despised *Jews*.

That attempts to minimize Voltaire's antisemitism are in error is further evidenced by the fact that Voltaire's contemporaries understood his anti-Jewish writings as attacks on Jews. As Arthur Hertzberg, the leading scholar on Voltaire and the Jews, has noted, Voltaire was understood by his contemporaries as being an enemy of the Jews, and antisemitic pamphleteers based their arguments against the Jews and Jewish emancipation on his antisemitic ideas.[7]

Gay's second explanation of Voltaire's anti-Jewish writings refers to the oft-commented-upon fact that Voltaire had suffered some severe financial reversals in dealings with Jewish bankers, which constituted in Gay's words, "experiences to which he did not bring his usual keen enlightened spirit."[8]

Here Gay dismissed Voltaire's statements as atypically irrational sentiments. Since the father of the Enlightenment could not possibly be deeply antisemitic, his vitriolic statements about Jews must be considered, at least when it is inconceivable to dismiss them as disguised attacks on Christianity, as personal, emotional, and irrational sentiments, but not as Voltaire's "considered reactions" to Jews and Judaism. It was the Jews' bad luck that Voltaire did not fare well in his financial dealings with some of them. Presumably had Voltaire had good experiences with Jewish bankers, or equally poor ones with Christians, he would have had more positive opinions about Jews.

Unfortunately for Gay, however, this thesis was specifically denied by Voltaire himself. He insisted that his antisemitism had nothing to do with his financial dealings with some Jews: "I have forgotten about much larger bankruptcies through Christians."[9]

The attempt to deny Voltaire's antisemitism is an exercise in wishful thinking. Voltaire despised the Jews and their religion. In his view, the Jews possessed a vile nature caused by Judaism and its laws which in turn reflect the hatred that Jews feel for other people. In fact, Voltaire's antisemitism was so strong that he attacked Judaism even when he agreed with it. His writings on torture in the *Dictionnaire* illustrate this point. Throughout his life Voltaire vigorously opposed institutional torture, such as Church torture of suspected heretics. Among Jews torture had always been illegal and unknown. Jewish law not only forbade torture, it rendered it pointless since it did not accept confessions, not voluntary ones, let alone forced ones, in capital cases. As this had been Jewish law for thousands of years one would have expected Voltaire to laud the Jewish prohibition of torture, or at the very least omit mention of it. Instead, Voltaire used the Jews' opposition to torture as an occasion to mock the Jews' concept of chosenness: "What is very odd is that there is never any mention of torture in the Jewish books. It is truly a pity that so gentle, so honest, so compassionate a nation did not know this means of finding out the truth. The reason for this, in my opinion, is that they did not need it. God always made it known to them as his cherished people. . . . thus torture cannot be in use with them. This was the only thing lacking in the customs of the holy people."[10]

Fundamental to the world views of Voltaire and the men of the Enlightenment was admiration for pagan culture. As Voltaire immersed himself in Greco-pagan literature, he became quite familiar with its anti-Jewish writings and often used them in place of Christian antisemitic arguments. He especially cited these pagan claims, with his own embellishments, that the Jews were deadly to the human race, and resurrected the pagan contempt for Judaism's lack of emphasis on the aesthetic.[11] Voltaire thus reintroduced the pre-Christian reasons to hate Jews, as well as introducing new Enlightenment ones.

Voltaire's anti-Jewish writings had profoundly negative effects. Hertzberg has documented how Voltaire served as the major link in Western intellectual history between the antisemitism of classical paganism and of the modern age. Voltaire saw himself as Cicero reborn, and "he ruled the Jew to be outside society and to be hopelessly alien even to the future age of enlightened man."[12] Voltaire played a major role in helping develop the idea that the admission ticket for a Jew into Western society was his willingness to stop being a Jew.

Had Voltaire been the one Enlightenment figure to have expressed hostility toward the Jew and Judaism, his contribution to modern antisemitism would have been substantial, considering the preeminent role he has played in modern intellectual history. But he was far from alone. "Only a few of the men of the Enlightenment were pro-Jewish. . . . [the great majority] had their own Enlightenment reasons for regarding Jews as no more within the pale of Culture than the ancient Romans regarded slaves to be when they talked of the rights of men in civilized society."[13]

Jean-Baptiste de Mirabaud, permanent secretary of the Académie française, and noted writer of antireligious works, contended that the universality of antisemitism proved that the Jews deserve to be hated: "Not only did all the nations despise the Jew; they even hated them and believed that they were as justified in hating as in despising them. They were hated because they were known to hate other men; they were despised because they were seen observing customs which were thought ridiculous."[14]

Paul Henri Dietrich d'Holbach was a German baron in Paris, who gave biweekly "philosophical dinners" attended by leading Enlightenment figures.[15] Baron d'Holbach published over fifty atheist and materialist works between 1760 and 1765; some were his own manuscripts, but most were books by other authors. Baron d'Holbach's publications on the Jews were among the most venomous anti-Jewish writings of the eighteenth century. He particularly emphasized the theme of Jews as enemies of mankind: "It must in fact be admitted that even while they perished the Jews were well avenged on the Romans, their conquerors. From the ruins of their country, a fanatic sect emerged which gradually polluted the whole Empire." We here encounter the theme, later expanded by nineteenth- and twentieth-century racists, of Jews as polluters of the world.

As d'Holbach was not a racial antisemite, he attributed the evil of Jews only to Judaism: "If, as cannot be doubted, honest and virtuous people can be found among them, it is because they do not conform to the principles of a law which is obviously calculated to make men unsociable and maleficent, an effect which the Bible and the saints it holds up as models must have produced."

Virtually every major figure of the French Enlightenment was hostile to Judaism. Even those who fought for the legal emancipation of the individual Jew and fought against antisemitism wished to see the Jews assimilate. Montesquieu, for example, powerfully denounced Christian antisemitism in his essay *The Spirit of Laws* by condemning the Portuguese Inquisition through the mouth of a persecuted Jew: "You put us to death, who believe only what you believe, because we do not believe all that you believe. We follow a religion, which you yourselves know to have been formerly dear to God. We think that God loves it still, and you think that he loves it no more; and because you judge this, you make those suffer by sword and fire, who hold an error so pardonable as to believe that God loves what he once loved."[18] In the very same essay, however, Montesquieu dismissed Judaism as a religion of ignorance, and called upon the Jews to cease being Jews and become Enlightened men and philosophers.

GERMANY

In Germany the situation was basically the same. With the exception of Gotthold Lessing, leaders of the German Enlightenment were divided between those who favored granting civil rights to assimilated Jews and those who opposed civil rights for any Jews.

An example of the latter was Johann Fichte, who pointed to Jewish values as the source of his antisemitism. "Give them civil rights?" asked Fichte in a book published in 1793. "I see no other way of doing this except to cut off all their heads one night and substitute other heads without a single Jewish thought in them. How shall we defend ourselves against them? I see no alternative but to conquer their promised land for them and to dispatch them all there. If they were granted civil rights they would trample on other citizens."[17] Reading Fichte's fears of the Jews' danger to Germany, it is easy to forget that the Jews numbered about 1 percent of Germany's population.

But, most important, is to understand the link between Fichte's thinking and Hitler's racial antisemitism. Fichte here paves the intellectual way to Hitler by theorizing that Jews are unchangeable, unassimilable, and unconvertible. The only way to solve the "Jewish Problem" is to "cut off all their heads" since they hold all those Jewish thoughts. Thus, for Fichte and, as we shall see, for Hitler, it is Jewish thoughts, not Jewish genes, that make the Jews Jewish.

Even Immanuel Kant, the major German thinker of the eighteenth century, though never calling for the persecution of Jews, did call for the end of Judaism and its laws: "The euthanasia of Judaism can only be achieved by means of a pure, moral religion, and the abandonment of all [its] old legal regulations."[18]

ENGLAND

The one major, though partial, exception to the antisemitism of the Enlightenment took place in England. There, as early as 1689, John Locke had written the first of his four *Letters on Toleration*, stating that "Neither pagan nor Mohametan [sic] nor Jew ought to be excluded from the civil rights in the commonwealth because of his religion."[19] Well before the French Enlightenment, this English thinker had formulated a theory of religious tolerance, though no state yet practiced it. Among those who shared Locke's tolerant views was the deist John Toland, who in 1714 published a pamphlet, *Reasons for Naturalizing the Jews in Great Britain and Ireland.*

On the other hand it would be an error to characterize the men of the English Enlightenment as particularly sympathetic to the Jews or Judaism. The dominant philosophy of the English Enlightenment, deism, held that knowledge of God's existence and belief in an immortal soul were sufficient to prompt moral behavior. Deists rejected religions based on revelation, and vigorously attacked Judaism for, among other things, introducing this idea to the West.

They downplayed the significance of the Bible and particularly the special role of the Jews. The early seventeenth-century deists Herbert of Cherbury and John Spencer contended that Jewish ideas were copied from the Egyptians. The eighteenth-century writer Anthony Collins argued that Greek wisdom was superior to Jewish wisdom, the Jews being "an illiterate, barbarous and ridiculous people." Matthew Tindal, in a similar vein, contrasted natural religion with Jewish "barbarism." The attacks of English deists on the Bible were important sources for Voltaire's attacks on the Bible.[20]

Since most Jews continued to believe in the Bible and to follow its tenets, they were consequently perceived by many men of the English Enlightenment as acting "barbarously." Thus, in England, as on the Continent, for a Jew to be accepted in enlightened society, he had "to disassociate himself explicitly from the Jews, disavow his despised Jewish past and even condemn it."[21]

CONCLUSION

No violence accompanied Enlightenment antisemitism. As befits Enlightened men and women, no violence against the Jew could be tolerated, let alone called for. But Enlightenment opposition to Judaism and its particularism (that is, Jewish peoplehood) helped to lay the philosophic basis for antisemitism in the modern secular world. The Jew as Jew continued to have few friends. Antisemitism now became even more broadly based, rooted now in Christianity, secular humanism, and nationalism, the new European faith which developed in the eighteenth and nineteenth centuries alongside or instead of Christianity. The manifestation of any of Judaism's components now had religious, secular, and nationalistic opponents. By the twentieth century virtually every popular ideology in Europe wanted the Jews to disappear.

ELEVEN

Leftist Antisemitism

MARXISM AND SOCIALISM, like Christianity, Islam, nationalism, and the Enlightenment, were born with Jew-hatred. Their two main ideological sources, Marx and the early French socialists, developed antisemitic ideas which have characterized much of the Left to this day.

KARL MARX

The father of Marxist ideologies, Karl Marx, was born in the German city of Trier in 1818. Though descended on both parents' sides from a long line of distinguished rabbis,[1] Marx was baptized a Lutheran when he was six years old. His father, who had converted to Christianity before Karl's birth in order to continue practicing law (forbidden to Jews by new Prussian laws), baptized his children so that they would not suffer from antisemitism. It was into this self-denying world that Karl Marx was born.

Given this background, it is not surprising that one of Marx's first major essays was *On the Jewish Question*. Marx ostensibly wrote the piece as a response to philosopher Bruno

Bauer's article, "The Jewish Question," in which Bauer virulently attacked the Jews and Judaism, and argued against
emancipation for the Jews until they abandon their "exclusive religion, morality and customs."[2]

Marx, in his response, though critical of some of Bauer's
conclusions, did not criticize Bauer's antisemitism. Indeed, he
far outdid Bauer in antisemitic vituperation. He criticized
Bauer for primarily attacking religious Jews, when all who
identify as Jews should be attacked: "Not only in the Penta-
teuch [Torah] and in the Talmud, but also in present-day society we find the essence of the modern Jew."[3] As historian
Robert Wistrich notes, "Marx's hatred was therefore focused
not [only] against Bruno Bauer's 'Sabbath-Jew' but rather
against contemporary Jewry."[4]

On the Jewish Question is filled with a hatred of Jews and
Judaism so extreme that at times it sinks to Nazi-like Jew-
hatred: "What is the secular cult of the Jew? *Haggling.* What
is his secular god? *Money.* Well then! Emancipation from
haggling and *money,* from practical, real Judaism would be
the self-emancipation of our time. . . ."[5] "Money is the jealous
God of Israel, beside which no other God may stand."[6]

In the closing passages of *On the Jewish Question,* Marx
goes so far as to identify the emancipation of humanity with
the abolition of Judaism.[7]

The blatant antisemitism of *On the Jewish Question* has always proved an embarrassment to Jewish socialists who have
retained a Jewish identity. For over a hundred years after its
writing, Jewish socialists, who translated almost all of Marx's
writings into Yiddish and Hebrew, refrained from translating
Marx's only essay devoted exclusively to the Jewish question.

Others, however, have been only too pleased to translate
and learn from Marx's Jew-hating essay. In 1963, for example,
the Ukrainian Academy of Sciences published *Judaism Without Embellishment* by Trofim K. Kichko, who liberally quoted
from *On the Jewish Question.* The book was so antisemitic
that international protests forced the Soviet government to
withdraw it from circulation. Adolf Hitler, too, claimed to
have learned from Marx's essay: "It is quite enough that the
scientific knowledge of the danger of Judaism is gradually

deepened and that every individual on the basis of this knowledge begins to eliminate the Jew within himself, and I am
very much afraid that this beautiful thought originates from
none other than a Jew."[8]

Nor was the Jew-hatred in *On the Jewish Question* an exception to Marx's views on the Jews. Marx's subsequent writings about Jews, even working-class Jews, remained uniformly contemptuous. For example, Marx described the
impoverished Jewish refugees from Poland in Germany as
"this filthiest of all races, [who] only perhaps by its passion for
greedy gain could be related to [the Jewish capitalists of]
Frankfort." The April 29, 1849 issue of *Neue Rheinische Zei-
tung*, which Marx then edited, accused Polish Jews of robbing
churches, burning villages, and beating defenseless Poles to
death—charges which were "outrageous slanders against a
people who lived in daily dread of the very crimes they were
accused of. . . ."[9]

A contemporary reader of Marx would conclude that
wealthy capitalist Jews destroy society and that poorer Jews
are too uncivilized to enter society.

Marx even dredged up the ancient libel of Manetho, who
had described the Jews' exodus from Egypt as "the expulsion
of a 'people of lepers' headed by an Egyptian priest named
Moses."[10] And in the 1850s, Marx ridiculed those who fought
for the right of Baron Rothschild to take the seat that he had
won in the British House of Commons: "It is doubtful
whether the British people will be very much pleased by ex-
tending electoral rights to a Jewish usurer."[11]

In keeping with his policy of equal antagonism toward rich
and poor Jews, Marx ignored the plight of Jewish workers,
though they lived near him in London. Likewise, he never
commented on the pogroms which swept through Russia in
1881, though he often wrote on behalf of victims of oppression. Throughout his life, Marx identified Jews and Judaism with all that he hated in capitalism.[12]

Historian Edmund Silberner has noted two negative influences of Marx's anti-Jewish writings. They provoked and
strengthened anti-Jewish prejudices among Christian Marxists, and they alienated Jewish Marxists from the Jewish peo-

ple.[13] The latter was evidenced most dramatically in 1891, when Abraham Cahan, a delegate to the Second Socialist International in Brussels, urged the International to condemn Europe's increasing antisemitism. To Cahan's shock, *both the Jewish and non-Jewish delegates opposed a resolution condemning antisemitism.* According to the socialists, echoing Christian, Muslim, and history's other antisemites (with the exception of the Nazis), the one answer to antisemitism was for all Jews to cease being Jews and adopt the antisemites' (in this case, socialist) identity. The final resolution of the Second International condemned "anti-Semitic and philo-Semitic [i.e., Jewish] outbursts as one of the means by which the capitalist class and reactionary governments seek to divert the socialist movement and divide the workers."[14] The socialists thereby nullified opposition to antisemitism by equating it with Judaism and labeling both as enemies of socialism.

THE FRENCH SOCIALISTS

Had Socialist antisemitism been promulgated on the Left only by Karl Marx and his followers, it would have caused serious problems for Jews. But the other founders of socialism, the French socialists, were even more anti-Jewish than Marx.

George Lichtheim, one of the foremost historians of socialism, has emphasized the relevance of French socialism to subsequent leftist antisemitism, since France "was the cradle of the socialist movement" where socialism developed a full generation before it developed in Germany."[15] Lichtheim documents how from its beginning in the early 1800s, French socialism was hostile to Jews.

Charles Fourier, one of the two founders of French socialism, regarded the Jews as "parasites, merchants, usurers," whose emancipation he termed "the most shameful of all recent vices of society."[16]

Henri de Saint-Simon, the other founder of French socialism, was sympathetic to Jews, acknowledging that the socialist mission was a form of messianism derived from the Jews.

Unfortunately, as Lichtheim documents, in the French social-ist community, the antisemitism of Fourier triumphed over the philosemitism of Saint-Simon.

In the decades after Fourier and Saint-Simon, strong anti-Jewish views were expressed by three leading French social-ists: Alphonse Toussenel, Pierre Leroux, and Pierre Joseph Proudhon.

In 1845, Toussenel published *Les Juifs, rois de l'époque* (*The Jews: Kings of the Epoch*) which was favorably reviewed by much of the Socialist press. In this essay he developed the theme of "the cosmopolitan Jew. . . . Europe is entailed to the domination of Israel. This universal domination, of which so many conquerors have dreamed, the Jews have in their hands."[17] Similar ideas were later expressed by Proudhon.

It thus appears that the belief in Jewish world domination, a belief spread during the twentieth century through *The Protocols of the Elders of Zion*, and used by the Nazis as a jus-tification for genocide, was first introduced into the West's consciousness not by racists, Fascists, or Nazis, but by the Left, by socialists in nineteenth-century France.

Pierre Leroux, creator of the term socialism, identified the Jews with the despised capitalism, regarded them as the in-carnation of *mammon*, and said that they lived by exploiting others. Leroux, a religious Christian, saw but one solution to the "Jewish Problem"—the conversion of all Jews to Chris-tianity.[18]

Pierre Joseph Proudhon, one of the most important theorists of early socialism, expressed his antisemitism in his public writings in a "moderate" manner and in a more ex-treme form in his journals, which were published posthu-mously. In the journals of this great socialist, we find Nazi-like sentiments regarding the Jews. In December 1847, he outlined a program for the disappearance of Jewry: "This race poisons everything by meddling everywhere without ever joining itself to another people. Demand their expulsion from France, with the exception of individuals married to Frenchwomen. Abolish the synagogues: don't admit them to any kind of employment, pursue finally the abolition of this

cult. . . . The Jew is the enemy of the human race. One must
send this race back to Asia or exterminate it. . . . By fire or fusion or by expulsion, the Jew must disappear. . . . What the
peoples of the middle ages hated by instinct I hate upon re-
flection, and irrevocably."[19]

It is no wonder that Proudhon's disciples justified the Russian pogroms. As Lichtheim notes: "Four years after [Proud-
hon's] death, in 1869, his pupil George Duchene . . . [de-
clared]: 'Citizens, when you hear it said that in a notoriously
barbarous country [Russia] the population treats the Jews
roughly, do not believe one treacherous word. What you have
is simply a case of honest people chasing rascals, usurers, and
exploiters of labor.'"[20]

Against this backdrop, the indifference of socialists to the
fate of Alfred Dreyfus, the Jewish army officer falsely accused
by the French government of having spied for Germany, becomes explicable. One might have expected that French socialists, hostile toward the government, Church, and military,
each of which led the attack on Dreyfus, would have risen to
his defense. But Dreyfus was a Jew; and for this reason alone,
on January 28, 1898, the French socialist press published a
manifesto calling for "non-participation in the Dreyfus Affair
on the grounds that while the reaction wishes to exploit the
conviction of one Jew to disqualify all Jews, Jewish capitalists
would use the rehabilitation of a single Jew to wash out 'all
the sins of Israel.' " Among the manifesto's signatories were
the leading Socialists of the age, including Alexandre Mil-
lerand, Marcel Sembat, Jules Guesde, and Jean Jaurès.[21]
When the socialists did subsequently take a stand on the
Dreyfus case, they made a point of declaring that the Jewish
aspect of the antisemitic affair was irrelevant.

Thus, the French socialists, with the exception of Saint-
Simon and a very few others, propounded antisemitism from
their very beginnings. Historian Zosa Szajkowski, in 1947,
concluded his painstakingly researched article, "The Jewish
Saint-Simonians and Socialist Anti-Semitism in France," by
noting that try as he could, he could not find a single word on
behalf of Jews in the whole of French socialist literature from
1820 to 1920.[22]

COMMUNISM AND THE JEWS
IN THE CONTEMPORARY WORLD

In the hundred years since Marx and the French socialists there have been different socialist responses to the Jews. Social Democrats, for example, have been among the strongest supporters of Jewish rights in the world. Between 1948 and 1977 the Jewish state itself, Israel, was governed by the Labor Party, which was founded on socialist principles.

But the further Left one goes, the greater the antisemitism. Wherever Marxists have come to power they have initiated government-supported antisemitism. In the Soviet Union and Eastern Europe the antisemitism has been expressed against native Jews and through support for those seeking to destroy Israel. And Third World Marxist countries in which no Jews live (such as China and Vietnam) support groups seeking to destroy Israel[23] and deny Jewish national rights (for example, voting for the United Nations resolution denouncing Zionism as racism). Marxists and Leftists in democratic societies likewise oppose Israel, Zionism, and Jewish nationalism.

Since the Communist revolution in 1917 the Soviet Union has been implacably hostile toward Jewish religious and national expressions (in 1919 Zionism was designated a counter-revolutionary movement and prohibited).[24]

Indeed, the Soviet Union's campaign to destroy the Jewish religion in the country has been largely successful. Between 1956 and 1965 the number of synagogues in Russia declined from an already very low 450 to 60. Today there may be fewer than five rabbis for the more than two million Soviet Jews, and there are no known rabbinic students. In many parts of the Soviet Union it is illegal for a male to pray in a synagogue until he has completed military service, and Soviet Jews are forbidden classes in Judaism or even the Hebrew language. The only permitted books on Judaism are printed by the party-controlled publishers and they depict Judaism as a vulgar and immoral anachronism. Characteristic of the only material about Judaism legally available in the Soviet Union is this insight into the Jews in Trofim Kichko's *Judaism and Zionism* (Kiev, 1968): "The chauvinistic idea of the god-chosenness of the Jewish people . . . the idea of ruling over the peoples of the world. . . . Such ideas of Judaism were inculcated into the Jews first by priests and later by the Rabbis . . . and are inculcated today by Zionists, educating the Jews in the spirit of contempt and hatred towards other people. . . . The ideologists of Judaism, through the 'Holy Scriptures' teach the observant Jew to hate people of another faith and even to destroy them."[25]

While the government prints such material against Judaism and the Jews, the Jewish community is forbidden to operate a single Jewish school, let alone publish pro-Jewish books. This governmental attempt to annihilate Judaism is almost without precedent in Jewish history. Christian and Muslim antisemites, and for that matter even the Nazis during the 1930s, permitted Jewish schools. As a result of the Soviet Communists' prohibition of Jewish education, the Jews of the USSR are probably the Judaically most ignorant Jews in history.

Having succeeded in stifling the God and law components of Judaism, Soviet antisemitism now primarily attacks Jewish nationalism. The *Great Soviet Encyclopedia* of 1952, *defines* Zionism as "a reactionary movement . . . which denies the class struggle and strives to isolate the Jewish working masses from the general struggle of the proletariat."

The Soviets attempt to destroy the Jewish national identity in a variety of ways. For example, well before neo-Nazi "historical revisionists" arose to deny the Holocaust, Soviet books and films on World War II have ignored, virtually to the point of denying, the Jews' Holocaust. To cite a typical instance, in a forty-minute Russian-language film shown to Soviet visitors at Auschwitz, Poland, where over three million Jews were murdered, the Jews are not mentioned.[26]

In order to obliterate Jewish nationalism, Soviet propaganda goes one step further and charges that Zionists, that is all identifying Jews, worked with the Nazis. In 1979, an art exhibit in Russia "featured a grotesque painting of Russian corpses being gloated over by a grinning Nazi soldier and a grinning

Jewish prisoner wearing a Star of David. The message: Nazis and Jews were collaborators."[27] Thus, the Soviets not only deny (by omission) the Holocaust, but actually use Nazi atrocities to increase antisemitism in the Soviet Union by identifying Nazism with Zionism.

Since the Six-Day War in 1967, all Soviet media constantly refer to the Jewish state as a Hitlerian state. The tone for this campaign was set by the late Soviet president and first secretary of the Communist party Leonid Brezhnev on July 5, 1967: "In their atrocities against the Arabs it seems they [the Israelis] want to copy the crimes of the Hitler invaders."[28] Two years later, Yury Ivanov published *Beware Zionism*, which was hailed by *Komsomolskaya Pravda* as "the first scientific and fundamental work on this subject." In this book, Ivanov describes Zionism as an ideological offshoot of Nazism.

Both of us have visited the Soviet Union (Dennis Prager, 1969, 1981; Joseph Telushkin, 1973) and have personally witnessed its antisemitism. When Dennis Prager was asked to smuggle out material by Russian Jews detailing governmental antisemitism, he asked one of the writers, Tina Brodetskaya, "If these letters are published in the West, won't you be sent to prison?" "Where do you think I am now?" she responded. In 1973, Joseph Telushkin danced with Russian Jews in front of the major synagogue on Simhat Torah, a joyous Jewish holiday. The dancing was violently stopped by the KGB, the Soviet secret police, and a Russian Jew, Dmitri Ramm, who had accompanied Telushkin to the synagogue was beaten and had his leg fractured. Both of us met Soviet Jews who had served long prison terms *solely* for seeking to learn about Judaism and/or for desiring to emigrate to Israel. In a recent case, Joseph Begun, a Jewish mathematician who taught an underground Hebrew class, was fired from his job, then convicted for not working and exiled to Siberia.

Government-inspired antisemitism, coupled with renewed Jewish pride after the Six-Day War, has led to a large migration of Soviet Jews, many of whom risked their lives to emigrate. Others did not succeed. In Novosibirsk, Siberia, in 1973, Telushkin met with a local Jew, Dr. Isaac Poltinnikov, who had been without work and, along with his wife, Irma, and daughter, Victoria, had been terribly harassed for the three years since he and his family had applied for a visa to Israel. Finally, in 1979, after nine years of refusals, the Poltinnikovs were given permission to emigrate, but Mrs. Poltinnikov and Victoria, believing it was just a KGB trick, refused to go (on previous occasions the KGB had arrested them, subjected them to long interrogations, and killed their dog). Dr. Poltinnikov did go, and flew to Israel. The Soviets then refused Mrs. Poltinnikov and Victoria permission to join him. Irma soon thereafter died of malnutrition, and Victoria then committed suicide.

In Eastern Europe, Communist antisemitism persists even though few Jews have remained there since the Holocaust. For example, in the early 1950s, thirteen leaders of the Czech Communist party, ten of them Jews, were accused of being "Zionist agents" and hanged. These trials were ordered as one of a series of antisemitic show trials culminating in 1953 in the Soviet Union's "Doctors' Plot" in which Stalin charged a group of doctors, mostly Jews, with plotting to poison the Soviet leadership. Stalin died before the trial, but it was subsequently revealed that he was preparing to use the "Doctors' Plot" as a pretext to expel over two million Jews to Siberia. In 1968, Poland's media were dominated by "the unmasking of Zionists in Poland," though fewer than one out of every fifteen hundred Poles was Jewish.

Because there are so few Jews in Eastern Europe and because Eastern European Communism has been less totalitarian than that of the Soviet Union, Jews there have encountered less government-inspired antisemitism. Communist antisemitism in Eastern Europe, with the exception of Romania, is primarily expressed through support for terrorists and governments seeking to destroy Zionism and the Jewish homeland.

Aside from the Soviet Union and Eastern Europe, few Jews live in Communist-ruled societies. Nonetheless, Leftist anti-Jewish hostility remains a worldwide phenomenon. The most serious antisemitic act of the 1970s, the United Nations General Assembly resolution declaring Zionism to be racism, was the product of an Arab, Muslim, and Leftist alliance. Whereas almost the only countries opposing the resolution were democracies, every Leftist government in the world (with the exception of Romania which absented itself from the vote) declared the Jews' national movement racist and therefore illegitimate. The idea for the resolution was originally the Soviets', and among the resolution's sponsors was Cuba.[29]

WESTERN LEFTISTS

The Left in the West is also almost uniformly hostile to Jews and Judaism, and the further Left one is on the political spectrum the more intense is the antisemitism. Not surprisingly, Western Leftists who officially identify as Communists are the most antagonistic. In the United States, for example, the Socialist Workers party has specified that "the major task confronting American revolutionaries [as regards the Middle East] remains that of educating the radicalizing youth . . . for destruction of the state of Israel."[30] In 1972, the party's paper, *The Militant*, criticized the Palestinian terrorists' murder of eleven Israeli athletes at the Munich Olympics only on the grounds that it made "the criminal look like the victim."[31] The Communist party U.S.A. differs from the Socialist Workers party in that it concedes Israel's right to exist, but typical of its view of Zionism is this statement in the party's journal by Hyman Lumer, the Communist Party U.S.A. theoretician on the Middle East: "Zionism is . . . in its very essence a racist ideology. It sets the Jewish people apart as a special people, a 'chosen' people—if you will, a superior people. In Israel, the Zionist rulers have created a racist state."[32]

Similar denunciations of Jewish nationalism are made today by other Communist parties in the West. Individuals on the revolutionary Left are even more aggressive. Vanessa Redgrave, for example, the Academy Award–winning actress and a member of the Central Committee of the British

Worker's Revolutionary party (a Trotskyite Communist organization) made a propaganda film for the PLO in the late
1970s. In it, Redgrave performs a sensuous dance with a PLO
machine gun. Under the guise of only attacking Zionists and
Zionism (the film uses the Arabic word for Jew, *Yahud*, but
the English subtitles speak of "Zionists"), the movie utilizes
some classic Jew-hating images. In one scene Redgrave asks a
young Arab girl, "What would you do if he [a Jewish soldier]
tried to kill you?" Marie Syrkin, in a critique of the film,
wrote: "At this point my mind wandered to the prioress of
The Canterbury Tales who devoutly recounts a medieval tale
of a Christian child murdered by the Jews. The killing of
children: the hoariest of antisemitic libels."[33]

The non-Communist far Left is similarly single-minded in
its attacks on Israel and all Jews who identify with it. Let us
cite a number of characteristic examples from the United
States. During the 1970s the left-wing National Lawyers
Guild sent a delegation to only one country in the world to
examine human rights—Israel. The delegation met with PLO
representatives, heard their story, and returned with a report
denouncing Israel. A Jewish lawyer in the group, Dickstein,
wrote a dissenting report, but the National Lawyers Guild
suppressed it.[34] At the Harvard Law School in 1979 leftist
Third World students sponsored a conference on "Human
Rights in the Third World." As Harvard law professor Alan
Dershowitz reported: "At that time there were massacres in
the Central African Republic, the blood of people killed by
Idi Amin was still fresh in people's minds, and the atrocious
record of Libya on human rights could well have been discussed. But only one item concerning human rights was
placed on the agenda: 'The So-Called Nation of Israel's Terrorism and Genocide.' "[35]

The title of the Harvard Leftists' "conference" exemplifies
two characteristics of contemporary left-wing antisemitism:
the denial of Jewish nationhood, hence the appellation "the
so-called nation of Israel," and the constant accusation of
genocide against the Jewish state. The charges are related in
an Orwellian manner. The denial of Jewish nationhood legiti-
mates all efforts at annihilating the Jewish state and Zionists,

what may be truly called genocide. But this genocidal attempt against Israel is then inverted and projected from the enemies of Israel onto Israel.

Thus it is not coincidental that on one issue, the annihilation of Israel, the far Left and Nazism agree. On April 14, 1970, *The New York Times* reported that the radical Black power leader Stokely Carmichael declared: "I have never admired a White man, but the greatest of them, to my mind, was Hitler." In Chicago in October 1970, a speech by Israel's foreign minister, Abba Eban, was picketed by the far Left Youth Against War and Fascism and by the American Nazi party.

Leftist antisemitism has also deeply infected left-wing Christians. Among Protestant groups, the World Council of Churches and affiliates such as the (American) National Council of Churches have been among the major advocates of recognition of the Palestine Liberation Organization, though its *raison d'être* has been to destroy Israel, and though it has been the world's leading supporter of terrorism against Western democracies. Similar support has been offered by the American Friends Services Committee which represents American Quakers.

In 1976 the pro-Third World *Christian Science Monitor* was the only one of the fifty major newspapers in the United States to condemn Israel's raid on Entebbe, Uganda's airport, where PLO terrorists were about to start murdering Jewish passengers of a hijacked plane.

The same situation holds for the Catholic Church wherein Leftist theologians, clergy, and lay leaders with Third World orientations combine traditional Church resentment of the "old Israel" with the Left's resentment of the new Israel. One man who combines both motifs in his antisemitism is Archbishop Hilarian Capucci, formerly of Jerusalem. On August 18, 1974, Israeli police caught Capucci smuggling weapons and explosives for terrorists to kill Israeli civilians. Though sentenced to twelve years in prison, Israel released him after less than three years at the specific request of Pope Paul VI. Upon his release Capucci declared: "Jesus Christ was the first *fedayeen* [Arab freedom fighter]. I am just following his example." A short time thereafter he celebrated a Mass "in protest against the genocide perpetrated against the Arab people." A Catholic journal, *Resumen*, responded to Capucci's activities with a denunciation of his "propaganda pamphlets which revive the myths which make Capucci a Jesus and the Israelis deicidal mercenaries." In January 1979 Archbishop Capucci attended meetings in Damascus of the Palestine National Council, the supreme authority of the PLO, which had earlier made him an honorary member.[36]

Whereas in the past Christian attitudes toward Jews were almost uniformly hostile, today such hostility emanates almost exclusively from Christianity's far Right and Left. On the other hand, moderate and conservative Christians in the United States are among the most aggressive supporters of Jewry and Israel's right to live.

CONCLUSION

The Left has opposed Jews both for their religion and nationality. The unique Jewish fusion of religion and nationality is anathema to the secularism and universalism of the Left. This partially explains why the Left, though so hospitable and supportive of the national liberation movements of almost all other peoples, is so antagonistic to the nationalism of the Jews. It was regarding this Leftist hatred of the Jews that Social Democrat Irving Howe wrote, "In the warmest of hearts there is a cold spot for the Jews."

From Marx and the French Socialists to the Soviets, the Third World, and Western Leftists today, an intense Jew-hatred has prevailed. As United States Senator Daniel Patrick Moynihan has said, "Antisemitism has become a unifying global ideology of the totalitarian Left."[37] And many on the non-totalitarian Left have been compromised by their "no enemies on the Left" attitude. Thus a movement founded, established, and supported in large part by Jews has come to constitute, along with the Arab/Muslim world, the Jews' greatest enemy at this time.

TWELVE

Nazi Antisemitism

PERHAPS NO UNDERSTANDING of an antisemitic ideology
is so widely held and unchallenged as that which ascribes
Nazi antisemitism to racism. The Nazis, so the belief goes,
were racists and therefore hated Jews and all other "non-
Aryans."

History and reason, however, point to a very different understanding of Nazi antisemitism. The Nazis were indeed racists when they claimed the inferiority of "non-Aryan races"
(though who was "non-Aryan" had little to do with race, and
much to do with politics—they did not, for example, racially
denigrate the Japanese or Arabs, both allies of the Nazis). But
Nazi antisemitism was not an outgrowth of racist ideology.
Racism was fundamentally irrelevant to Nazi antisemitism.
Attempts to subsume Nazi antisemitism under the heading of
racism is another mistaken endeavor to dejudaize Jew-hatred.

The commonly accepted view of Nazi antisemitism as an
expression of racism must be questioned on two scores. First,
and most basic, why did the Nazis label the Jews a race?
There are Jews of every race; and since anyone of any race
can become a Jew, Jews can hardly constitute a race. The entire racial claim needs explanation. Why did the Nazis need

151

it? After all, thousands of years of pre-Nazi antisemites needed no racial basis to hate the Jews. For some reason the Nazis found in racism an explanation of antisemitism which no other ideology could supply.

Second, if racism was the basis of the Nazis' world view, why did Nazi hatred focus on the Jews to the virtual exclusion of all other "races"—including the Gypsies, who though murdered en masse were, quite unlike the Jews, incidental to the Nazi world view and not the objects of genocide?[1] And if race was the issue, why did the Nazis show such fondness for that other Semitic "race," the Arabs?

In holding the simplistic view that the Nazis hated Jews because of racism, we once again commit the fundamental error (wishful thinking?) of other modern explanations of antisemitism: we dejudaize it. In this instance it seems logically irresistible to do so: the Nazis hated "non-Aryans"; the Jews were "non-Aryans"; therefore, the Nazis hated the Jews. Yet, the Jews were the only "non-Aryans" whom the Nazis attempted to annihilate, and antisemitism, not anti-non-Aryanism, was the essence of Nazism.

It was not because of racism that Nazis hated Jews but because of their hatred of Jews that the Nazis utilized racist arguments. The Jew-hatred came first. Racial Jew-hatred was needed in order to explain the one new belief of Nazi antisemitism. Whereas former antisemites believed that a Jew could change and become like them, Hitler and the Nazis denied this possibility. Once a Jew, always a Jew. As Hitler wrote in *Mein Kampf*, "In his new language [the Jew] will express the old ideas; his inner nature has not changed . . . the Jew . . . can speak a thousand languages and nevertheless remains a Jew. His traits of character have remained the same. . . . It is always the same Jew."[2] The Jews seek to dominate the non-Jewish world through various instruments: Christianity, Marxism, socialism, capitalism, democracy. All are products of Jews and their values no matter what their non-Jewish guises.

Hitler viewed himself as insightful and courageous enough to conclude what previous antisemites had either not realized or shirked from concluding. A Jew cannot become a non-Jew any more than a Black man can become white; the Jews' permanent "traits of character" render them a "race." Therefore any campaign directed against Jews must be directed against all of them no matter what non-Jewish religious or national identity they may hold. Their non-Jewish identity is irrelevant; they remain Jews because they have fixed characteristics that only members of a race possess. These fixed characteristics are alien Jewish ideas.

Nazi antisemitism was before all else hatred of the Jewish character, not hatred of the Jews' "non-Aryan" blood. It was, like all other forms of antisemitism, hatred of the challenges posed by Jews and Jewish values. This Jewish challenge formed the basis of the Nazi beliefs that mankind's ultimate conflict is between the Jews and the Aryans and that only one of them could survive.

By Hitler's own account in his autobiography *Mein Kampf,* he was first an antisemite, not a racist. His innovation was to amalgamate the two and develop a new program to solve "the Jewish Question" once and for all. Only racial antisemitism could correctly understand and deal with the "Jewish Problem." All other forms of antisemitism were in error. Prior to racial antisemitism, antisemites had assumed that Jews who abandoned Judaism and adopted the antisemites' values and identity could fully assimilate and become non-Jews. Antisemitic Christians believed that Jews could really become Christians; the secular nationalists expected the Jews to abandon their national identity and identify only with the nation in which they lived; and the Left demanded that Jews give up their particularism and become universalists.

To Hitler, however, all attempts to solve the "Jewish Problem" through conversion/assimilation were futile. No matter what new identity a Jew may assume, he carries subversive Jewish values with him and merely uses his new guise as a Christian, or Marxist, or German to spread his values. As Hitler put it, "the Jews speak German, but they think Jewish."

Apparently no Nazi ever stopped to question how a race

could be defined by something so unbiological as ideas and "traits of character."* Yet this notion typified Nazi thinking about the Jews. On August 23, 1936, SS-Oberscharführer Schröder, Eichmann's superior at the time, issued a statement typical of innumerable Nazi statements: "Wherever [the Jew] tries to transmit his work, his influence and his world outlook to the non-Jewish world, he discharges it in hostile ideologies, as we find in Liberalism . . . in Marxism, and not least in Christianity. These ideologies then accord with a broader concept of Jewish mentality."[3]

To cite but one other example, *Schwarze Korps*, the official publication of the SS, said in its May 15, 1935, issue: "The as-similationist minded Jews deny their race and insist on their loyalty to Germany or claim to be Christians, because they have been baptized, in order to subvert National-Socialist principles."[4]

Hitler and the Nazis had to account for the extraordinary fact that Jews have fixed "traits of character." Only race could explain this phenomenon. Once this was understood, the age-old solution to the Jewish challenge, converting the Jews to the majority identity, became utterly untenable. If you want to rid the world of the Jews' "hostile ideologies," then you must physically rid the world of the Jews. The Nazi conclusion was as rationally thought out as the means they ul-timately adopted for implementing it. Every other solution had been tried and had failed; the Nazis would implement the "Final Solution."

Racism is one of two commonly held explanations for Nazi antisemitism which deny its explicitly anti-Jewish character. The second is the scapegoat thesis. According to this explana-tion, in order to attain power, Hitler and the Nazis needed a

---

* Hitler himself is reported as having told his intimate associate, Hermann Rauschning: "I know perfectly well that in the scientific sense there is no such thing as a race. As a politician I need a concep-tion which enables the order which has hitherto existed on a historic basis to be abolished and an entirely new order enforced and given an intellectual basis. And for this purpose the conception of race serves me well." Hermann Rauschning, *Hitler Speaks* (London: T. Butter-worth, 1939), p. 229.

scapegoat upon whom to blame the ills of Germany, and the Jews served this purpose most conveniently. The Nazis attacked the Jews not because attacking Jews was central to the Nazi world view, but because attacking the Jews was the politically wise thing to do.

The historical record unambiguously affirms the *opposite* of the scapegoat thesis. The Nazis did not attack the Jews in order to achieve power; rather they wanted power in large measure to attack the Jews.

This point is hardly a revelation. It has been most recently documented by the Holocaust historian Lucy Dawidowicz in *The War Against the Jews, 1933–1945:* "Serious people, responsible people, thought that Hitler's notions about the Jews were, at best, merely political bait for disgruntled masses, no more than ideological window dressing to cloak a naked drive for power. Yet precisely the reverse was true. Racial imperialism and the fanatic plan to destroy the Jews were the dominant passions behind the drive for power."[5]

To Hitler, the "Final Solution" to the "Jewish Problem" was more important than winning World War II. Late in the war, when the Nazis were losing, German troops were taken from the Allied fronts and deployed to murder Jews. In July 1944, when the Germans needed every train to begin their evacuation of Greece, not a single train was diverted from those taking Jews to death camps. When the Germans declared a ban on all nonmilitary rail traffic in order to free trains for a summer offensive in southern Russia, the only trains exempted were those transporting Jews to death camps.[6]

A second fact which negates the scapegoat thesis was the Nazi policy of murdering Jews. Considering the Nazis' severe manpower shortages, they should have used the Jews as slave laborers, not murdered them—that is, if the Jews were scapegoats, or even hated political enemies. Instead, the Nazis murdered the overwhelming majority of Jews who fell into their hands. Even those few Jews who were used as slave labor were usually so mistreated that they died in a matter of weeks or months. When a Nazi general, Kurt Freiherr von Grienanth, gingerly noted in September 1942 that "the principle should be to eliminate the Jews as promptly as possible without impairing essential war work," he was demoted by Heinrich Himmler, the chief of the Gestapo, who denounced the general's proposal as a subtle effort to support the Jews.[7] To most German military leaders Germany's primary war was against the Allies, but for the Nazis, it was the war against the Jews.

A third fact undermining the scapegoat thesis is that in the early years of the Third Reich the Nazis did not want the Jews to remain in Germany where they could have been used as scapegoats; indeed, the Nazis encouraged Jews to leave Germany. In what now reads as incredible, in January 1935, Reinhard Heydrich, head of the SA, issued a directive to the Bavarian political police to cooperate with German Zionists. "The activity of the Zionist oriented youth organizations [in encouraging Jews to emigrate to Palestine] . . . lies in the interest of the National Socialists States' leadership."[8] Two months later the Nazis forbade Jewish organizations from encouraging Jews to stay in Germany. All of this was rather strange behavior toward "scapegoats."

A fourth error in the scapegoat thesis is the premise upon which it rests: that antisemitism was so politically effective in Germany that the Nazis needed to use it to achieve power. On the contrary, the major appeal of the Nazis to the German electorate was not the party's antisemitism, but its promise of economic improvement, its appeals to patriotism, and its promises to avenge Germany's humiliation from the Versailles Conference which concluded World War I. While it is true that the people who voted for the Nazis were at best indifferent to the fate of Jews, most of them did not vote for the Nazis because of the Nazis' antisemitism.[9] The most important factor in Nazi success at the polls was the economic situation in Germany.

The final refutation of the scapegoat thesis was delivered by Adolf Hitler himself in his final message to the German people. In this message, delivered just prior to committing suicide, Hitler spoke of that which was most important to him. The subject which gripped Hitler's attention to the last moments of his life was the Jews. On April 29, 1945, Adolf

Hitler addressed his final words to the German people:
"Above all I charge the leaders of the nation and those under
them to scrupulous observance of the laws of race and to the
merciless opposition to the universal poisoner of all peoples,
international Jewry" (emphasis ours).[10] Scapegoats to the
end?

IDEOLOGICAL ROOTS OF NAZI ANTISEMITISM

Nearly every popular ideology in German history helped
provide ideological soil for Nazi antisemitism: Christianity,
the Enlightenment, Marxism, nationalism, and racism. The
antisemitism of the first three has been discussed in separate
chapters. Let us now discuss the antisemitic elements in German nationalism and racism and see how our general thesis
applies to them.

German nationalist antisemites argued that German Jews
had failed to fulfill their part of the bargain implicit in emancipation—that in return for citizenship, they cease being a
distinct people. As German nationalism intensified, any manifestation of the Jews' national identity increased antisemitism.* In 1879, the leading historian of modern Germany,
Heinrich von Treitschke, a man with both a wide scholarly
and political following, published *A Word About Our Jewry,*
an essay in which he set forth the conditions under which
German Jews could be accepted in Germany. "What we have
to demand from our Jewish fellow citizens is simple: That
they become Germans, regard themselves simply and justly as
Germans. . . ." They could continue practicing Judaism,
Treitschke wrote, but restrict it to the private domain, and

---

* So strong was this German hostility to Jewish peoplehood that
many German Jews decided to drop the national component of Judaism and to identify themselves as "Germans of the Mosaic persua-
sion," Jews whose one and only national identity was German. Many
German Jews so feared accusations of "dual loyalties" that the most
important nineteenth-century leader of Reform Judaism in Germany,
Abraham Geiger, opposed the intervention of world Jewry on behalf
of Jews in Damascus, Syria, who were victims of a "blood libel."

not try and influence Germany with Jewish values: "We do not want an era of German-Jewish mixed culture to follow after thousands of years of German civilization."[11]

In addition, Treitschke accused the Jews of having contempt for Germans. As an example, he accused the leading Jewish historian of the time, Heinrich Graetz, of preaching in his *History of the Jews,* "Deadly hatred . . . of the purest and most powerful exponents of German character, from Luther to Goethe, and Fichte. . . . And this stubborn contempt for the German *goyim* is not at all the attitude of a single fanatic." Treitschke then cites another "fanatic" Jew who, not having an exclusive German national identity, was a hostile "outsider": "Borne [an early nineteenth-century Jewish writer] was the first to introduce into our journals the peculiar shameless way of talking about the Fatherland offhand, and without any reverence, like an outsider, as if mocking of Germany did not cut deeply into the heart of every German."

It was in response to these perceived threats to German values that Treitschke wrote what later became the slogan of the Nazis: "Even in the best educated circles . . . we hear today the cry, as from one mouth 'the Jews are our misfortune.' "

Within a year of *A Word to Our Jewry*'s publication, a German students association distributed an "Anti-Semites' Petition." The petition demanded that Bismarck achieve the "emancipation of the German People from a form of Alien domination which it cannot endure for any length of time." The petition demanded an end to, or at least great restrictions on, Jewish immigration, the exclusion of Jews from government and teaching positions, and the resumption of a Jewish census. The petition was circulated mainly in Prussia where it received 225,000 signatures. A counterpetition circulated by liberal students did poorly. At the University of Göttingen, for example, the petition demanding an end to equal rights for Jews received more than twice as many signatures as the petition requesting that Jews merely be allowed to retain their equal rights.

Alongside this rising nationalist sentiment in Germany was

the racist movement which promulgated a philosophy of German/Aryan superiority counterpoised against Jewish decadence. Its most influential exponent was the English expatriate, Houston Stewart Chamberlain, who in 1899 published *Foundations of the Nineteenth Century*, one of the most important racist and antisemitic works in modern history, and one well received by many intellectuals of the day. *The London Times Literary Supplement* (December 1919) called it "unquestionably one of the rare books that really matter."

According to *Foundations*, the future of humanity will be determined by the outcome of the epochal struggle between two "races": the Teutonic ("Aryan") and the Jewish ("Semitic"). The racial thesis of *Foundations* notwithstanding, Chamberlain's real opposition was to the Jews' values and theology, not to their race and biology.

This fact is repeatedly made clear throughout his two-volume work. One would expect a racial antisemite to hate all Jews, but Chamberlain painstakingly disassociates himself from such "crude" antisemitism: he repeatedly denied any "personal animus against individuals belonging to the Jewish nation."[12] In fact, Chamberlain dedicated *Foundations of the Nineteenth Century* to a Jew, Julius Wiesner, once his professor at the University of Vienna.

It was not hatred of the Jews as a race that animated the foremost evangelist of racial antisemitism. He hated what the Jews stood for and their success in overturning others' values: "I cannot help shuddering . . . at the portentous, irremediable mistake the world made in accepting the traditions of this wretched little nation . . . as the basis of its belief."[13] He hated the Jews for their monotheism and moral values which prevented the natural human being from possessing unrestricted freedom: "The Jew came into our gay world and spoiled everything with his ominous concept of sin, his law, and his cross."[14]

The success of Chamberlain's Aryan versus Jew interpretation of history was remarkable. Within a few years of publication the book went through eight editions and "became the Bible of hundreds of thousands of Germans." Kaiser William II read it aloud to his children and sent it to all the army officers and libraries in Germany. In a letter to Chamberlain the Kaiser wrote, "You explain what was obscure, you show the way of salvation to Germany and all the rest of mankind."[15]

Throughout the late nineteenth and early twentieth centuries antisemitic ideologies proliferated in Germany. In addition to traditional Christian sources of antisemitism, anti-Jewish attacks now emanated from virtually all sources, including anti-Christian ones. The latter focused their animus against Judaism for, among other things, bringing forth Christianity. The very creator of the term "anti-Semitism" and founder of the Anti-Semites League, Wilhelm Marr, denounced Christianity as a "disease of the human consciousness" which was but one more manifestation of Judaism.[16] Eugen Dühring, the prominent racist of the late 1800s, argued that "Christianity is itself semitic" and that all monotheistic religions preach hatred of life.[17] Richard Wagner called for a new German religion with no Jewish or Christian influence: "Emancipation from the yoke of Judaism appears to us the foremost necessity."[18]

Hatred of Judaism for subverting pagan values and unleashing Christianity was later expressed in a song of the Hitler Youth: "Pope and Rabbi shall be no more. We want to be pagans once again. No more creeping to Churches. We are the joyous Hitler Youth. We do not need any Christian virtues. Our leader, Adolf Hitler, is our Savior."[19]

Despite such anti-Christian attitudes, however, there was always a crucial distinction between the racists' anti-Judaism and their anti-Christianity. They held all Jews accountable for alien Jewish values, including Jews who were nonreligious and assimilated. Racists held that Jewish values were embedded in Jewish blood. Christians, however, could cease being Christians and become good German Aryans by adopting an Aryan Christianity with an Aryan Jesus (Chamberlain, for example, claimed that Jesus was an Aryan completely devoid of Jewish blood), Aryan disciples, and the removal of all Jewish concepts in Christianity, such as monotheism and its universal moral code.

To most contemporary readers one of the most shocking aspects of the racist campaign against the Jews is the success it achieved in academic and educated circles. Yet the fact is that advocacy of nationalist and racist antisemitism was as widespread among intellectuals as among other Germans. A Jewish writer, B. Segel, described this in the early 1920s: "In Berlin I attended meetings which were entirely devoted to the *Protocols* [*of the Elders of Zion*]. The speaker was usually a professor, a teacher, an editor, a lawyer, or someone of that kind. The audience consisted of members of the educated class, civil servants, tradesmen, former officers, ladies, above all students.... Passions were whipped up to the boiling point. There in front of one, in the flesh, was the cause of all those ills [the Jews], those who made the war and brought about the defeat and engineered the revolution.... I observed the students. A few hours earlier they had perhaps been exerting all their mental energy in a seminar under the guidance of a world famous scholar, in an effort to solve some legal or philosophical or mathematical problem. Now young blood was boiling, eyes flashed, fists clenched, hoarse voices roared applause or vengeance.... Whoever dared to express a slight doubt was shouted down, often insulted and threatened.... German scholarship allowed belief in the genuineness of the *Protocols* and in the existence of a Jewish world conspiracy to penetrate ever more deeply into all the educated sections of the German population, so that now [1924] it is simply ineradicable.... None of the great German scholars (save for the late lamented Strack) rose to unmask the forgery."[20]

Nine years after this typical meeting in Berlin, Adolf Hitler was chancellor of Germany, and soon the Holocaust, the consequence of all these various German and European ideologies, was under way. When the antisemitism of these ideologies, whether Christian, nationalist, universalist Enlightenment, or racist, is understood, the Nazi destruction of European Jewry can no longer be regarded as some psychological aberration, Machiavellian need for scapegoats, or racist eruption, but as a logical consequence of Jew-hatred.

THE UNIVERSALITY AND DEPTH
OF EUROPEAN ANTISEMITISM

The German brew of antisemitic ideologies was a unique one and it culminated in Germany's unleashing of the "Final Solution" of the "Jewish Problem." But thanks to the virtual universality of antisemitism, the Germans found fertile fields to sow the Holocaust throughout nearly all of Europe. The six million Jews murdered by the Nazis came from twenty-one European countries. Hitler's goal was to render at least Europe *judenrein* (free of Jews), and by 1945, he had murdered almost seven out of every ten Jews on the European Continent. In some countries, the Nazis murdered nearly every Jew. To cite the two most extreme examples, in Poland, the Nazis murdered 3 million Jews out of a prewar Jewish population of 3.3 million, and in Latvia, Lithuania, and Estonia, 228,000 out of 253,000.

The major reason for the Nazis' success in murdering Europe's Jews was the cooperation they received from citizens of Nazi-occupied countries. This is proven by the fact that, except in Holland, wherever the local populations refused to cooperate the percentage of Jews murdered was considerably smaller than elsewhere, and in two instances almost all the Jews were saved.

One example was Denmark whose prewar Jewish population of eight thousand was mainly composed of Jews well integrated into Danish society. After the Nazi takeover in April 1940, Himmler and other top German officials repeatedly pressured Denmark to take actions against its Jewish citizens. Lucy Dawidowicz describes the events: "After Denmark came under martial law, Best [the German minister in charge of Denmark] tried to deport the Danish Jews. His plans . . . were reported on September 28 [1943] to Danish Social Democratic leaders. The Germans had scheduled the roundup of the Jews for October 1, 1943, but in an extraordinary operation involving the whole Danish people and the agreement of the Swedish government, nearly all Danish Jews were hidden and then ferried across to Sweden, where they remained in safety until the end of the war. The Germans managed to round up some four hundred Jews, whom they sent to Theresienstadt [a concentration camp in Czechoslovakia]. The internment of the Danish Jews in Theresienstadt agitated the Danish government which repeatedly requested permission to inspect the camp. In June, 1944, such permission was granted, and the visit was made by delegates of the Danish Red Cross. As a consequence of persistent Danish interest in the deported Jews, none was sent to Auschwitz. At the end of the war, fifty-one had died in Theresienstadt of natural causes."[21]

Finland provides a second example of a Nazi-occupied nation being able to save its Jews. When Himmler visited Helsinki in July 1942, he pressured the Finns to deport their Jews to German concentration camps. The Finnish foreign minister, Rolf Witting, simply refused to consider the matter, and no Finnish Jews were murdered.

A third example of a country (in this instance an ally of Germany) where the Nazis encountered stiff resistance to the Final Solution from the populace and leadership is Bulgaria. After Bulgaria's political leaders halted the deportation of Bulgarian Jews, though not of refugee Jews living in Bulgaria, "the Germans continued to exert pressure to deport the Jews, but the counterpressure of Bulgarian opinion, especially the Bulgarian Orthodox Church, restrained the government from compliance. King Boris III, too, was opposed to deporting any but 'Communist elements.' "[22] As a result, 50,000 of the 64,000 Jews in Bulgaria survived the war.

In most of the countries the Nazis occupied, however, they received enormous local support in locating, arresting, and in Eastern Europe, even murdering the Jews. It was this support, offered enthusiastically in countries with large Jewish populations, that enabled the Final Solution to achieve its demonic success.

In Poland, with its long history of antisemitism and its large Jewish population (one-tenth of Poland's population), the Nazis were constantly aided in their program to murder all Polish Jews. When Poland became independent in 1919 it marked the event with a series of pogroms.* During the years between the wars, severe quotas were placed on Jews in universities, and discriminatory economic regulations impoverished many Jews.[23]

The record of Polish support for Nazi actions against the Jews is recorded in many sources, nowhere more vividly than in *The Warsaw Diary of Chaim A. Kaplan.*[24] Kaplan, a German-born Jew living in Poland, meticulously recorded Jewish life in Poland under Nazi rule. His published diary runs from September 1, 1939, the day of the German invasion, until Kaplan's own deportation on or about August 4, 1942. Throughout the journal Kaplan writes of Poles' support for the Nazis' anti-Jewish policies. When, for example, the Nazis ordered the confiscation of almost all the Jews' property and money, Jews pleaded with longtime Christian friends to accept sums for safekeeping, but, writes Kaplan, "the Christian 'friends' refused, because their merchants association had forbidden its members to give assistance to Jews in any form whatsoever" (October 16, 1939).

The depth of Polish Jew-hatred is particularly evident in Kaplan's description of the expulsion of the Jewish community of Pultusk. The entire community, including "old men with canes and sick people on the point of death" were exiled to Poplawy. "The rabbi went with the exiles. . . . That night the Polish inhabitants of the village attacked the rabbi, beat him up, and stole his last pennies. They stole the money from the rest of the exiles as they were leaving the village. The crowd cheered them all and emptied their pockets" (October

---

* A popular Jewish joke of the interwar period bears witness to the depth of Polish antisemitism. "Ignace J. Paderewski, post-war premier of Poland, was discussing his country's affairs with the late President Wilson. 'If all our demands are not granted at the peace conference,' said Mr. Paderewski, 'I can foresee serious trouble in my country. Why, my people will be so irritated that many of them will go out and massacre the Jews.' 'And what will happen if your demands are granted?' asked Mr. Wilson. Replied Paderewski, 'Why, my people will be so happy that many of them will get drunk and go out and massacre the Jews.' " (S. Felix Mendelsohn, *The Jew Laughs,* p. 46.)

26, 1939). To cite one other example, Kaplan notes that in the early days of the occupation before the Nazis had ghettoized the Jews, when Jews and Poles waited on bread lines for food, the Poles, "Even though . . . they do not know German . . . have nevertheless learned to say 'Ein Jude' in order to get [a Jew] thrown out of line" (October 5, 1939).

But what may most reveal the depth of Polish antisemitism is that most of the Poles in the anti-Nazi underground refused to help Polish Jews even during the latter's revolt in the Warsaw Ghetto. And a few months after the revolt's failure, on September 15, 1943, General Tadeusz Bor-Komorowski of the Armia Krajowa, the main Polish underground force, ordered that Jewish anti-Nazi fighters be liquidated.[25] Though moving individual instances of Poles risking their lives to save Jews are recorded, such as the seven Poles who smuggled arms into the Warsaw Ghetto, Poles overwhelmingly reacted to the Nazi genocide of the Jews with, at best, indifference, and very often, support. Only with Polish cooperation could the Nazis have murdered over 90 percent of the three million Jews of Poland. And it is not coincidental that every major Nazi death camp was located in Poland.

Hitler's actions against the Jews were also abetted by his ally from 1939 to 1941, Joseph Stalin. When Nazi foreign minister Joachim von Ribbentrop met with Stalin to discuss the Russian-German partition of Poland, they also discussed Germany's treatment of the Jews. Von Ribbentrop reported Stalin's response: "The Polish national problem might be dealt with as Germany saw fit," a statement which the Germans understood as supportive of their anti-Jewish actions.[26] Though Stalin knew about Nazi persecution of Polish Jews from 1939 on, he kept this information secret. As a consequence, when the Germans broke their alliance with the Communists and invaded Russia in 1941, Russian Jews had no idea that the Nazis intended to murder them. The effects of this ignorance were catastrophic. Oblivious to the Nazi designs, the Jews in occupied Soviet territories at first made no attempt to resist the Nazis or even flee. When the Nazis ordered local Jewish leaders to gather all the Jews for resettlement to a "Jewish region," the Jews obeyed. When the Jews did gather, *Einsatzgruppen*, Nazi mobile killing units, together with "local Ukrainian, White Russian, or Latvian militia would transport the Jews outside the town and murder them all—men, women, and children—by machine-gun fire within abandoned dugouts and ravines."[27]

The Nazis were able to rely on local support of this kind throughout Eastern Europe. As soon as the Nazis captured Kovno, Lithuania, gangs of Lithuanians murdered 3800 Jews on June 25 and 26, 1941. Upon capturing Lvov, in the Ukraine, the Nazis immediately organized a Ukrainian militia which murdered 7000 Jews on July 2 and 3. Historian Shmuel Ettinger has noted that the actions of the Ukrainians were so immediate and precipitate that "the murders were halted by order of the Germans" who wished to bring greater order to the genocide campaign. That fall, at the end of September, on Yom Kippur, 1941, Germans and Ukrainians murdered at least 34,000 Jews in Babi Yar, near Kiev.

The Romanians also participated in the murder of the Jews. On June 28, 1941, bloody pogroms were carried out there, and 7000 Jews were murdered. Later, the Romanians established concentration camps for the Jews. By the war's end 300,000 Romanian Jews had been murdered through the joint efforts of the Nazis and Romanians.

In March 1942, the leader of the Slovak People's party, Father Joseph Tiso, a Catholic priest, agreed to expel the Jews of Slovakia. After his Fascist Hlinka Guard conducted massive manhunts for Jews, 35,000 were sent eastward to be murdered in the death camps. A Slovakian rabbi went to Archbishop Kametko and asked him to influence his former private secretary Tiso to stop the expulsions. The archbishop responded: "This is no mere expulsion. There you will not die of hunger and pestilence; there they will slaughter you all, old and young, women and children, in one day. This is your punishment for the death of our Redeemer. There is only one hope for you—to convert all to our religion. Then I shall effect the annulling of this decree."[28]

In the fall of 1944, Rabbi M. D. Weissmandel escaped while en route to a concentration camp, and met with the papal nuncio, describing for him the horrors of the Jews in temporary camps awaiting deportation to Auschwitz. He begged the papal nuncio to intervene with Tiso. The papal nuncio answered: "This, being a Sunday, is a holy day for us. Neither I nor Father Tiso occupy ourselves with profane matters on this day." Weissmandel persisted, arguing that the lives of innocent human beings, including infants and children, were not a profane matter. The papal nuncio responded: "There is no innocent blood of Jewish children in the world. All Jewish blood is guilty. You have to die. This is the punishment that has been awaiting you because of that sin" [the death of Jesus].

Shmuel Ettinger has summarized the support given by the people of Eastern Europe in the Nazi war against the Jews: "The most active accomplices of the Germans in these acts of extermination were the Ukrainians and Lithuanians, but they had many helpers among the Croatians, Rumanians, Hungarians and Slovaks. . . . Their police personnel were willing to search tirelessly for days and even weeks in order to hunt down one concealed Jewish child. Though Poland was notorious for her antisemitism, it is a fact that the number of Jews hidden and saved there by the local population was many times higher than in Soviet Ukraine and Soviet White Russia. . . . [But] it is not by chance that Poland was chosen as the country of extermination. The Polish people . . . [did not] lift a finger to help the Jews, even in the worst days of mass murder, or during the Warsaw ghetto uprising. There were many Poles who handed escaping Jews over to the Nazis. Nevertheless, there were some Poles, mainly in the monasteries, who were shocked at the brutal murders, and particularly the slaughter of young children, and attempted to save them. Through them several thousand Jewish children were saved in Poland."[29]

There is no question that in Western Europe the Nazis took greater care in carrying out the Final Solution, knowing that anti-Jewish feelings were less intense there. As a result, except for Holland, the percentage of Jews murdered in Western Europe was considerably less than in Eastern Europe. Nonetheless, the Nazis were also extended extensive cooperation in Western Europe as well. In France, for example, the

Nazis required French cooperation to carry out the Jewish deportations, since the Germans lacked the manpower to do it alone. On June 11, 1941, the Nazis formulated plans to round up all Jews between the ages of sixteen and forty. Pierre Laval, vice-prime minister in Vichy, unoccupied France, informed the Germans that he would not use French police to round up Jews who were French citizens. But he did order the French police to turn over to the Nazis the 64,070 Jewish refugees in Paris, including children under sixteen years of age. By mid-July French police had delivered 4051 Jewish children under the age of sixteen into the hands of the Nazis, Jews whom the Nazis themselves had not ordered rounded up. These children were subsequently sent to Auschwitz.[30]

Virtually every ideology and nationality in Europe had been saturated with Jew-hatred by the time the Nazis developed the Final Solution. Over the preceding decades and centuries essential elements of Christianity, Marxism and socialism, nationalism, and Enlightenment and post-Enlightenment thought had ruled the existence of the Jews to be intolerable. In the final analysis they all would have opposed what Hitler had done, but without them Hitler could not have done it.

THIRTEEN

Anti-Zionist Antisemitism

UNTIL THE HOLOCAUST, enemies of the Jews, whether pagans, Christians, Muslims, men of the Enlightenment, Leftists, or Nazis, proudly and publicly espoused their opposition to the Jews.[1] Since the revelations of the Nazi crimes, however, it has become taboo to call oneself an opponent of the Jews, and today, for the first time in history, antisemites deny that they are antisemites. In fact, contemporary antisemites often go one step further and insist that they actually like Jews. The Soviet Union, one of the most antisemitic governments and societies in the world, not only denies being antisemitic, but boasts of being the only society to have actually eliminated antisemitism, and the only one to have outlawed it in its constitution, an act initiated by the well-known patron of the Jews, Joseph Stalin. Similarly, Arabs whose proclaimed policy it is to destroy the Jewish homeland often claim to be friends and admirers of Jews. If one is to take such people by their words, there are no more antisemites on the face of the earth. Since the revelations of the Holocaust the most hated people in history no longer have a single enemy.

It is clear that what has taken place among antisemites is only a change in rhetoric. Hitler and Eichmann have ren-

dered the term antisemite universally ugly and therefore un-
usable, at least for the time being. Those who prior to the
Holocaust would have called themselves, and certainly been
called by others, antisemites, now utilize the term "anti-
Zionist." Thus the Soviets, when they jail Jews for Jewish activities, claim to be only "anti-Zionist," and those who seek to
destroy the Jewish state and deny the Jews their national
identity likewise call themselves only anti-Zionist. They deny
hating all Jews, only those Jews who insist upon retaining
their Jewish national beliefs and homeland.*

Yet this claim of anti-Zionists that they do not hate all Jews
is not new to anti-Zionists. Virtually all modern antisemites
have claimed that they only oppose Jews who affirm Jewish
nationhood. Only Hitler and the Nazis, among modern antisemites, have hated all Jews. Now, unless the Nazis are to be
considered the only antisemites in modern history, anti-
Zionists are as antisemitic as every other type of antisemite.
Like all other antisemites, anti-Zionists are at war with nearly
every identifying Jew.

Anti-Zionism is unique in only one way: it is the first form
of Jew-hatred to deny that it hates Jews. Accordingly, any discussion of anti-Zionism must begin by explaining why it is
antisemitism.

Anti-Zionism as Antisemitism in Theory

Can someone deny that Italians are a nation, work to destroy Italy, and all the while claim that he is not an enemy of
the Italian people because he does not hate all Italians? The

---

* The Jews have always been both a nation and a religion, but in
order to legitimize their denial of the Jews' right to Israel, anti-
Zionists deny that the Jews are a nation or a people, and assert that
they are members only of a religion. A typical such denial of Jewish
peoplehood is this statement from the charter of the Palestine Liberation Organization: "Judaism, in its character as a religion, is not a nationality with an independent existence. Likewise the Jews are not
one people . . ." (Article 20 of the Palestine National Covenant).

question is obviously absurd. If you deny Italian nationhood and any Italian rights to their homeland, and seek to destroy Italy, no matter how sincerely you may claim to love some Italians, you are an enemy of the Italian people. The same holds true for those who deny Jewish nationhood and the Jews' right to their state, and who advocate the destruction of Israel. Such people are enemies of the Jewish people and the term for their attitudes, even when espoused by people who sincerely like some Jews, is antisemitism.

An anti-Zionist would likely respond that the analogy between Italy and Israel is invalid, because Italian has meaning as a nationality, while Judaism has meaning only as a religion. And since Judaism is only a religion and Zionism is a national movement, one can oppose Zionism without being an enemy of the Jews or Judaism.

In addition to reasons already presented, this argument is false on four scores.

First, it makes the extraordinary assumption that non-Jews can tell Jews what it means to be Jewish. As the prominent Jewish theologian Rabbi Emanuel Rackman wrote: "I am a Jew and a Zionist. For me the two commitments are one. Furthermore, I hold this to be the position of historic Judaism. . . . I must firmly ask [non-Jews] to respect my religious convictions as I see them and not as they see them."[2]

Throughout its long history, Judaism has held that Jewish nationhood is, along with God and Torah, the basis of Judaism. In the words of an ancient Jewish text, "God, Torah and Israel are one." The Jews' self-definition as a nation with a homeland in Israel is not some new political belief of contemporary Jews, but the essence of Judaism since biblical times.

Second, the contention that anti-Zionists are not enemies of the Jews, despite their advocacy of policies which would lead to the mass murder of Jews, is, to put it as generously as possible, disingenuous. If anti-Zionism succeeded in its goal of destroying Israel, nearly all of Israel's three million Jews plus an untold number of non-Israeli Jews, would die in their effort to maintain Israel. Both the Israelis and their Arab enemies know this. The Arabs, some Western-oriented propaganda notwithstanding, have repeatedly called for the destruction of the Jews in Israel during a war with Israel. The Israelis for their part would fight to the last, both to keep Israel alive and because they have reason to believe that death is a preferable fate to capture by the Arabs. In the words of the Israeli *leftist* writer, Amos Kenan: "Shukairy [the head of the Palestine Liberation Organization before Yasir Arafat] used to say that the Jews should be driven into the sea. After the 1967 defeat, it became apparent that a slogan of this sort was not good public relations for the Arab cause. So today, only the Zionists are to be thrown into the sea. The only trouble is that when the Arabs get through pushing all the Zionists into the sea, there won't be a Jew left in Israel. For not a single Jew in Israel will agree to less than political and national sovereignty."[3]

Given, then, that if anti-Zionism realized its goal, another Jewish holocaust would take place, attempts to draw distinctions between anti-Zionism and antisemitism strike most Jews as demagogic.

Third, it was possible before the establishment of Israel in 1948 to oppose the Zionist movement and not be an enemy of the Jews, just as prior to 1776 one could have opposed American statehood without being an enemy of Americans. Once the United States was established, however, anyone advocating its destruction would obviously be considered an enemy of Americans. So, too, once Israel was established, anyone advocating its destruction is considered an enemy of the Jews.

Fourth, anti-Zionists would be hard put to find any affirmatively identifying Jew who would not view them as mortal enemies. Studies and opinion polls have shown that 99 percent of American Jewry identifies with the right of Jews to the Jewish state.[4]

For religious Jews, as we have seen, Israel and Jewish nationhood are part of their religious creed. An anti-Zionist is therefore an enemy of religious Jews.[5] As for secular and less religious Jews, anti-Zionists oppose the one aspect of Judaism which they passionately affirm—Israel.

ANTI-ZIONISM AS ANTISEMITISM IN PRACTICE

Though they constantly deny being antisemites, in their writings and speeches anti-Zionists rarely draw distinctions between Zionists and Jews. In order to hide their antisemitism, enemies of the Jews nearly always use the word "Zionist" when they mean Jew. This substitution often becomes ludicrous. As noted earlier, on October 21, 1973, the Soviet ambassador to the United Nations, Yakov Malik, declared: "The Zionists have come forward with the theory of the Chosen People, an absurd ideology." This is a typical example of antisemitism masquerading as anti-Zionism. An attack on Jewish chosenness is not an attack on Zionism: chosenness plays no role in Zionism. It is a basic doctrine of Judaism. Malik's attack was consistent with Soviet, Arab, and Leftist opponents of the Jews who disguise their attacks on Jews and Judaism as attacks on Zionism. In the Museum of Religion and Atheism in Leningrad, an exhibit about Zionism and Israel designates the following as anti-Soviet *Zionist* material: Jewish prayer shawls, *tefillin* (phylacteries) and Passover Haggadahs,[6] all *religious* items used by Jews for thousands of years.

A similar and characteristic use of anti-Zionism to disguise antisemitism was made in the *Black Panther* (August 25, 1970), the newspaper of the late radical black organization. Writing about the trials of Panther leader Huey Newton and of the "Chicago Eight" the paper concluded: "It was a Zionist judge, Judge Freedman, who sentenced Huey P. Newton to fifteen years in jail. It was a Zionist judge, Judge Hoffman who allowed the other Zionists to go free but has kept Bobby Seale in jail. . . . The other Zionists in the Conspiracy 8 trial were willing and did sacrifice Bobby Seale. . . . Once again we condemn Zionism as a racist doctrine." The men denounced as Zionists include Jerry Rubin, Abbie Hoffman, and William Kunstler, people who could best be described as non-Jewish Jews. The *Black Panther* attacked them because they are Jews (by birth), not because they are Zionists.[7]

In the Arab world, "anti-Zionists" have adopted the calumnies of antisemitism and now spread them under the guise of anti-Zionism. The late president of Egypt, and the leading political figure in the Arab world, Gamal Abdel Nasser, repeatedly cited the *Protocols of the Elders of Zion* to document his charge that three hundred Zionists rule the world. King Faisal, leader of Saudi Arabia until his death in 1975, repeatedly publicized his accusation that Jews kill non-Jews and drink their blood. The Arab writer, Saluk Dasuki, published *America—A Zionist Colony*, which was widely distributed both in the Arab world and in the Soviet Union. In an anti-Zionist expression of Nazi theory on Jews, Dasuki noted that "Jews, whether they have preserved their religion, or whether they have adopted other religions, are known in the United States under the collective name Zionists." Basing their statistics on Dasuki's work, the Soviets published an article in the journal of the Young Communist League which asserted that in the United States, 70 percent of the lawyers, 69 percent of the physicists, 43 percent of the industrialists, and 80 percent of the owners of publishing houses were Zionists.[8]

Moral leaders of various faiths have repeatedly warned that anti-Zionism is antisemitism in practice. The late Dr. Martin Luther King, Jr., said, upon hearing a Black student at Harvard launch a tirade against Zionists: "When people criticize Zionists they mean Jews. You're talking antisemitism."[9] In a similar vein, the president of the United Church of Christ, Dr. Robert Moss, commented on the anti-Zionist resolution passed by the United Nations General Assembly in 1975: "We should not be deceived by the use of the term Zionism. The sponsors of this resolution mean by it Jews and Judaism as well as the state of Israel." The UN delegate from Costa Rica noted that the resolution was an invitation to genocide against the Jewish people.[10]

Whether the destruction of the Jewish national movement and the Jewish state, a holocaust of the three million Jews of Israel, and the subsequent abandonment of world Jewry to the goodwill of the world with no refuge of its own are carried out in the name of anti-Zionism or antisemitism is quite irrelevant to Jews. That the people who want to do these things now call themselves anti-Zionists instead of antisemites is an interesting historical fact. There may be some differences in what aspects of Jewish life anti-Zionists and anti-semites hate. But these differences are of interest only to historians. For Jews the consequences are identical.

PART THREE

What Is
to Be Done?

FOURTEEN

What Is to Be Done?

WHAT IS TO BE DONE?

Jew-hatred has existed for thousands of years, from Hellenic and Roman society to the leaders of the Enlightenment,
throughout Christendom and Islam, in Communist and Fascist societies, from ancient times until today. There is little
reason to suppose that antisemitism, humanity's most enduring hatred, will soon disappear.

What then is to be done? What, if anything, can Jews do to
eradicate, diminish, or at the very least, individually avoid
antisemitism?

One possible response to antisemitism is assimilation. If
one is no longer a Jew, in most cases he will no longer suffer
antisemitism.

A second option for a Jew is to leave the antisemitism of
non-Jewish society and go to live among Jews in the Jewish
state, Israel.

A third possible way to help prevent antisemitism is to
convert many non-Jews to Judaism. The great German-Jewish
leader, Rabbi Leo Baeck, noted after the Second World War
that had many Germans had Jewish relatives (meaning Ger-

mans who had converted to Judaism), the Holocaust might never have occurred.

A fourth and most obvious Jewish response to antisemitism is to fight it whenever it manifests itself—through all appropriate means from political to physical.

A fifth response to antisemitism is for Jews, from within Judaism, to influence non-Jews to live according to moral values which are consonant with those of Judaism.

ASSIMILATION

A Jew who wants to cease suffering Jew-hatred can often do so by the logical device of ceasing to be a Jew. Such a decision is tragic from the perspective of the Jewish people, but for a Jew unconcerned with Jewish survival it is neither illogical nor unworkable. Indeed for such Jews antisemitism makes a powerful case on behalf of assimilation.

Many Jews deny that assimilation is possible, recalling that the Nazis checked for "Jewish blood" and murdered assimilated Jews as readily as they murdered affirmative Jews.

As true as these facts about Nazi Germany are, however, they ignore the fact that millions of Jews have assimilated in the past, many of them since the second half of the seventeenth century, and that assimilation is possible for a Jew today. The Nazis were unique in their rejection of Jews who adopted the non-Jewish majority's national and religious identity. Throughout Jewish history Jews who assimilated escaped antisemitic persecution. Even Jews who were forcibly converted have eventually successfully assimilated. Over a hundred thousand Jews who were forcibly converted to Catholicism during the Spanish Inquisition in the fifteenth century have disappeared as Jews.

Hitler was alone among the major antisemites of history in denying that Jews could become non-Jews. The argument that Hitler "proves" that Jews cannot assimilate is simply wrong. What people who hold this view really mean is that under a racial antisemite like Hitler, assimilation is impossible. But unless one posits that in the coming generation a

Hitlerian antisemite will come to power and attempt to murder all of a country's Jews, including, for example, Christian children of Jews who converted to Christianity, pointing to Hitler to deny the possibility of a Jew assimilating is pointless.

In fact, the Holocaust can lead to precisely the opposite conclusion. That antisemitic violence will one day be unleashed against one's children is an eloquent argument *for* attempting to assimilate. Many marginal Jews would sooner try assimilation than bequeath to their children or grandchildren a fate of torture and murder. Boris Pasternak, recipient of the Nobel Prize for literature, and a Jew who converted to Russian Orthodoxy, eloquently made this case in *Dr. Zhivago:* "In whose interests is this voluntary martyrdom? . . . Dismiss this army which is forever fighting and being massacred, nobody knows for what. . . . Say to them: That's enough. Don't hold on to your identity. Don't all get together in a crowd. Disperse! Be with all the rest."[1]

The fact is that an American or French or Uruguayan native-born Jew can assimilate and virtually assure that his children do. Of course, true assimilation usually necessitates converting to the majority's religion, and may also involve changing one's name and perhaps even one's residence, but it can be accomplished, as it is every day throughout the world. One must not ignore the first step, however. Most Jews who abandon their Jewish identity do not convert to the majority religion, and in the eyes of the non-Jews they remain Jews.

Two factors, however, invalidate assimilation as a solution to antisemitism. First, it is applicable only to individuals, not to the Jewish people as a whole. Many Jews will never assimilate, which alone invalidates assimilation as a solution to antisemitism. Moreover, even if all the Jews of some nation would try to assimilate at one time, it is doubtful they would be fully accepted. Many Jewish individuals, perhaps even an entire Jewish community, could assimilate over the course of generations, but it is unlikely that an entire community could at one time. Second, no matter how successful, assimilation could never be considered a solution to antisemitism. A solution to antisemitism must by definition include the survival of

Jewry, just as a solution to an illness must by definition include the survival of the patient. We seek solutions to antisemitism which enable Jews to live as Jews.

Nevertheless, it bears repeating that while tragic from Jewry's perspective and a victory for antisemitism, assimilation is a rational and viable way to escape antisemitism for individual Jews.

ZIONISM

A second response, and one which has offered itself as a solution to antisemitism, is Zionism, the return of the Jews to their own state, Israel. Zionism affords Jews the opportunity to cease being minorities everywhere, and to live in the one state wherein they cannot be persecuted by fellow citizens for being Jews. Zionism is, at least in theory, an ideal solution to antisemitism.

In fact, Theodor Herzl founded the modern Zionist movement first and foremost as a solution to antisemitism.[2] Herzl, an assimilated Hungarian Jew, had at first advocated Jewish assimilation, including conversion to Christianity, as the solution to the Jewish question. Only when Herzl concluded that Jews could not assimilate into the European nations did he formulate the Zionist solution to antisemitism. What reinforced Herzl in that conclusion was the Dreyfus trial in 1894. After witnessing the virulent antisemitism that accompanied the trial in supposedly enlightened France, Herzl concluded that the only solution to antisemitism was for the Jews to cease living among non-Jews. The Jews must live in their own state.

The founders of Zionism held that the fundamental cause of antisemitism is the Jews' uniquely unnatural position as a "nation within a nation," whereby the Jews' commitment to Jewish peoplehood is often viewed as a challenge to the nationalism of the non-Jews among whom Jews live. Only by living in their own nation can the Jews become like other nations and no longer cause Jew-hatred.

Zionism thus offers entire Jewish communities as well as individual Jews a possible solution to antisemitism. Should all the Jews of a given country make *aliyah* (move to Israel), as have the Jews of Yemen, there will obviously be no more Jews in that country to suffer antisemitism. If that country then continues to oppose Jews, that opposition will focus on Israel which is in an immeasurably superior position to defend itself than are persecuted Jews in a hostile non-Jewish society.

And that is not all. In addition to providing Jews with a haven from Jew-hatred and potentially reducing antisemitism through "normalizing" the Jews' situation, Zionism also helps to protect Diaspora Jewish communities against antisemitic outbreaks. The establishment of Israel has meant that Jews who continue to live among non-Jews now have a country to help defend their rights and to which they may flee if necessary. Israel has served both functions for Jews in Arab countries and the Soviet Union.

These facts notwithstanding, Zionism alone cannot solve antisemitism. Like assimilation, *aliyah* can solve antisemitism for individual Jews and for some Jewish communities, but not for the Jewish people as a whole. First, there is simply no prospect of all the Jews making *aliyah*. More important, even if every Jew in the world moved to Israel, there is no reason to assume that Jew-hatred will disappear.

Contrary to the theoretical bases and great hopes of Zionism, the creation of Israel has not reduced antisemitism— neither for world Jewry nor even for Israeli Jewry. Indeed, the Jewish state has actually exacerbated antisemitism. In addition to having to suffer traditional antisemitism, Diaspora Jews now have to contend with Israel's mortal enemies who hate Jews everywhere who affirm Jewish nationhood; and they now have to endure the new antisemitic charge that Diaspora Jewry's commitment to Israel means that Jews are disloyal citizens of the countries they inhabit. As for Israel itself, it has become the focus of intense worldwide hatred. While few Jews in the world are as secure to express their Jewish identity as are the Jews of Israel, few Jews in the world are as isolated and despised as the Jews of Israel.

Zionism, whose major aim was to end Jew-hatred through the establishment of the Jewish state, has produced the most

hated state in the world. This development would have
shocked the secular founders of Zionism who regarded the
Jews as being different from other nations primarily in their
not having their own state; who regarded Jew-hatred as basically a reaction to this one abnormality of the Jews, and who
accordingly regarded the end of this abnormality, through the
Jews living in their own state, as the solution to antisemitism.

But for those who understand that the Jews are different
from other nations in ways far deeper than their not having
their own state, and who understand why Jew-hatred has
been humanity's deepest hatred, it was to be expected that
the Jewish state would be as hated among states as Jews have
been among peoples.

Theodor Herzl founded Zionism to end antisemitism. Since
its creation in 1948, Israel has given Jewry a self-respect it
had not known in nearly two thousand years; it has afforded
Jews the one place where they can lead a fully integrated
Jewish life; it has been a haven for hundreds of thousands of
Holocaust survivors and other oppressed Jews of various
lands; it has given Jews hope after Auschwitz. It has, in short,
done virtually everything for the Jewish people except the
one thing Zionism's founders expected it to do: end antisemitism.

SEEKING CONVERTS

A third possible way to prevent antisemitism, particularly
in the United States today, is to increase the number of Jews
through converting many non-Jews to Judaism. This helps
prevent antisemitism in four ways. First, by increasing the
number of Jews, the Jews become stronger and less likely to
be attacked. Second, it ensures that many non-Jews have Jewish relatives. Third, serious conversions ideally spread Jewish
values. And fourth, by making it known that Jews welcome
converts, Jews can help destroy such antisemitic beliefs as
that Jews think they are an inherently superior race, or that
Jews are ethnic chauvinists.

Such an approach to helping prevent antisemitism has

rarely been suggested. This, too, has a number of reasons. First, Jews have rarely lived in societies where they were unharassed, let alone free to convert non-Jews to Judaism. Second, many Jews have come to believe that seeking converts would provoke antisemitism. And third, many Jews believe that Judaism does not seek converts.

The first problem does not exist for American Jews, for they are free to advocate Judaism. As for the fear of incurring antisemitism, it needs to be stressed that we are not speaking here of converting Christians, but rather of the tens of millions of unchurched non-Jews in the United States. Nor does seeking converts imply missionizing in the traditional Christian sense. As Judaism does not hold that it is the only way to God, such missionizing is neither necessary nor desirable. Rather we are for making it known that Jews accept and desire converts, and for educating the general public about Judaism with its distinctive values and way of life.

Such an approach to seeking converts would not only not increase antisemitism, it would decrease it, for a major source of hostility to Jewry emanates from the perception that Jews consider themselves a superior race and constitute a closed ethnic club.

Now the only question remaining is does Judaism seek converts?

The answer is yes. This surprises most Jews, who for so long have believed that Judaism discourages people from converting. But the reasons for this Jewish policy are historical, not theological, and they were brought about by non-Jews. For nearly fifteen hundred years Jews have lived in Christian and Muslim societies which often made conversion to Judaism a capital offense—both for the convert and for the Jews involved in the conversion. It was only for this reason that Jews adopted their policy of discouraging conversion. *Judaism desires converts*, and when Jews were free to do so they actively encouraged would-be converts.

In the Talmud, Rabbi Eleazar ben Pedat went so far as to claim that the exile of the Jews from Israel, the most destructive event in ancient Jewish history, had one constructive purpose: "The Holy One, praised be He, exiled Israel among the nations for the purpose of gaining converts" (*Pesachim* 87B). In fact, of several dozen statements in the Talmud concerning converts and seeking converts, all but four are highly positive.[3] The *Avot de Rabbi Nathan* (chap. 12), an early rabbinic work, encouraged Jews to emulate Abraham, who alone with his wife Sarah, spread the monotheist ideal: "Every Jew should endeavor to actively bring men under the wing of God's presence even as Abraham did." The model of Abraham was used not only to encourage Jews to seek converts, but also to encourage potential Gentile converts: "If a man wishes to convert to Judaism, but says, 'I am too old to convert,' let him learn from Abraham, who when he was ninety-nine years old, entered God's covenant" (*Tanhuma B, Lekh Lekha* 40). Some rabbis went so far as to proclaim that converts were the greatest of Jews: "Said Resh Lakish: the convert is dearer than the Jews who stood before Mount Sinai. Why? Because had they [the Jews] not seen the thunder and the lightning and the mountains quaking and the sounds of the horn, they would not have accepted the Torah. But this one, who saw none of these things, came, surrendered himself to the Holy One and accepted upon himself the kingdom of heaven. Could any be dearer than he?" (*Tanhuma B, Lekh Lekha* 6).

In espousing these beliefs about Jews influencing non-Jews, the rabbis were faithfully reflecting the Hebrew Bible's attitude. The prophet Isaiah dreamed of the day when all the nations of the world would declare: "Come, let us go up to the Mount of the Lord, to the House of the God of Jacob; that he may instruct us in His ways and that we may walk in His path. For out of Zion shall go forth the Torah, and the word of God from Jerusalem" (*Isaiah* 2:3).

Judaism bestowed what may be considered its highest honor upon a convert. Jewish tradition holds that the Messiah will be of the family of Ruth (ancestress of King David), a woman who converted to Judaism and for whom a book of the Bible is named.

That Jews attempted to implement Judaism's wish to seek converts is recorded in non-Jewish and Jewish sources. The New Testament states that in the Roman Empire the Jews would "sail the seas and cross whole countries to win one convert" (*Matthew* 23:15). Judaism had become so popular among segments of the Roman intelligentsia that Juvenal, the great Roman writer, wrote a satire about Roman fathers who eat no pork, observe the Sabbath, worship only the heavenly God, and whose sons undergo circumcision, despise Roman laws, and study the Jews' Torah. The Jewish historian Josephus wrote in the first century: "The masses have long since shown a keen desire to adopt our religious observances; and there is not one city, Greek or barbarian, nor a single nation, to which our customs of abstaining from work on the seventh day has not spread, and where the fasts and lighting of [Sabbath] lamps and many of our prohibitions in the matter of food are not observed" (*Contra Apion* 2:39).

When the Roman Empire became Christian, however, the situation was altered radically. Conversion to Judaism became a crime, soon a capital one, for both the convert and the Jews involved in the conversion.[4]

One would expect the Jews, now faced with capital punishment, to have ceased their efforts to spread Judaism. Yet, in general, they did not; and this persistence constitutes the most convincing evidence of how powerful was the Jews' desire to gain converts. As George Foot Moore, the great Harvard historian of religions, has written: "Against all such attempts of pagan or Christian rulers to shut up Judaism in itself and prevent its spread, the Jews persisted in their missionary efforts to make the religion God had revealed to their fathers the religion of all mankind."[5]

Nevertheless, as the persecution of the Jewish community increased, the price for accepting converts became increasingly onerous. Often, whole communities would be punished for one Christian's conversion to Judaism. To cite but one example, in 1012, a German priest, Vicilinus of Mainz, became a Jew and then wrote essays in which he used the Bible to demonstrate the continuing validity of Judaism. Within a few months Emperor Henry II expelled the entire Jewish population of Mainz.

The Jews therefore had no choice but to change their attitudes toward encouraging conversion to Judaism. The point

cannot be overemphasized that Jews stopped seeking converts to Judaism only because they were forced to, and only
then did vigorous discouragement of would-be converts become the official Jewish policy. In the words of Rabbi Solo-
mon Luria (1510–1573), perhaps the leading European Talmud scholar of the sixteenth century: "Under the present
conditions, when we live in a country that is not ours, like
slaves under the rod of a master, if a Jew encourages someone
to become a proselyte he becomes a rebel against the government, subject to the death penalty. . . . Therefore, I caution
anyone against being a party to such activity when the law of
the state forbids it, for he thereby forfeits his life."[6]

Jewish reluctance to seek converts under such conditions
was highly understandable. But why have Jews been reluctant to seek converts in a society such as the United States
where converts and Jews who facilitate conversions are not
made to suffer at all? One reason is simple inertia. A communal attitude which is nearly one thousand years old is not easily broken. A second reason is that over the last century and a
half much of the Jewish community has become secular and
ethnic. Obviously secular Jews are unable to encourage conversion to a religion which they do not practice. A characteristic example of the inability of secular Jews to advocate Judaism is offered in the recently published and widely praised
book, *Letters to an American Jewish Friend: A Zionist's Po-
lemic* by Hillel Halkin, a secular Jew. Halkin relates the following: "A Jewish girl whom I knew was thinking of marrying a non-Jewish boy and wanted him to become a Jew. She
asked me if I would talk to him; I agreed. . . . His first question was, 'tell me, apart from my future mother-in-law's feelings, why should I become a Jew?' . . . And there wasn't a single reason I could think of. . . . This encounter happened with
a non-Jew, but had it been with an assimilated Jew or with a
Jew who wished to know why he should feel more committed
to his Jewishness than he did, I could not have answered any
differently. I don't know why one should be a Jew."[7]

A third reason why Jews do not encourage converts is that
many unfortunately still believe that a convert to Judaism is
not "really" Jewish (thus, unwittingly disqualifying Abraham,

the first Jew). Fourth, even religious Jews generally lack the ability to articulate Judaism to non-Jews, or for that matter, to irreligious Jews. Finally, some conversions devoid of meaning have given conversions to Judaism a bad name. We are referring here to hasty *pro forma* "conversions" made more to alleviate the bad feelings of anxious in-laws than to help create a new committed Jew. While Jews must enthusiastically welcome converts to Judaism, such sign-on-the-dotted-line conversions are not the way.

There are then any number of obstacles to overcome in beginning a program to seek converts to Judaism. But there is little question that among other benefits to Jewry, more converts would be a most effective tool in the fight against antisemitism.

COMBATING OUTBREAKS OF ANTISEMITISM

By far the most common Jewish response to antisemitism is to fight it whenever it erupts and attempt to identify and suppress its sources before it erupts. Since the Holocaust, Jews, particularly those living in democracies, have effectively prevented major antisemitic attacks in their countries and have achieved a success, unparalleled by any other religious or ethnic group, in helping their fellow Jews in nondemocratic countries, particularly the USSR.

In the United States, for example, groups such as the Anti-Defamation League of B'nai B'rith (ADL) and the American Jewish Committee have vigilantly monitored the far Right and Left for signs of antisemitism and have generally effectively silenced Jew-haters through public exposure. Other Jewish groups have led the fight against Soviet antisemitism, and against the persecution of Jews in Ethiopia (though this movement is only beginning), Syria, and elsewhere.

With regard to combating antisemitism and its anti-Zionist incarnation, free Jewry has functioned since the Holocaust like a finely tuned watch. Jews have learned how to use media effectively, petition public officials, demonstrate, help to elect candidates sympathetic to the fight against domestic

and international enemies of the Jews. In a world which revolves to a substantial extent around power and public per-
suasion, the access to power of Jews and non-Jews who are
committed to fighting antisemitism has been of great importance to Jewish survival.

Given the success of American Jewish groups in helping to
combat outbreaks of antisemitism in the West, we only wish
to add the following points.

First, the case against antisemitism and for Israel must be
made before all Americans, not only in Washington. The
struggle for America's continuing support for Israel will ultimately be won or lost back in the home districts of congressmen, not in Washington alone. American Jews must earn
the support of their fellow Americans for Israel, Soviet Jewry,
and Jewish causes by taking their case directly to the American people. For this, Jewry needs not only good lobbyists who
can effectively make Jewry's case before policy makers and
legislators, but eloquent spokesmen in leadership positions
who can engender goodwill directly from the American
people.

Second, American Jews must understand their stake in
modern politics, and should not, both for their sake and
America's, identify with, or strengthen, the far Left or the far
Right. Third, American Jews should not equate the death of
religion with Jewish security. That some American Jews and
some Jewish institutions have been among the leaders against
virtually any public manifestation of religion in the United
States may ultimately backfire against Jewish, not to mention
American society's, better interests.

Finally, as all Jews must recognize, virtually all their efforts to combat antisemitic outbreaks deal with the symptoms
rather than the causes of Jew-hatred. This is why no matter
how effective these efforts, they cannot solve antisemitism.
These efforts are important and effective—but only in a society relatively free of antisemitism. When a Jewish group
publicly condemns someone for antisemitism, that condemnation is effective only if the society has values that hold antisemitism contemptible. Thus, the only *solution* to antisemi-

tism is for Jews to affect the values of non-Jews. All other attempts to end antisemitism are doomed to failure. They only buy time until the next eruption.

A SOLUTION TO ANTISEMITISM

Zionism seeking converts to Judaism and combating antisemitism when it arises are each critically important, and together could help prevent future antisemitic outbreaks. But if the goal is to put an end to antisemitism, then Jews must also attempt to influence the moral values of non-Jews so that no aspect of Judaism any longer threatens the non-Jews' values. If the Holocaust taught anything, it is that in order to prevent another one, the Jews have no choice but to influence their neighbors' moral values.

Jews must therefore resume their original task of spreading ethical monotheism. The Jewish role is not to bring mankind to Judaism, but to universal moral law. *It is the exquisite irony of Jewish history that this task, which has been the ultimate cause of antisemitism, must be fulfilled in order to end antisemitism.*

This means in essence that the Jews must make the world aware of two basic principles: ethics need God, and God's major demand is ethics. The Jewish people in the tradition of ethical monotheism's greatest advocates, the Jewish Prophets, must therefore oppose religionists of any religion who advocate God without depicting goodness as God's central concern; and likewise oppose secularists who advocate a value system devoid of religious moral values. In the first case God is rendered morally irrelevant and religion becomes a superstitious refuge from the moral demands of this world. In the second instance, ethics become relative, rarely transcending personal taste. God without ethics has led to crusades and Qaddafi; ideologies without God have led to Gulag and Auschwitz.

While many secular Jews may find this prospect most unappealing, there is really little choice. For even these Jews recognize that if antisemitism is a moral failing, only the moral values of non-Jews can prevent antisemitism. The only questions regarding antisemitism over which Jews might then differ is not whether Jews ought to influence the moral values of others but through which values. In the United States Jews have tended to push secular liberal values, trusting that these would constitute a bulwark against antisemitism. Jewish history has taught Jews well the dangers of reactionary religious and political ideologies, and the need for pluralism and a nondogmatic approach to religious beliefs. But American Jews are increasingly aware of the dangers on the Left as well, despite their tendency to sympathize with whoever opposes the Right. The breakdown of many traditional values and of a sense of obligation to something higher than the self, poses as great a threat to the Jews' well-being as does the extreme Right. Thus secular values, as indispensable as they are to the proper functioning of government, are not enough to ensure the moral vitality of the society, and only a morally strong society will not be hostile to Jews and Israel.

The time may be uniquely ripe for Jews, especially in the United States and Israel, to influence the world by communicating not only humanist, liberal, conservative, or socialist values, but Jewish and ethical monotheist values. As we have seen, Leftist, Rightist, secularist, socialist, and even humanist ideologies emanating from the Enlightenment have often been saturated with antisemitism. For Jews to attempt to eliminate antisemitism through ideologies which themselves have easily led to antisemitism is obviously an exercise in self-destruction.

Israel and America offer contemporary Jews unique opportunities to reduce antisemitism and to "perfect the world under the rule of God." Indeed, as thousands of years of Jew-hatred have shown, *the tasks are identical.* As Jews have believed since antisemitism began, only in a world guided by ethical monotheism will Jews be able to live in peace.

It is not the purpose of this book to delineate these values or how to communicate them. Those are critical subjects worthy of their own extended analysis.[8] Our concern has been only to show that Jewish religious and moral values are both the ultimate cause of and solution to antisemitism.

"The Jews," said the great modern Jewish thinker Abraham Joshua Heschel, "are a messenger who forgot his message." For the Jews' sake, as well as for humanity's, Jews ought to remember that message.

The Meaning
of Antisemitism
for Non-Jews

ANTISEMITISM IS A JEWISH PROBLEM, but non-Jews make a most self-destructive error when they dismiss it as only the Jews' problem. For reasons explained in this book, treatment of the Jews has served as one of humanity's moral barometers. Watch how a nation, religion, or political movement treats Jews, and you have an early and deadly accurate picture of that group's intentions toward others.

Moral non-Jews who fail to act against antisemites inevitably suffer from them. Nothing about Jew-hatred is clearer than this. Jew-haters begin with Jews but never end with Jews, as antisemitism is ultimately a hatred of higher standards. The antisemites first wish to destroy the perceived embodiment of that higher call to the good, the Jews. But they do not hate the Jews alone. They hate whatever and whoever represents a higher value, a moral challenge. Whoever sees antisemitism as only some aberrational hatred on the part of an otherwise morally acceptable group does not understand antisemitism. So long as there are good people, the Jews will never be the only targets of antisemites.

A particularly clear contemporary example of one such target is the United States. Those who hate the Jewish nation are often the most likely to hate America as well. And almost as consistently as Jew-hatred, America-hatred has become a moral litmus test of nations, regimes, and individuals. America represents freedom, a higher quality of life, and a willingness to fight for its values. These qualities are despised by regimes characterized by tyranny and socioeconomic failure, and by individuals in the West who support such regimes or who wish to denigrate America for reasons akin to those of antisemites in their denigration of Jews. Both supporters and haters of America know that with all its flaws it alone stands between democracy and the ascent of tyranny throughout the world.

Thus, it is small surprise that among tyrannical regimes and their defenders, America and Israel are so often identified as the same enemy. This is not merely a consequence of America's standing alone behind Israel; the United States has aided various Arab countries very generously, and it has on some critical occasions backed Arab regimes (such as Nasser's Egypt in 1956 and Saudi Arabia in 1981) against Israel. This hostility is aroused largely because America and Israel represent democracy, a higher quality of life, and a willingness to confront despotism.

Likewise, within the democratic West itself, so often the individuals who smear America's name attempt to do the same to Israel's. For example, The Village Voice's Alexander Cockburn, a leftist columnist widely known for his scathing attacks on America, has compared Israel in Lebanon to the Nazis in Poland.[1] There is a desire among opponents of Israel (and America), in the eloquent words of The New Republic's editor Martin Peretz, "to try to establish a parity of immorality,"[2] between Israel and its enemies. The reason for this is that the Jewish nation (again, like America) has offered itself, and is perceived, as a moral beacon; hence many individuals wish to portray it as negatively as possible. This explains the unparalleled preoccupation with Israel's (and America's) flaws. And the Jews continue to be aware of their moral challenge: In July 1982, Newsweek's James Pringle asked an Israeli soldier guarding PLO and Syrian prisoners how the latter were treated. "There is no torture," answered the

Israeli soldier, "because we are Jews and Jewish people have hearts." [3]

The same mentality which compares a Lyndon Johnson to Nazi war criminals compares a Menachem Begin to Yasser Arafat. Through such exercises of "parity of immorality" America is made to appear morally indistinguishable from the other superpower, the Soviet Union, and Israel is depicted as morally little better than its enemies. To cite one other example, the nationally renowned political cartoonist Conrad depicted these moral equivalences during one week's cartoons in the *Los Angeles Times*. He showed Menachem Begin staring into a mirror which reflected the face of Arafat (July 9, 1982). Later in the week (July 11), the Pulitzer Prize–winning cartoonist drew the Iron Curtain in the form of an American flag. Israel is morally equivalent to the PLO; America is the moral equivalent of the Soviets.

Yet despite all this hatred, America remains the dreamed-for haven of the world's oppressed; and Israel remains an embattled democracy in the midst of authoritarian states, and the birthplace of the kibbutz to which tens of thousands of youth from around the world turn for a living lesson in human equality.*

America today with all its imperfections represents a model of something better, fighting for its ideals and in so doing constituting a moral challenge to others. But the Jews have played this role for millennia. The Jews might be described as humanity's miner's canary. Just as the death of canaries warns miners of noxious fumes, so the death of Jews warns civilized nations of noxious moral fumes. But despite

---

* There is another parallel between Jew-hatred and America-hatred. Both are often perceived as emanating from antagonism to Jews' and Americans' wealth. We have seen how this perception is false regarding Jew-hatred. It is also false as regards America-hatred. Were wealth the major reason for hating a nation, then Switzerland ought to be at least as deeply hated as America, and certainly the Arab oil-exporting nations, whose wealth has increased in direct proportion to a decrease in Third World wealth, should be particularly hated. Yet America, like Israel and the Jews, is hated far more than are these countries. It is what America represents, not merely its wealth, that is loathed.

these universal ramifications of Jew-hatred few heed these warnings. Examples abound.

Many in the Western democracies dismissed the Nazis' antisemitism as a bad feature of people who otherwise could be lived with. But had the antisemitism of Hitler and the Nazis been perceived to be the evil it was, had therefore Hitler and the Nazis been perceived to be the evil they were, then good nations would have opposed Hitler earlier and saved not only six million Jews but tens of millions of others.

Before Idi Amin began to butcher hundreds of thousands of Ugandan Christians, he announced his hatred of Israel and his admiration for Hitler's "Final Solution." But only Jews, and America, whose ambassador protested, listened; the rest of the world ignored Amin's antisemitism—that was the Jews' problem. But, as then United States ambassador to the United Nations Daniel Patrick Moynihan pointed out: "It is no accident" that the "racist murderer" Idi Amin called for the extinction of Israel. "For Israel is a democracy and it is simply the fact that despotisms will seek whatever opportunities come to hand to destroy that which threatens them most, which is democracy." [4]

One of the first acts of the Ayatollah Ruhollah Khomeini after assuming power in Iran was the takeover of the Israeli embassy in Tehran. That too was dismissed as the Jews' problem—until the Iranians did the same thing to the American embassy.

The Arab and Muslim hatred of Israel has long been dismissed by many in the West as a Jewish problem which ultimately reveals little about the Arabs or Muslim states. But gradually it has become clear that the hatred of Jewish independence displayed by the Arab Muslim states is not some unrepresentative quirk, but a moral indicator of some precision. As the Christians of Lebanon, who have suffered far worse from Muslim hatred than have the Jews of Israel, have learned, Arab leaders who call for wars to annihilate Zionism are not otherwise tolerant, democracy-loving gentlemen. Indeed, there is often a direct correlation between the ferocity of a Muslim leader's hatred of the Jewish state and his hatred of democracy and other Western values. Iran's Khomeini,

Libya's Qaddafi, and Iraq's Hussein are three such examples. Conversely, Arab and other Middle Eastern Muslim societies that are less characterized by despotism and wanton cruelty, such as Tunisia and Turkey, are also characterized by a greater tolerance of the Jews.

The Soviet Union provides another contemporary example of a state whose hostility to Jews is both an indicator of its immoral nature and a warning of the threat it poses to those societies which hold democracy and justice as primary values. Those in the West who regard the Soviet Jewish problem as solely a Jewish problem do a terrible disservice to the other religious groups and nationalities in the Soviet Union whose plights are not as publicized; and they do the West a disservice by preventing it from confronting the evil nature of the Soviet regime.

Jew-hatred and its latest incarnation, Israel-hatred, are the price Jews pay for their role in history. They pay it often unwillingly and they live the role, for the most part, unwittingly. But as the great French Catholic theologian Jacques Maritain noted: "Israel . . . is to be found at the very heart of the world's structure, stimulating it, exasperating it, moving it. Like an alien body, like an activating ferment injected into the mass, it gives the world no peace, it bars slumber, it teaches the world to be discontented and restless as long as the world has not God, it stimulates the movement of history. . . . It is the vocation of Israel which the world hates." [5]

And moral non-Jews who do not heed the universal implications of this hatred are destined to be its victims.

Notes

PART ONE
WHY THE JEWS? THE EXPLANATION

ONE: *Why Jew-Hatred Is Unique*

1. The term anti-Semitism was coined in 1879 by Wilheim Marr, an anti-Jewish spokesman in Germany, as a euphemistic substitute for *judenhass*, Jew-hatred. The term is a misnomer, of course, since it has nothing to do with Semites. Therefore, in order to avoid any confusion we have adopted the approach of the distinguished historian James Parkes, who has suggested that antisemitism be written as one word. Emil Fackenheim, the Jewish philosopher, has also adopted this spelling, explaining ". . . the spelling ought to be antisemitism without the hyphen, dispelling the notion that there is an entity 'Semitism' which 'anti-Semitism' opposes" (Emil Fackenheim, "Post-Holocaust Anti-Jewishness, Jewish Identity and the Centrality of Israel," in *World Jewry and the State of Israel*, ed. Moshe Davis, p. 11, n. 2).

2. Pogrom is not the only word bequeathed by antisemitism to the contemporary vocabulary. Other terms include *genocide*, stemming from the Nazi attempt to murder all Jews; *Holocaust*, the Nazi murder of six million Jews between 1939 and 1945; and *ghetto*, the name given to the enclosed areas where Jews were forced to live in parts of Europe until the twentieth century. (See "The Origin of the Ghetto,"

in Cecil Roth's *Personalities and Events in Jewish History,* pp. 226–36).

3. The Russian expression was *"Byay Zhidov Spassai Rossiyu"* ("Beat the Zhids and save Russia"). This phrase is so well known among the Russians that Yevgeny Yevtushenko quoted it in his most famous poem, "Babi Yar," written in protest against contemporary Soviet antisemitism.

4. The lack of documentation in Egyptian and Persian sources in no way disproves that such anti-Jewish campaigns were conducted. These countries might well have been embarrassed by their ineffectual efforts to wipe out the Jews. Even today, despite the vast pictorial and eyewitness proofs, the testimony of tens of thousands of survivors, and the confessions of thousands of perpetrators, dozens of books, pamphlets, and articles have been published denying the Germans' attempt to annihilate the Jews.

5. We do not use the commonly utilized term *exterminate* in referring to Hitler's murder of the Jews, as this was the word used by the Nazis in order to equate the murder of Jews with the extermination of vermin.

6. N. Hanover, *Yeven Mezulah,* pp. 31–32, cited in H. H. Ben-Sasson et al., *A History of the Jewish People,* p. 656.

7. Bernard Glassman, *Anti-Semitic Stereotypes Without Jews: Images of the Jews in England,* 1290–1700. See particularly pp. 37–40 and 67–70.

8. See Paul Lendvai, *Anti-Semitism Without Jews.*

9. Salo Baron, *The Russian Jew Under Tsars and Soviets,* pp. 49–50

TWO: *Antisemitism: The Hatred of Judaism and Its Challenge*

1. *The New York Times,* November 30, 1974.

2. Ernest van den Haag, *The Jewish Mystique,* pp. 60–61.

3. Reported by the first-century Egyptian Jewish philosopher Philo, and cited in Vamberto Morais, *A Short History of Anti-Semitism,* p. 28.

4. Quoted from a personal conversation with Hitler by Hermann Rauschning in *The Ten Commandments,* ed. Armin Robinson, pp. IX–XIII.

5. Cited in Ernst Christian Helmreich's *The German Churches Under Hitler,* p. 201.

6. See Maimonides, *The Commandments,* vol. 1, Positive Commandments, no. 9, pp. 12–13, in the translation of Charles B. Chavel. Regarding the other laws of monotheism, see Maimonides' *Sefer ha-Mada (Book of Knowledge),* introduction to "Fundamentals of the Torah" and "Idolatry and Heathenism."

7. In the two biblical depictions of Utopia, the Garden of Eden and the messianic days, all creatures are depicted as herbivorous (*Gen.* 1:27–29; *Isa.* II:6,7,9). In addition, the Talmud (*Sanhedrin* 59b) explicitly states that human beings are allowed to eat meat only as a concession to man's lust for meat.

8. For a fuller explanation of Kashrut see Dennis Prager and Joseph Telushkin, *The Nine Questions People Ask About Judaism*, pp. 57–64.

9. The Talmud records one telling exception to the prohibition on attending public events on the Sabbath, which also serves to illustrate the moral gulf which existed between Jewish and Roman law and society. The rabbis permitted Jews to attend gladiator fights on Sabbaths and any other day so that they could vote at the end of each fight to spare the life of the defeated gladiator (*Tosefta, Avodah Zarah*).

10. This seems to have departed from the views of Jesus. Jesus is cited in the New Testament as stressing the need to observe Jewish law: "Do not imagine that I have come to abolish the law or the prophets. I tell you solemnly, till heaven and earth disappear, not one dot, not one little stroke, shall disappear from the law until its purpose is achieved. Therefore, the man who infringes even the least of these commandments and teaches others to do the same will be considered the least in the kingdom of heaven; but the man who keeps them and teaches them will be considered great in the kingdom of heaven" (*Matt.* 5:17–9). According to the New Testament, Jesus' early Disciples observed Jewish law. Acts 10:14 records Peter's observance of Kashrut; Acts 15:1 records that "some men came down from Judea" to teach followers of Jesus that 'unless you have yourselves been circumcised in the tradition of Moses, you cannot be saved.' In Acts 21:24, James (Jesus' brother) says to Paul, ". . . Let everyone know that there is no truth in the reports that they have heard about you, and that you still regularly observe the law."

11. Cited in Rosemary Reuther, *Faith and Fratricide*, p. 150.

12. The name Israel, which literally means "wrestle with God," was given to the patriarch Jacob (*Gen.* 32:29). Hence the term "children of Israel" is the biblical term for the Jewish nation.

13. Reform Judaism, begun in Germany, was characterized in its early period as much by its dropping of Jewish nationhood as by its dropping of much of Jewish law. The first major Reform prayer book published in Breslau in 1818 deleted all prayers for the coming of the Messiah and for the return of the Jews to Israel, on the grounds that the Jews needed neither. They were fully content as Germans and could fulfill all their national aspirations as Germans in Germany. The Reform abandonment of Jewish peoplehood spread to the United States. The 1885 convention of the American Reform rabbinate declared: "Judaism is only a religion. We Jews are not a nation." Reform

Judaism has since returned to the normative Jewish view of Judaism, and today affirms the national component at least as strongly as the other components.

14. That the Jews are a nation defined by religion is acknowledged by both secular and religious Jews. This was demonstrated by a 1963 Israeli Supreme Court case. Daniel Rufeisen, a German Jew who converted to Catholicism, applied for Israeli citizenship under Israel's Law of Return, which offers any Jew immediate citizenship upon arrival and application in Israel. He contended that being born into the Jewish nation rendered his religious identity irrelevant; just as one could be a German of any faith, one could be a Jew of any faith. The secular Supreme Court of Israel ruled against Rufeisen, ruling that a Jew who adopts another *religion* automatically leaves the Jewish *nation*. (This explains why Jews regard fringe groups such as "Jews for Jesus" as having left the Jewish people.)

15. Clermont-Tonnerre's speech is reprinted in *The Jew in the Modern World,* ed. Paul R. Mendes-Flohr and Jehuda Reinharz, pp. 103–5.

THREE: *The Chosen People Idea as a Cause of Antisemitism*

1. The Malik statement is a prime example of anti-Judaism hiding behind the cover of anti-Zionism (see chap. 13). The attack on chosenness is purely an attack on a basic Jewish religious belief: chosenness is not a component of the secular Zionist movement.

2. The study appears in Gertrude Selznick and Stephen Steinberg, *The Tenacity of Prejudice,* p. 6.

3. The story of this document which claims to outline the program of a Jewish world conspiracy is recounted in an important work of scholarship, *Warrent for Genocide: The Jewish World Conspiracy and the Protocols of the Elders of Zion* by Norman Cohn. Though the *Protocols* had been definitively proven to be a forgery by the *London Times* in 1921, it continued to be utilized by antisemites and believed by millions of people. In the United States, Henry Ford had tens of millions of copies rewritten under the title *The International Jew* and distributed through his newspaper, the *Dearborn Independent*. While Ford eventually apologized to the Jewish community, his antisemitic publications were used by Adolf Hitler throughout the Nazi era. During the 1960s the *Protocols* were republished by President Gamal Abdel Nasser of Egypt, and were distributed by King Faisal of Saudi Arabia in the 1970s.

4. For a discussion of Shaw's hostility to the doctrine of chosenness, see Hayim Greenberg's essay, "The Universalism of the Chosen People," reprinted in the *Hayim Greenberg Anthology,* ed. Marie Syrkin.

5. *Religion in Life,* Summer 1971, p. 279.

6. *Sabbath Prayer Book,* Jewish Reconstructionist Foundation, p. XXIV.

7. See Mordecai Kaplan's essay in *The Condition of Jewish Belief,* ed. Milton Himmelfarb, p. 121.

8. The implication by Rabbi Jacob Agus, *ibid.,* pp. 13–14 that historically the Jews did see themselves as superior to the nations surrounding them is misleading. The Jews saw their superiority as an existential fact, not a theological premise, as Jewish life-style, not Jewish chosenness. They saw—how could they not—that they lived a morally better life than did the societies around them (see chap. 4). In a comparable manner, Paul and his disciples thought that they were living morally superior lives to most of the Romans around them.

9. Louis Jacobs, *A Jewish Theology,* p. 274.

FOUR: *The Higher Quality of Jewish Life as a Cause of Antisemitism*

1. Thomas Sowell, *Ethnic America: A History,* p. 94.

2. The Church, in fact, long discouraged Catholics from reading the Bible on their own. It was only Martin Luther's fifteenth-century translation of the Bible into German that widely popularized Bible study among literate Germans.

3. *Talmud Bava Bathra,* 21A.

4. Moses Maimonides, *Laws of Torah Study* I:1–10 (emphasis ours).

5. Cited in Beryl Smalley, *The Study of the Bible in the Middle Ages,* p. 52.

6. Cited in S. D. Goitein, *Methods of Education,* p. 66. Cited in *A History of the Jewish People,* ed. H. H. Ben-Sasson, p. 521.

7. *A History of the Jewish People,* ed. H. H. Ben-Sasson, p. 521.

8. Abraham Joshua Heschel, *The Earth Is the Lord's,* p. 46.

9. See the discussion of the extremely high Jewish representation in the status professions in Ernest van den Haag, *The Jewish Mystique,* chaps. 10–11. This was the source for the above stated statistics.

10. In the 1970s the following percentages of different religious groups attended college: Baptists 28 percent, Methodists 45 percent, Episcopalians 65 percent, and Jews 88 percent. Cited in Andrew Greeley, *The American Catholic: A Social Portrait,* p. 41.

11. By the mid-fifties the percentage of Jews in the Ivy League schools was 23 percent: Nathan Glazer and Daniel P. Moynihan, *Beyond the Melting Pot,* 2d ed. rev., p. 157. In 1981, with the Jews composing only 2.6 percent of the American population, the Jewish percentage at Harvard was estimated at between 28 to 40 percent, Richard Reeves, *American Journey,* p. 280.

12. U.S. Bureau of Census and the National Jewish Population Survey, cited in Sowell, *Ethnic America,* p. 5.

13. Raphael Patai, *The Jewish Mind*, p. 441.
14. Charles R. Snyder, *Alcohol and the Jews*, p. 4.
15. *Hos.* 4:11, *Isa.* 5:11 and 28:7; *Prov.* 20:1; 21:17; 23:19–21, and 23:29–35; 31:4–5.
16. The material contained herein is drawn, unless otherwise noted, from Raphael Patai, *The Jewish Mind*, pp. 433–47.
17. Snyder, *Alcohol and the Jews*, pp. 85, 92, 98, 101.
18. Stephen D. Isaacs, *Jews and American Politics*, pp. 6, 119–20.
19. Israel Abrahams, *Jewish Life in the Middle Ages*, pp. 325ff.
20. Chaim Bermant, *The Jews*, p. 243.
21. Lancelot Addison, *The Present State of the Jews* (London, 1675), chap. 25; cited in Abrahams, *Jewish Life*, p. 307.
22. Moses Maimonides, *Code of Jewish Law, Gifts to the Poor*, chap. 7; *Jewish Encyclopedia* 3:669–70 and *Encyclopedia Judaica*, 8:281–86.
23. *Plutarch's Lives*, "Lycurgus," p. 61.
24. Diogenes Laertius, *Lives of Eminent Philosophers*, 2 vols. (Cambridge, Mass.: Harvard University Press, n.d.), VI, 72; VII, 33 and 131.
25. Abba Hillel Silver, *Where Judaism Differed*, pp. 48–49.
26. 1 *Cor.* 7:1–2; 6–7.
27. Origen's statement is cited in Silver, *Judaism Differed*, p. 221.
28. *Shabbat* 31A, *Kiddushin* 20B, *Yoma* 1:1.
29. Gershom Scholem, *Major Trends in Jewish Mysticism*, pp. 105–6.
30. Patai, *Jewish Mind*, pp. 493–94.
31. See Glazer and Moynihan, *Melting Pot*, p. 165; and T. P. Monaham and W. Kephart, "Divorce and Desertion by Religious and Mixed Religious Groups," *American Journal of Sociology* #50, no. 5 (March 1954): pp. 454–65.
32. The studies are cited in Marshall Sklare, *America's Jews*, p. 95.
33. Glazer and Moynihan, *Melting Pot*, p. 165.

FIVE: *Non-Jewish Jews and Antisemitism*

1. The term "non-Jewish Jew" is taken from Isaac Deutscher's autobiographical essay, *The Non-Jewish Jew*. In the essay, the noted Marxist historian described his abandonment of God, law, and Jewish nationhood, and his subsequent identification with "humanity" rather than with any particular people or country.
2. It is true that Marx converted to Christianity at the age of six. But this was a *pro forma* conversion done by his father to avoid Prussian anti-Jewish legislation. Marx was an atheist and opponent of religion who did not consider himself a Christian, and was regarded by his opponents, both in his own time and until today, as a Jew.

3. Ernest van den Haag, *The Jewish Mystique*, pp. 96–97.

4. As regards the heritage of the Jewish mission, modern historian Walter Laqueur writes: "One explanation of the Jewish inclination toward left-wing radicalism . . . is that it is an outgrowth of Jewish messianism" (*Out of the Ruins of Europe*, p. 478). And concerning the distorted moral passion, George Mosse, one of the foremost scholars of modern German history, writes: "Jewish monotheism meant a social conscience imbued with personal responsibility and a love for one's fellow man. . . . For many young Jews this commitment to a left-wing idealism provided a new religion" (*Germans and Jews*, p. 206).

5. See Stanley Rothman and S. Robert Lichter, *Roots of Radicalism: Jews, Christians, and the New Left*, p. 81.

6. Seymour Martin Lipset, "The Left, the Jews and Israel," *Encounter*, December 1969.

7. Peter G. J. Pulzer, *The Rise of Political Anti-Semitism in Germany and Austria*, p. 261.

8. In the words of Irving Howe, radical Jews "yearn to bleach away their past and become men without, or above, a country" (*World of Our Fathers*, p. 93).

9. Cited in Robert Wistrich, *Revolutionary Jews from Marx to Trotsky*, p. 189.

10. Cited in Rothman and Lichter, *Roots of Radicalism*, p. 111.

11. *Ibid.*, p. 93.

12. *Ibid.*, p. 89.

13. Istvan Deak, *Weimar Germany's Left-Wing Intellectuals: A Political History of the Weltbuhne and Its Circle*, p. 24.

14. In the words of Columbia professor and historian of the period, Fritz R. Stern, the Leftist intellectuals who attacked the foundations of Weimar Germany "were not concerned with compromise . . . they sought to destroy the present" (*The Politics of Cultural Despair: A Study in the Rise of Germanic Ideology*, p. 268.)

15. Kurt Tucholsky, *Gesammelte Werke*, II:1086. Cited in Deak, *Weimar Germany's*, p. 43.

16. Deak, p. 43.

17. Mosse, *Germans and Jews*, p. 214.

18. *Die Weltbuhne*, May 31, 1932, p. 835. Cited in George Mosse, *Masses and Man*, p. 311.

19. Mosse, *ibid.*, p. 310.

20. Rothman and Lichter, *Roots of Radicalism*, pp. 81–82.

21. Simon Karlinsky, "Dostoevsky as Rorschach Test," *The New York Times Book Review*, June 13, 1971.

22. Noam Chomsky, *Towards a New Cold War*, p. 254.

23. The quote is from Chomsky's article "On Resistance," *The New York Review of Books*, December 1967.

24. Martin Peretz, *The New Republic*, January 3–10, 1981, p. 38. See also Nadine Fresco, "The Denial of the Dead: The Faurisson Affair—and Noam Chomsky," *Dissent*, Fall 1981, pp. 467–83.

25. *Commentary*, October 1968.

26. In conversation with Philip Nobile, *Intellectual Skywriting*, p. 145.

27. *The New York Review of Books*, August 2, 1967.

28. *Commentary*, September 1967.

29. Quoted in Nobile, *Intellectual Skywriting*, p. 96.

30. *Ibid.*, p. 98.

31. Ben Stein, *The View from Sunset Boulevard*, pp. 39, 126–27.

32. Norman Mailer, *The Presidential Papers*, pp. 69–70.

33. The essay is contained in Laqueur's book *Out of the Ruins of Europe.*

34. *Commentary*, December 1981.

SIX: *Other Theories of Antisemitism*

1. A recent example of an attempt to dejudaize the Jewish experience, though the subject was not antisemitism, was supplied by a Jewish academic, Stephen Steinberg, professor of sociology at Queens College, New York. He has written a book, *The Ethnic Myth*, which concentrates on the Jews, in order to debunk the "myth" that "there are ethnic reasons for ethnic success, and the causes are to be found within the groups themselves." The biggest myth of all, according to Steinberg, is that there are Jewish reasons for the Jews' success. The notion that specifically Jewish values may be at the root of Jewish achievements in America repulses Professor Steinberg. Thus, he reduces the Jews' achievements in America to a series of fortuitous socioeconomic circumstances. This even includes the Jews' commitment to education: "But were these values [on education] distinctively part of a religious and cultural heritage, or were they merely cultural responses of a group that had acquired the economic prerequisites for educational mobility at a time when educational opportunities abounded?" (p. 137).

2. Maurice Samuel, *The Great Hatred*, p. 48.

3. That economic factors do not cause Jew-hatred does not mean that they do not cause some ethnic rivalry or some resentment of Jews. But such feelings of resentment are one thing and Jew-hatred is quite another. This book is concerned with the Jew-hatred that has existed for over two thousand years, and *that* has not been caused by Jews who lead lives of conspicuous consumption.

4. Hannah Arendt, *The Origins of Totalitarianism*, p. 4.

5. Arthur Hertzberg, *The French Enlightenment and the Jews*, p. 7.

6. *Ibid.*

7. T. W. Adorno; Else Frenkel-Brunswick; Daniel J. Levinson; and R. Nevitt Sanford, *The Authoritarian Personality*.
8. From the Max Horkheimer preface to *The Authoritarian Personality*, p. ix.
9. Gordon Allport, *The Nature of Prejudice*, pp. xv–xvi.
10. Adorno et al., *Authoritarian Personality*, p. 1.
11. Originally published as *Reflexions sur la Question Juive* (Paris: Paul Morihein, 1946), the book was translated and published in the United States in 1948 by Schocken. It is currently in its *thirteenth* printing as a Schocken paperback. Citations are from that edition.
12. Sartre, *Anti-Semite*, p. 54.
13. *Ibid.*, p. 53.
14. *Ibid.*, pp. 13, 67, 91.
15. *Ibid.*, p. 135.

PART TWO
THE HISTORICAL EVIDENCE
SEVEN: *Antisemitism in the Ancient World*

1. Philostratus, *The Life of Apollonius of Tyana*, translated by F. G. Conybeare; cited in Menachem Stern, *Greek and Latin Authors on Jews and Judaism*, 2:341.
2. Yizhak Heinemann in *Anti-Semitism*, Jerusalem, Keter Publishing, 1974, p. 3.
3. Josephus, *Against Apion*, II:65.
4. Cited in Josephus, *Against Apion* I, 304–11.
5. The Jews' successful revolt against Antiochus' attempt to destroy Judaism is commemorated by the holiday of Chanukah.
6. Victor Tcherikover, *Hellenistic Civilization and the Jews*, p. 478, n. 39; see also pp. 195–96, 199.
7. Josephus, *Against Apion* I, 91–96.
8. Tacitus' extensive writings on the Jews, the most detailed account of Judaism and Jewish history in classical Latin literature, have been collected in *Greek and Latin Authors on Jews and Judaism*, edited with introductions, translations, and commentary by Menachem Stern, 2:1–93. Concerning the impact on Tacitus' description of the Jews, Stern notes: "Since this description is found in the works of the greatest historian of Rome, its subsequent influence, especially after the revival of interest in Tacitus in the sixteenth century, may be considered out of all proportions to its inherent merits" (p. 1).
9. See Philo, *Embassy to Gaius*, Loeb edition, vols. IX–X, trans. F. H. Colson. Cited in Vamberto Morais, *A Short History of Anti-Semitism*, p. 28.
10. A discussion of the Jewish population in the Roman Empire is in Salo Baron, *A Social and Religious History of the Jews*, I:370–72.
11. Cited in Stern, *Greek and Latin Authors*, 1:431.

12. Josephus, *Antiquities*, vol. 20.5 1–3 and *The Jewish War*, 2.12.2.
13. Stern, *Greek and Latin Authors*, 2:26.
14. Baron, *Social and Religious History*, 1:194.
15. Rosemary Reuther, *Faith and Fratricide*, pp. 24–25.
16. This dislike was not motivated by any distinctive Jewish economic status. Historians Marcel Simon in *Versus Israel* and J. Juster in *Les Juifs dan L'Empire Romain* have both documented that the pagan world did not associate the Jews with distinctive economic roles or with wealth. See Edward Flannery, *The Anguish of the Jews*, chap. 1.

EIGHT: *Christian Antisemitism*

1. See note on p. 93. See also Hyam Maccoby, *Revolution in Judaea*, for a full discussion of Jesus the Jew.
2. Whereas other Gospel writers had usually attacked Jewish authority figures, John uses the term "the Jews" almost exclusively (some sixty times) for his condemnation (see Rosemary Reuther, *Faith and Fratricide*, pp. 115–16).
3. See R. S. Storrs, *Bernard of Clairvaux* (New York, Gordon Press, n.d.), p. 357, and J. H. Newman, *Historical Sketches* (Westminster, Md.: Christian Classics, 1970), II: 234. Both of these works are cited by the Catholic historian Malcolm Hay in his *Europe and the Jews*, p. 27.
4. Citations from the speeches and writings of St. John Chrysostom are in Hay, *Europe*, pp. 26–31.
5. *Ibid.*, pp. 30–31.
6. St. Ambrose wrote two accounts of this, one sent as a letter to the emperor, the other as a letter to his sister. Both are in Jacob Marcus, *The Jew in the Medieval World*, pp. 107–10.
7. The facts and contemporary chronicles of the Crusades are in Leon Poliakov, *The History of Anti-Semitism: From the Time of Christ to the Court Jews*, pp. 41–56. The complete Jewish chronicles from the Crusader period have been translated and edited by Professor Shlomo Eidelberg in *The Jews and the Crusaders: the Hebrew Chronicles of the First and Second Crusades*.
8. Poliakov, *Time of Christ to the Court Jews*, p. 45.
9. *Ibid.*, p. 47, n. 6.
10. *Ibid.*, p. 48.
11. See Hay, *Europe*, pp. 127–28; for methods of torture used, see pp. 132–33.
12. We are indebted in this section to a remarkable work of contemporary scholarship, *The Devil and the Jews: The Medieval Conception of the Jew and Its Relation to Modern Antisemitism* by Joshua Trachtenberg. The relevant pages of Trachtenberg's book are pp. 97–155.
13. Trachtenberg, *Devil and the Jews*, p. 130.

14. *Ibid.*, p. 131.
15. Charles Lamb, "Imperfect Sympathies," *Essays of Elia.* Cited in Hay, *Europe*, p. 126.
16. In F. J. Child's *The English and Scottish Popular Ballads* (Magnolia, Mass.: Peter Smith, 1965), the compiler quotes twenty-one versions of the ballad about Hugh of Lincoln. See Marcus, *Jew in the Medieval World*, p. 126.
17. Trachtenberg, *Devil and the Jews*, p. 135.
18. Haim Hillel Ben-Sasson, *Trial and Achievement: Currents in Jewish History*, p. 247.
19. James Parkes, *The Foundations of Judaism and Christianity*, p. 247. Malcolm Hay places much of the blame for the continued popularity of the blood libel in modern times on a faction in the Vatican: "Although Pope Innocent IV in the 13th century had decreed that no one was to accuse the Jews of using human blood in the religious rites, this prohibition did not prevent the publication of the old calumnies by the semi-official journal of the Vatican, *La-Cruila Cattolica*, in a series of articles . . . [that] appeared between February, 1881 and December, 1882. Characteristic of its articles is this selection from the March 4, 1882 issue: 'Every practicing Hebrew worthy of that name is obliged even now, in conscience, to use in food, in drink, in circumcision, and in various other rites of his religious and civil life the fresh or dried blood of a Christian child, under pain of infringing his laws and passing among his acquaintances for a bad Hebrew . . . all this is still true and faithfully observed in the present century' " (*Europe*, pp. 311–12).
20. The blood libel had been introduced into the Muslim world by Christian missionaries in the nineteenth century. See Hay, *Europe*, p. 310.
21. Professor Jacob Milgrom of the University of California at Berkeley has noted: "This prohibition is not found anywhere else in the ancient Near East. . . . That none of Israel's neighbors possess this absolute and universal binding prohibition means that it cannot be a vestige of a primitive taboo, but the result of a deliberate reasoned enactment. This is clear from the rationale appended to the law: "blood is life" (*Lev.* 17:11, 14 and *Deut.* 12:23. Milgrom's conclusion appears in the *Encyclopedia Judaica*, 4:1115).
22. Ahad Ha-Am, *Selected Essays*, pp. 203–4.
23. James Parkes, *The Jew in the Medieval Community*, p. 50.
24. Trachtenberg, *Devil and the Jews*, p. 97.
25. *Ibid.*
26. Trachtenberg, *Devil and the Jews*, p. 99.
27. Ben-Sasson, *Trial and Achievement*, pp. 254–55.
28. Trachtenberg, *Devil and the Jews*, p. 114.
29. Raul Hilberg, *The Destruction of the European Jews*, p. 4.
30. Hilberg, *Destruction*, pp. 4–6. In each instance we have cited

only the first date on which any given law was enacted. Most of the laws were reenforced many times.

31. Cited in Hilberg, *Destruction,* p. 12.

32. See A. Roy Eckhardt, *Your People, My People,* p. 24.

33. *Mein Kampf,* p. 213.

34. Cited in Friedrich Heer, *God's First Love,* p. 286.

35. Hay, *Europe,* p. 286.

36. This pamphlet is reprinted in *The Jew in the Medieval World,* ed. Jacob Marcus, pp. 167–69.

37. See Eliezer Berkovits, *Faith After the Holocaust* (New York: Ktav, 1973), for a scathing and brilliant assessment of Christian responsibility for the Holocaust.

38. Cited in Heer, *God's First Love,* after dedication page.

NINE: *Islamic Antisemitism*

1. Salo Baron, *A Social and Religious History of the Jews,* 3:94.

2. S. D. Goitein, *Jews and Arabs,* p. 84. Goitein's book is the best survey of Jews under the Arabs and Islam. *The Jews of Arab Lands,* by Norman A. Stillman, complements Goitein's work, with over 300 pages of documents from Jewish life in the Islamic world.

3. Goitein, *Jews and Arabs,* pp. 58–59.

4. The translations used in this chapter are taken from The Koran, translated by the noted Arab scholar N. J. Dawood (New York: Penguin, 1964).

5. Walter Kaufmann, *Religions in Four Dimensions,* p. 186.

6. *Ibid.*

7. Goitein, *Jews and Arabs,* p. 64.

8. Christians, too, were accused of omitting from the New Testament a prophecy of Jesus relating to Muhammad: "And of Jesus, who said to the Israelites: 'I am sent forth to you by Allah to confirm the Torah already revealed and to give news of an apostle that will come after me whose name is Ahmed [another name of Humammad's] . . .' " (61:6).

9. See Joel Kramer, "War, Conquest and the Treatment of Religious Minorities in Medieval Islam," in *Violence and Defense in the Jewish Experience,* ed. Salo Baron and George Wise, p. 150.

10. *Ibid.,* pp. 151–52.

11. The complete text of the Pact of Umar is printed in *Islam,* vol. 2: *Religion and Society,* ed. and trans. Bernard Lewis, pp. 217–19.

12. Goitein, *Jews and Arabs,* pp. 67–68.

13. Both the regulation and the quote from Baron are in Baron, *Social and Religious History,* 3:167.

14. *Ibid.,* p. 168. Baron noted that this procedure was regarded as so degrading that when Muslims imposed this on Christians in Jerusalem in 758, many Christians fled to Byzantium.

15. *Ibid.*, p. 171.
16. Kraemer, "Treatment of Religious Minorities," p. 153.
17. See Raul Hilberg, *The Destruction of the European Jews*, p. 5.
18. Baron, *Social and Religious History*, 3:141.
19. *Ibid.*, p. 140.
20. This description of Jewish life in Yemen is taken from Goitein, *Jews and Arabs*, pp. 74–78.
21. The quotation appears in Lane's book, *An Account of the Manners and Customs of the Modern Egyptians* (Magnolia, Mass.: Peter Smith, n.d.) on pp. 512–13, and is cited in Shimon Shamir, "Muslim-Arab Attitudes Towards Jews in the Ottoman and Modern Periods," in *Violence and Defense in the Jewish Experience*, ed. Salo Baron and George Wise, p. 195.
22. See *A History of the Jewish People*, ed. H. H. Ben-Sasson, pp. 847–48.
23. See Shamir, "Muslim-Arab Attitudes," p. 195.
24. See "Palestine Before the Zionists" by Harvard historian David Landes, *Commentary*, February 1976, pp. 47–56.
25. James Finn, *Stirring Times*, I:118–19.
26. Albert Memmi, *Jews and Arabs*, pp. 32–33.
27. *Ibid.*, p. 33.
28. Yehoshafat Harkabi, *Arab Attitudes to Israel*, p. 221.
29. Cited in Elias Cooper, "Forgotten Palestinian: The Nazi Mufti," *The American Zionist*, March-April 1973, p. 26.
30. Among the war criminals welcomed to Nasser's Egypt were Leopold Gleim, head of the Gestapo in Poland; Hans Eichler, who served in Buchenwald; Heinrich Willerman; a doctor who experimented on human guinea pigs in Dachau; and Alois Moser who took part in the massacre of hundreds of thousands of Jews in the Ukraine. In Syria, the Nazis include Franz Rademacher, head of the German foreign office department dealing with Jews, and Otto Ernst Remer, the former military governor of Berlin. The Egyptians also employed several hundred Nazi technicians to develop its missile and aircraft industry, while the Syrians used Nazis to develop their secret police and assist in producing anti-Jewish propaganda. (See Julian J. Landau, *Israel and the Arabs*, p. 173.)
31. Cited in Landau, *ibid.*, p. 175.
32. Cited in Harkabi, *Arab Attitudes*, p. 279.
33. See Moshe Ma'oz, "The Image of the Jew in Official Arab Literature and Communications Media," in *World Jewry and the State of Israel*, ed. Moshe Davis, p. 45.
34. Cited in Landau, *Israel and the Arabs*, p. 177.
35. Cited in Ma'oz, "Image of the Jew," p. 46.
36. *Ibid.*, p. 38.
37. Cited by Landau, *Israel and the Arabs*, p. 40.
38. Ma'oz, "Image of the Jew," p. 44. In Cairo in 1974, Dennis

Prager saw Arab translations of *The Protocols* in nearly every bookstore he visited.

39. Harkabi, *Arab Attitudes*, p. 241.

TEN: *Enlightenment Antisemitism*

1. Except where otherwise noted the quotations from the *Dictionnaire Philosophique* are cited in Leon Poliakov's *The History of Anti-Semitism: From Voltaire to Wagner*, pp. 88–89. Poliakov has, in the main, relied on the J. Benda. Naves edition of 1936 which follows the 1769 edition of the *Dictionnaire*.

2. From the entry on Jew in the *Dictionnaire*, 1756 edition, cited in *A History of the Jewish People*, ed. H. H. Ben-Sasson, p. 745.

3. Poliakov, *From Voltaire to Wagner*, p. 87.

4. Peter Gay, a professor at Yale University, has authored the following volumes on the Enlightenment: *The Enlightenment: vol. 1: The Rise of Modern Paganism; vol. 2: The Science of Freedom*. Also *The Party of Humanity: Essays in the French Enlightenment*, and *The Enlightenment: An Anthology*.

5. Gay, *Party of Humanity*, pp. 103, 105.

6. Gay, *ibid.*, pp. 44, 53.

7. Arthur Hertzberg's *The French Enlightenment and the Jews*, pp. 286, 287, 288, 289–90. We are indebted to Professor Hertzberg's work for documenting the profound influence of eighteenth-century Enlightenment thinking on modern antisemitism.

8. Gay, *Enlightenment: Anthology*, p. 746.

9. Cited in Hertzberg, *French Enlightenment*, p. 284.

10. Poliakov, *From Voltaire to Wagner*, p. 491, n. 38.

11. Hertzberg, *French Enlightenment*, pp. 297, 300, 301.

12. *Ibid.*, p. 10.

13. *Ibid.*, p. 299.

14. Poliakov, *From Voltaire to Wagner*, p. 119.

15. The material cited from d'Holbach comes from Poliakov, *ibid.*, pp. 120–24.

16. Montesquieu, *L'Esprit des lois*, XXV, 13: "A Most Humble Remonstrance to the Inquisitors of Spain and Portugal." Cited in Poliakov, *ibid.*, p. 82.

17. Ben-Sasson, *History of the Jewish People*, p. 745.

18. Cited in Ben-Sasson, *ibid.*, p. 746.

19. Cited in Ben-Sasson, *ibid.*, p. 742.

20. Hertzberg, *French Enlightenment*, pp. 38–39.

21. Shmuel Ettinger, "The Origins of Modern Anti-Semitism," in *The Catastrophe of European Jewry*, ed. Yisrael Gutman and Livia Rothkirchen, p. 12.

ELEVEN: *Leftist Antisemitism*

1. "Almost all the rabbis of Trier from the sixteenth century onwards were ancestors of Marx," notes Marx biographer David McLellan, *Karl Marx: His Life and Thought*, p. 3.

2. Quoted in Nathan Rotenstreich, "For and Against Emancipation: The Bruno Bauer Controversy," in *Yearbook IV* of the Leo Baeck Institute, pp. 7–8.

3. *On the Jewish Question* appears in Karl Marx's *Early Writings*, ed. Quintin Hoare, and trans. Rodney Livingston and Gregor Benton, pp. 211–41. The quote is on p. 241.

4. Robert Wistrich, *Revolutionary Jews from Marx to Trotsky*, p. 33.

5. *On the Jewish Question*, p. 236.

6. *Ibid.*, p. 239.

7. "The social emancipation of the Jews is the emancipation of society from Judaism." *Ibid.*, p. 241.

8. Cited in Julius Carlebach, *Karl Marx and the Radical Critique of Judaism*, pp. 355–56.

9. Max Geltman, "On Socialist Anti-Semitism," *Midstream* 23, no. 3 (March 1977): 25. The earlier citations in the paragraph are on pp. 24–25.

10. Written in a letter to Friedrich Engels on May 10, 1861. In this letter, Marx attacked his political opponent Ferdinand Lasalle as being a descendant of one of these leprous Jews.

11. Cited in Edmund Silberner's "Inaugural Lecture" delivered at the Hebrew University on January 4, 1953, and subsequently reprinted under the title *The Anti-Semitic Tradition in Modern Socialism*.

12. In recent years, Arnold Kunzli has attempted a posthumous psychoanalysis of Marx's antisemitism. Kunzli concludes that Marx's identification of Jews and Judaism with capitalism was a way of distancing himself from Jews. We know, in fact, that Marx virulently reacted against any mention of his Jewish origins. This desire to distance himself would also explain why he ignored the Jewish working class, and why he took no notice of Socialist movements among Jewish workers. "Marx must, therefore, have experienced the emergence of a Jewish socialism as a vexation, for thereby the legitimacy of his system, into which he had . . . forced Judaism was made questionable, and his alibi destroyed and he himself again brought into association with his Judaism." (See Arnold Kunzli, *Karl Marx-Eine Psychographie*, p. 209, cited in Leon Poliakov, *The History of Anti-Semitism: From Voltaire to Wagner*, p. 556, n. 148. See also above, chap. 5, on revolutionary non-Jewish Jews.)

13. Edmund Silberner, "Was Marx an Anti-Semite?" *Historica Judaica*, April 1949, p. 52.

14. Nora Levin, *While Messiah Tarried*, pp. 100–1.

15. The most important assessment of the French socialists' attitudes toward the Jews was written by Lichtheim in the essay "Socialism and the Jews," reprinted in his *Collected Essays*, pp. 413–47.

16. Cited in Jacob Katz, *From Prejudice to Destruction: Anti-Semitism, 1700–1933*, p. 121.

17. Alphonse Toussenel, *Les Juifs, rois de l'époque* (1845), pp. 73–74. Cited in Lichtheim, "Socialism and the Jews," p. 422.

18. Lichtheim, *ibid.*, p. 424.

19. *Carnets de P. J. Proudhon: Texte inédit et integral*, ed. Pierre Haubtmann, II: 337–38. Quoted in Lichtheim, p. 425.

20. Lichtheim, *ibid.*, p. 426.

21. Jean Juarès subsequently had a change of heart, and argued that Socialists should protest this injustice. See Edmund Silberner, "French Socialists and the Jews," *Historica Judaica*, April 1957, pp. 13–14.

22. *Jewish Social Studies*, January 1947.

23. In 1972, the Politburo of the North Vietnamese Communist party hailed the Black September (a wing of the Palestine Liberation Organization) murder of the Israeli athletes at the Olympics in Munich.

24. See Bernard Weinryb, "Antisemitism in Soviet Russia," in *The Jews in Soviet Russia Since 1917*, ed. Lionel Kochan, p. 326. Kochan's book and William Korey's *The Soviet Cage: Anti-Semitism in Russia* are the two most comprehensive works on Soviet antisemitism.

25. Quoted in Zev Katz, "After the Six-Day War," in Kochan, *Jews in Soviet Russia*, p. 335.

26. Witnessed by Dennis Prager, who speaks Russian, in 1972.

27. George Will, *Los Angeles Times*, October 9, 1979.

28. *Pravda*, July 6, 1967. Cited in Kochan, *Jews in Soviet Russia*, p. 347.

29. *American Jewish Year Book 1976*, vol. 76, ed. Morris Fine and Milton Himmelfarb, pp. 93–94.

30. *Intercontinental Press*, September 6, 1971. Cited in *Facts*, November 1972, p. 550.

31. *Ibid.*, p. 551.

32. Cited in Arnold Foster and Benjamin Epstein, *The New Anti-Semitism*, p. 147.

33. Marie Syrkin, "Redwashing Terrorism," in *The State of the Jews*, p. 210. Syrkin notes that before its showing in the United States some of the PLO's and Redgrave's more extreme antisemitic positions were censored. In the original version of the movie, for example, PLO leader Yasir Arafat declared: "The only solution to the Middle East problem is the liquidation of the state of Israel." To which Redgrave responds, "Certainly" (p. 211).

34. See Alan Dershowitz, "Now Jews Must Overcome," *ADL Bulletin*, April 1981, p. 10.

35. *Ibid.*, p. 8.

36. See the article by Father Leo Rudloff, "Capucci, Terrorism and the Vatican," *ADL Bulletin*, November 1981.

37. Cited in *ADL Bulletin*, October 1981, p. 7.

TWELVE: *Nazi Antisemitism*

1. "There were Gypsy tribes that were murdered and there were others that were protected. Individual Gypsies living among the rest of the population were not ferreted out and many even served in the Nazi army. It appears that the Nazis were ambivalent about what to do with them, but those who were murdered were the victims more of a campaign against so-called 'asocials' than against the Gypsy people as such." Yehuda Bauer, *The Holocaust in Historical Perspective*, p. 36.

2. Adolf Hitler, *Mein Kampf*, p. 312.

3. Cited in Lucy Dawidowicz, *The War Against the Jews*, p. 86.

4. Cited in Dawidowicz, *ibid.*, p. 84.

5. Dawidowicz, *ibid.*, p. 4.

6. *Ibid.*, pp. 141–42.

7. Lucy Dawidowicz, *A Holocaust Reader*, p. 85.

8. Cited in Dawidowicz, *War Against the Jews*, p. 191.

9. "Regional analyses of the Nazi party have appeared which trace in detail its evolution from a fringe group to a mass movement. They have focused primarily upon the novel structure and propaganda techniques of the party, and have in several cases cast strong doubts upon the significance of antisemitism in drawing recruits to the party and in attracting voters after 1929. In the case of Northeim, for example, historian W. A. Allen has argued that many who flocked to National Socialism just 'ignored or rationalized' its hatred of Jews; similarly, in . . . Bavaria." Geoffrey G. Field, *Evangelist of Race: The Germanic Vision of Houston Stewart Chamberlain*, p. 457.

10. Cited in Dawidowicz, *War Against the Jews*, p. 22.

11. Treitschke's account is in *Modern Jewish History: A Source Reader*, ed. Robert Chazan and Marc Lee Raphael, pp. 80–84.

12. Cited in Field, *Evangelist of Race*, p. 186.

13. Letter to Harriet Chamberlain, June 7, 1896, cited in *ibid.*, p. 107.

14. Cited in Will Herberg, *Judaism and Modern Man*, p. 274.

15. Poliakov, *The Aryan Myth*, p. 319.

16. Quoted in Uriel Tal, "Anti-Christian Anti-Semitism," in *The Catastrophe of European Jewry*, ed. Yisrael Gutman and Livia Rothkirchen, p. 94.

17. *Ibid.*, p. 95.
18. Cited in Dawidowicz, *War Against the Jews*, pp. 32–33.
19. Cited in Carl Friedrich, "Anti-Semitism: Challenge to Christian Culture," in *Jews in a Gentile World: The Problem of Anti-Semitism,* ed. Isacque Graeber and Steuart Henderson Britt, p. 8.
20. Cited in Norman Cohn, *Warrant for Genocide,* pp. 136–37.
21. Dawidowicz, *War Against the Jews,* pp. 373–74.
22. *Ibid.*
23. Celia Heller's *On the Edge of Destruction* details the sufferings of Polish Jewry between the two world wars.
24. *The Warsaw Diary of Chaim A. Kaplan* has been translated and edited by Abraham I. Katsh.
25. Yehuda Bauer, *A History of the Holocaust,* p. 285.
26. John Toland, *Adolf Hitler,* p. 797.
27. Shmuel Ettinger, "The Modern Period," in *A History of the Jewish People,* ed. H. H. Ben-Sasson, p. 1025. Unless otherwise noted all the factual evidence about Eastern European cooperation with the Nazis comes from pp. 1023–35.
28. Both this and the following instance are told in Rabbi M. D. Weissmandel's autobiographical account of the Holocaust years, *Min Hamezar,* pp. 24–25, and are cited in Eliezer Berkovits, *Faith After the Holocaust,* pp. 16–17.
29. Shmuel Ettinger, "Modern Period," p. 1034.
30. Raul Hilberg, ed., *Documents of Destruction: Germany and Jewry, 1933–1945,* pp. 152–53.

THIRTEEN: *Anti-Zionist Antisemitism*

1. An earlier version of this chapter appeared in chap. 6 in *The Nine Questions People Ask About Judaism,* by Dennis Prager and Joseph Telushkin.
2. *American Zionist,* March 1971.
3. Amos Kenan, "New Left Go Home," in *The New Left and the Jews,* ed. Mordecai S. Chertoff, p. 311.
4. See Norman Podhoretz, "Now, Instant Zionism," in *The New York Times Magazine,* February 3, 1974, p. 39.
5. There is a fringe group of several hundred ultra-Orthodox Jews in Israel, known as the *neturei karta,* who are well-known enemies of Israel and of Zionism. At first, one might think that their positions are consistent with anti-Zionists. But this is not so. These Jews believe that the Jews are a nation (Am Yisrael) and there should be a Jewish state. They insist, however, that this state should not come into existence until the Messiah personally establishes it, and since this was not the case with Israel (and furthermore, since the leaders of the state do not abide by the religious practices of the *neturei karta*), they do not recognize the current state of Israel. In any case, the *neturei*

karta Jews are as representative of Jews as the snake-handling sects are of Christians.

6. Cited in William Korey's "Updating the Protocols," *Midstream*, May 1970, p. 17.

7. While the Left's antisemitism generally masquerades under the guise of anti-Zionism, the anti-Jewish writings of the Fascist Right usually acknowledge their animosity toward the Jews, seeing Zionism correctly as a manifestation of Judaism. The late Gerald L. K. Smith, the major disseminator of antisemitic writings in the United States over the past four decades, wrote in the *Gerald L. K. Smith Newsletter* of April 19, 1973: "The enemies of Christ are determined to capture the world—not through the United Nations, not through what people call a World Government, but through the manipulating, financial and military power of World Zionism."

8. See William Korey, "Updating Protocols," *Midstream*, May 1976, p. 6.

9. See Seymour Martin Lipset, "The Socialism of Fools: The Left, the Jews and Israel," in Chertoff's *New Left*, p. 104.

10. See Sidney Liskofsky, "U.N. Resolution on Zionism," in the *American Jewish Year Book, 1977*, vol. 77, ed. Morris Fine and Milton Himmelfarb, p. 109.

PART THREE
WHAT IS TO BE DONE?

FOURTEEN: *What Is to be Done?*

1. Boris Pasternak, *Dr. Zhivago*, pp. 117–18.

2. We say *modern* Zionist movement because the Jews' goal of returning to Zion (Israel) is as old as the Jews' exile (starting in 586 B.C.E.).

3. The four statements reflect annoyance with converts whose motives for conversion were insincere, or disappointment with converts who deserted the Jewish community during periods of persecution.

4. See George Foot Moore, *Judaism in the First Centuries of the Christian Era*, I:352–53; and Andrew Sharf, *Byzantine Jewry from Justinian to the Fourth Crusade*, pp. 19ff.

5. Moore, *ibid.*

6. Commentary to *Yevamot* 49A; cited in Ben-Zion Bokser, *Jews, Judaism and the State of Israel*, p. 134.

7. Hillel Halkin, *Letters to an American Jewish Friend*, pp. 239–40.

8. See, for example, Dennis Prager and Joseph Telushkin, *The Nine Questions People Ask About Judaism*.

EPILOGUE: *The Meaning of Antisemitism for Non-Jews*

1. *The Wall Street Journal,* July 22, 1982.
2. *The New Republic,* August 2, 1982.
3. *Newsweek,* July 26, 1982.
4. Cited in *Midstream,* May 1976, p. 21.
5. Jacques Maritain, *A Christian Looks at the Jewish Question,* pp. 29–30.

Bibliography of Cited Works

Abrahams, Israel. *Jewish Life in the Middle Ages*. Philadelphia: Jewish Publication Society, 1896; New York: Atheneum (pbk.), 1969.

Adorno, T. W.; Else Frenkel-Brunswick; Daniel J. Levinson; and R. Nevitt Sanford. *The Authoritarian Personality*. New York: W. W. Norton (pbk.), 1969.

Allport, Gordon W. *The Nature of Prejudice*. Reading, Mass.: Addison-Wesley (pbk.), 1979.

Arendt, Hannah. *The Origins of Totalitarianism*. New York: Harcourt Brace Jovanovich, Harvest Books, 1973.

Baron, Salo. *The Russian Jew Under Tsars and Soviets*. New York: Macmillan, 1976.

———. *A Social and Religious History of the Jews*. 2d ed. New York: Columbia University Press, vol. I: 1952; vol. III: 1957.

———, and George Wise. *Violence and Defense in the Jewish Experience*. Philadelphia: Jewish Publication Society, 1977.

Bauer, Yehuda. *A History of the Holocaust*. New York: Franklin Watts, 1982.

———. *The Holocaust in Historical Perspective*. Seattle: University of Washington Press, 1978.

Ben-Sasson, Haim Hillel, ed. *A History of the Jewish People*. Cambridge, Mass.: Harvard University Press, 1976.

———. "The Middle Ages." In *A History of the Jewish People*, ed. H. H. Ben-Sasson. Cambridge, Mass.: Harvard University Press, 1976.

————. *Trial and Achievement: Currents in Jewish History.* Jerusalem: Keter Publishing House, 1974.

Berkovits, Eliezer. *Faith After the Holocaust.* New York: Ktav, 1973.

Bermant, Chaim. *The Jews.* New York: New York Times Books, 1977.

Bokser, Ben-Zion. *Jews, Judaism and the State of Israel.* New York: Herzl Press, 1973.

Carlebach, Julius. *Karl Marx and the Radical Critique of Judaism.* London: Routledge and Kegan Paul, 1978.

Chertoff, Modecai, S., ed. *The New Left and the Jews.* New York: Pitman Publishing, 1971.

Chomsky, Noam. *Towards a New Cold War.* New York: Pantheon Books, 1982.

Cohn, Norman. *Warrant for Genocide: The Jewish World Conspiracy and the Protocols of the Elders of Zion.* New York: Harper and Row, 1966, 1967.

Cooper, Elias. "Forgotten Palestinian: The Nazi Mufti." *The American Zionist,* March-April, 1973.

Dawidowicz, Lucy. *A Holocaust Reader.* New York: Behrman House, 1976.

————. *The War Against the Jews.* New York: Holt, Rinehart and Winston, 1975.

Deak, Istvan. *Weimar Germany's Left-Wing Intellectuals: A Political History of the Weltbuhne and Its Circle.* Berkeley: University of California Press, 1968.

Dershowitz, Alan. "Now Jews Must Overcome." *ADL Bulletin,* April 1981.

Deutscher, Isaac. *The Non-Jewish Jew and Other Essays.* London: Oxford University Press, 1968.

Eckhardt, A. Roy. *Your People, My People.* New York: Quadrangle, 1974.

Eidelberg, Shlomo. *The Jews and the Crusaders: The Hebrew Chronicles of the First and Second Crusades.* Madison: University of Wisconsin Press, 1977.

Encyclopedia Judaica. 16 vols. Jerusalem: Keter Publishing House, 1972.

Ettinger, Shmuel. "The Modern Period." In *A History of the Jewish People,* edited by H. H. Sasson, pp. 727–1096. Cambridge, Mass.: Harvard University Press, 1976.

————. "The Origins of Modern Anti-Semitism." In *The Catastrophe of European Jewry,* edited by Yisrael Gutman and Livia Rothkirchen. New York: Ktav, n.d.

Fackenheim, Emil. "Post-Holocaust Anti-Jewishness, Jewish Identity and the Centrality of Israel." In *World Jewry and the State of Israel,* edited by Moshe Davis. New York: Arno Press, 1977.

Field, Geoffrey G. *Evangelist of Race: The Germanic Vision of Hous-*

ton Stewart Chamberlain. New York: Columbia University Press, 1981.

Finn, James. Stirring Times. London: C. Kegan Paul, 1878.

Flannery, Edward. The Anguish of the Jews. New York: Macmillan, 1965.

Flavius, Josephus. Against Apion, Antiquities, and The Jewish War are all available in the Loeb Classical Library. 9 vols. Translated by H. St. J. Thackeray, Ralph Marcus, and Louis Feldman, 1926–1965.

Foster, Arnold, and Benjamin Epstein. The New Anti-Semitism. New York: McGraw-Hill, 1974.

Frank, Anne. The Diary of Anne Frank. Garden City, N.Y.: Doubleday, 1952; New York: Simon and Schuster, Pocket Books (pbk.), 1963, 1974.

Fresco, Nadine. "The Denial of the Dead: The Faurisson Affair and Noam Chomsky." Dissent, Fall 1981.

Friedrich, Carl. "Anti-Semitism: Challenge to Christian Culture." In Jews in a Gentile World, edited by Isacque Graeber and Steuart Henderson. New York: Macmillan, 1942.

Gay, Peter. The Enlightenment. 2 vols. New York: Knopf, vol. I, 1966; vol. II, 1969.

———. The Enlightenment: An Anthology. New York: Simon and Schuster, 1973.

———. The Party of Humanity: Essays in the French Enlightenment. Princeton, N.J.: Princeton University Press, 1959; New York: W. W. Norton (pbk.), 1971.

Geltman, Max. "On Socialist Anti-Semitism." Midstream, March 1977.

Glassman, Bernard. Anti-Semitic Stereotypes Without Jews: Images of the Jews in England, 1290–1700. Detroit: Wayne State University Press, 1975.

Glazer, Nathan. The Social Basis of American Communism. 1st ed. New York: Harcourt, Brace, 1961.

———, and Daniel Patrick Moynihan. Beyond the Melting Pot. 2d ed. rev. Cambridge, Mass.: M.I.T. Press, 1970.

Goitein, S. D. Jews and Arabs: Their Contacts Through the Ages. New York: Schocken Books (pbk.), 1964.

Greeley, Andrew. The American Catholic: A Social Portrait. New York: Basic Books, 1977.

Gutman, Yisrael, and Livia Rothkirchen, eds. The Catastrophe of European Jewry. New York: Ktav, n.d.

Ha-Am, Ahad. Selected Essays. Translated by Leon Simon. New York: Meridian Books, 1962.

Halkin, Hillel. Letters to an American Jewish Friend. Philadelphia: Jewish Publication Society, 1977.

Harkabi, Yehoshafat. *Arab Attitudes to Israel.* Jerusalem: Keter Publishing House, 1972.
Hay, Malcolm. *Europe and the Jews.* Boston: Beacon Press (pbk.), 1961.
Heer, Friedrich. *God's First Love.* New York: Weybright and Talley, 1967.
Heller, Celia. *On the Edge of Destruction.* New York: Columbia University Press, 1977.
Helmrich, Ernst Christian. *The German Churches Under Hitler.* Detroit: Wayne State University Press, 1979.
Herberg, Will. *Judaism and Modern Man.* Philadelphia: Jewish Publication Society, 1951; New York: Atheneum (pbk.), 1970.
Hertzberg, Arthur. *The French Enlightenment and the Jews: The Origins of Modern Anti-Semitism.* New York: Columbia University Press, 1968; New York: Schocken (pbk.), 1970.
Heschel, Abraham Joshua. *The Earth Is the Lord's.* New York: Henry Schuman, 1950; New York: Harper and Row, Harper Torchbook (pbk.), 1966.
Hilberg, Raul. *The Destruction of the European Jews.* New York: Quadrangle, 1961.
————. *Documents of Destruction: Germany and Jewry, 1933–1945.* Chicago: Quadrangle, 1971.
Himmelfarb, Milton. *The Condition of Jewish Belief.* New York: Macmillan, 1969.
Hitler, Adolf. *Mein Kampf.* Translated by Ralph Manheim. Boston: Houghton Mifflin, Sentry Edition, 1971.
Howe, Irving. *World of Our Fathers.* N.Y.: Harcourt Brace Jovanovich, 1976.
Isaacs, Stephen D. *Jews and American Politics.* Garden City, N.Y.: Doubleday, 1974.
Jacobs, Louis. *A Jewish Theology.* New York: Behrman House, 1973.
Jewish Encyclopedia. 12 vols. New York: Funk and Wagnalls, 1901–1905.
Katsh, Abraham, trans. and ed. *The Warsaw Diary of Chaim A. Kaplan.* New York: Macmillan, 1965; New York: Collier (pbk.), 1973.
Katz, Jacob. *From Prejudice to Destruction: Anti-Semitism, 1700–1933.* Cambridge, Mass.: Harvard University Press, 1980.
Katz, Zev. "After the Six-Day War." In *The Jews in Soviet Russia Since 1917,* edited by Lionel Kochan. New York: Oxford University Press (pbk.), 1978.
Kaufmann, Walter. *Religions in Four Dimensions.* New York: Reader's Digest Press, 1976.
Kenan, Amos. "New Left Go Home." In *The New Left and the Jews,* edited by Mordecai S. Chertoff. New York: Pitman Publishing, 1971.

Kochan, Lionel, ed. *The Jews in Soviet Russia Since 1917*, New York: Oxford University Press (pbk.), 1978.

The Koran. Translated by N. J. Dawood. New York: Penguin Books (pbk.), 1974.

Korey, William. *The Soviet Cage: Anti-Semitism in Russia.* New York: Viking Press, 1973.

————. "Updating Protocols." *Midstream*, May 1976.

————. "Updating the Protocols." *Midstream*, May 1970.

Kraemer, Joel L. "War, Conquest and the Treatment of Religious Minorities in Medieval Islam." In *Violence and Defense in the Jewish Experience*, edited by Salo Baron and George Wise, pp. 143–59. Philadelphia: Jewish Publication Society, 1977.

Landau, Julian J. *Israel and the Arabs.* Jerusalem: Israel Communications, 1971.

Landes, David. "Palestine Before the Zionists." *Commentary*, February 1976, pp. 47–56.

Laqueur, Walter. *Out of the Ruins of Europe.* New York: Library Press, 1971.

Lendvai, Paul. *Anti-Semitism Without Jews: Communist Eastern Europe.* 1st ed. Garden City, N.Y.: Doubleday, 1971.

Levin, Nora. *While Messiah Tarried.* New York: Schocken, 1977.

Lewis, Bernard. *Islam.* Vol. II, *Religion and Society.* New York: Harper and Row, 1974.

Lichtheim, George. *Collected Essays.* New York: Viking Press (pbk.), 1973.

Lipset, Seymour Martin. "The Left, the Jews and Israel." *Encounter*, December 1969.

————. "The Socialism of Fools: The Left, the Jews and Israel." In *The New Left and the Jews*, edited by Mordecai S. Chertoff. New York: Pitman Publishing, 1971.

Lukofsky, Sidney. "U.N. Resolution on Zionism." In *American Jewish Yearbook 1977*, edited by Morris Fine and Milton Himmelfarb. Philadelphia: Jewish Publication Society, 1976.

Maccoby, Hyam. *Revolution in Judaea.* New York: Taplinger, 1980.

McLellan, David. *Karl Marx: His Life and Thought.* New York: Harper and Row, 1973.

Mailer, Norman. *The Presidential Papers.* New York: Putnam, 1963.

Maimonides, Moses. *The Commandments.* Translated by Charles B. Chavel. London: Soncino Press, 1967.

Ma'oz, Moshe. "The Image of the Jew in Official Arab Literature and Communications Media." In *World Jewry and the State of Israel*, edited by Moshe Davis. New York: Arno Press, 1977.

Marcus, Jacob, ed. *The Jew in the Medieval World.* New York: Union of American Hebrew Congregations, 1938; New York: Harper and Row, Harper Torchbooks (pbk.), 1965.

Maritain, Jacques. *A Christian Looks at the Jewish Question.* New York: Longmans, 1939.

Marx, Karl. "On the Jewish Question." In *Early Writings.* Translated by Rodney Livingston and Gregor Benton. New York: Random House, Vintage Books (pbk.), 1975.

Memmi, Albert. *Jews and Arabs.* Chicago: O'Hara, 1975.

Mendelsohn, S. Felix. *The Jew Laughs.* Chicago: L. M. Stein, 1935.

Mendes-Flohr, Paul R., and Jehuda Reinharz, eds. *The Jew in the Modern World.* New York: Oxford University Press, 1980.

Moore, George Foot. *Judaism in the First Centuries of the Christian Era.* 3 vols. Cambridge, Mass.: Harvard University Press, 1927–30.

Morais, Vamberto. *A Short History of Anti-Semitism.* New York: W. W. Norton, 1976.

Mosse, George. *Germans and Jews: The Right, the Left, and the Search for a Third Force in Pre-Nazi Germany.* New York: Howard Fertig, 1970.

———. *Masses and Man,* New York: Howard Fertig, 1980.

Nobile, Philip. *Intellectual Skywriting: Literary Politics and The New York Review of Books.* New York: Charterhouse, 1974.

Parkes, James. *The Foundations of Judaism and Christianity.* London: Vallentine, Mitchell, 1960.

———. *The Jew in the Medieval Community.* 2d ed. New York: Hermon Press, 1976.

Pasternak, Boris. *Dr. Zhivago.* Translated by Max Hayward and Manya Harari. New York: Pantheon, 1958.

Patai, Raphael. *The Jewish Mind.* New York: Scribner, 1977.

Plutarch. *Plutarch's Lives.* New York: The Modern Library, n.d.

Podhoretz, Norman. "Now Instant Zionism." *The New York Times Magazine,* February 3, 1974.

Poliakov, Leon. *The Aryan Myth.* New York: Basic Books, 1974.

———. *The History of Anti-Semitism: From the Time of Christ to the Court Jews.* New York: Viking Press, 1965; New York: Schocken (pbk.), 1974.

———. *The History of Anti-Semitism: From Voltaire to Wagner.* New York: Vanguard Press, 1975.

Prager, Dennis, and Joseph Telushkin. *The Nine Questions People Ask About Judaism.* New York: Simon and Schuster, 1981.

Pulzer, Peter G. J. *The Rise of Political Anti-Semitism in Germany and Austria.* New York: John Wiley (pbk.), 1964.

Rauschning, Hermann. *Hitler Speaks,* London: T. Butterworth, 1939.

Reeves, Richard. *American Journey.* New York: Simon and Schuster, 1982.

Reuther, Rosemary. *Faith and Fratricide.* New York: Seabury Press, 1974.

Robinson, Armin, ed. *The Ten Commandments.* Preface by Herman Rauschning. New York: Simon and Schuster, 1944.

Rotenstreich, Nathan. "For and Against Emancipation: The Bruno Bauer Controversy." *Yearbook IV* of the Leo Baeck Institute, East and West Library, London.

Roth, Cecil. *Essays and Portraits in Anglo-Jewish History.* 1st ed. Philadelphia: Jewish Publication Society, 1962.

———. *Personalities and Events in Jewish History.* Philadelphia: Jewish Publication Society, 1953.

Rothman, Stanley, and S. Robert Lichter. *Roots of Radicalism: Jews, Christians, and the New Left.* New York: Oxford University Press, 1982.

Rudloff, Leo. "Capucci, Terrorism and the Vatican." *ADL Bulletin,* November 1981.

Samuel, Maurice. *The Great Hatred.* New York: Knopf, 1941.

Sartre, Jean-Paul. *Anti-Semite and Jew.* New York: Schocken, 1948; (pbk.), 1965.

Scholem, Gershom. *Major Trends in Jewish Mysticism.* 3d ed. New York: Schocken Books, 1954.

Selznick, Gertrude, and Stephen Steinberg. *The Tenacity of Prejudice.* New York: Harper and Row, 1969.

Shamir, Shimon. "Muslim Arab Attitudes Toward Jews in the Ottoman and Modern Periods." In *Violence and Defense in the Jewish Experience,* edited by Salo Baron and George Wise, pp. 191–203. Philadelphia: Jewish Publication Society, 1977.

Sharf, Andrew. *Byzantine Jewry from Justinian to the Fourth Crusade.* London: Routledge and Kegan Paul, 1971.

Silberner, Edmund. "French Socialists and the Jews." *Historica Judaica,* April 1957.

———. "Was Marx an Anti-Semite?" *Historica Judaica,* April 1949.

Silver, Abba Hillel. *Where Judaism Differed.* New York: Macmillan, 1956; (pbk.), 1972.

Sklare, Marshall. *America's Jews.* New York: Random House, 1971.

Smalley, Beryl. *The Study of the Bible in the Middle Ages.* Notre Dame, Ind.: University of Notre Dame Press (pbk.), 1970.

Snyder, Charles R. *Alcohol and the Jews.* Arcturus (pbk.), 1978. (Reprint of the edition published by Free Press, Glencoe, Illinois, in 1958 which was issued as number 1 of the monographs of the Yale Center of Alcohol Studies.)

Sowell, Thomas. *Ethnic America: A History.* New York: Basic Books, 1981.

Stein, Ben. *The View from Sunset Boulevard.* New York: Basic Books, 1979.

Steinberg, Stephen. *The Ethnic Myth.* New York: Atheneum, 1981.

Stern, Fritz. *The Politics of Cultural Despair: A Study in the Rise of*

Germanic Ideology. Garden City, New York: Doubleday (Anchor Books), 1965.

Stern, Menachem. *Greek and Latin Authors on Jews and Judaism.* Jerusalem: The Israel Academy of Sciences and Humanities, vol. I: 1974; vol. II: 1980.

Stillman, Norman. *The Jews of Arab Lands.* Philadelphia: Jewish Publication Society, 1979.

Stone, Isidor F. *The Hidden History of the Korean War.* New York: Monthly Review Press, 1969.

Syrkin, Marie, ed. *Hayim Greenberg Anthology.* Detroit: Wayne State University Press, 1968.

————. "Redwashing Terrorism." In her book *The State of the Jews.* Washington, D.C.: New Republic Books, 1980.

Szajkowski, Zosa. "The Jewish Saint-Simonians and Socialist Anti-Semitism in France." *Jewish Social Studies.* January 1947.

Tacitus. *The Histories.* New York: Penguin Books (pbk.), 1964.

Tal, Uriel. "Anti-Christian Anti-Semitism." In *The Catastrophe of European Jewry,* edited by Yisrael Gutman and Livia Rothkirchen. New York: Ktav Publishing House, n.d.

Tcherikover, Victor. *Hellenistic Civilization and the Jews.* Philadelphia: Jewish Publication Society, 1959.

Toland, John. *Adolf Hitler.* 1st. edition. Garden City, New York: Doubleday, 1976.

Trachtenberg, Joshua. *The Devil and the Jews: The Medieval Conception of the Jew and its Relation to Modern Antisemitism.* New Haven: Yale University Press, 1943; Cleveland and New York: Meridian Books (pbk.), 1961.

von Treitschke, Heinrich. "A Word About Our Jewry." Translated by Robert Chazan and Marc Lee Raphael, eds. In *Modern Jewish History: A Source Reader.* New York: Schocken Books, 1974.

van den Haag, Ernest. *The Jewish Mystique.* 2nd edition. New York: Stein and Day, 1977.

Weinryb, Bernard. "Antisemitism in Soviet Russia." In *The Jews in Soviet Russia Since 1917,* edited by Lionel Kochan. New York: Oxford University Press (pbk.), 1978.

Wistrich, Robert S. *Revolutionary Jews From Marx to Trotsky.* New York: Barnes and Noble Books, 1976.

Index